IMAGES
of America

ORANGEBURG

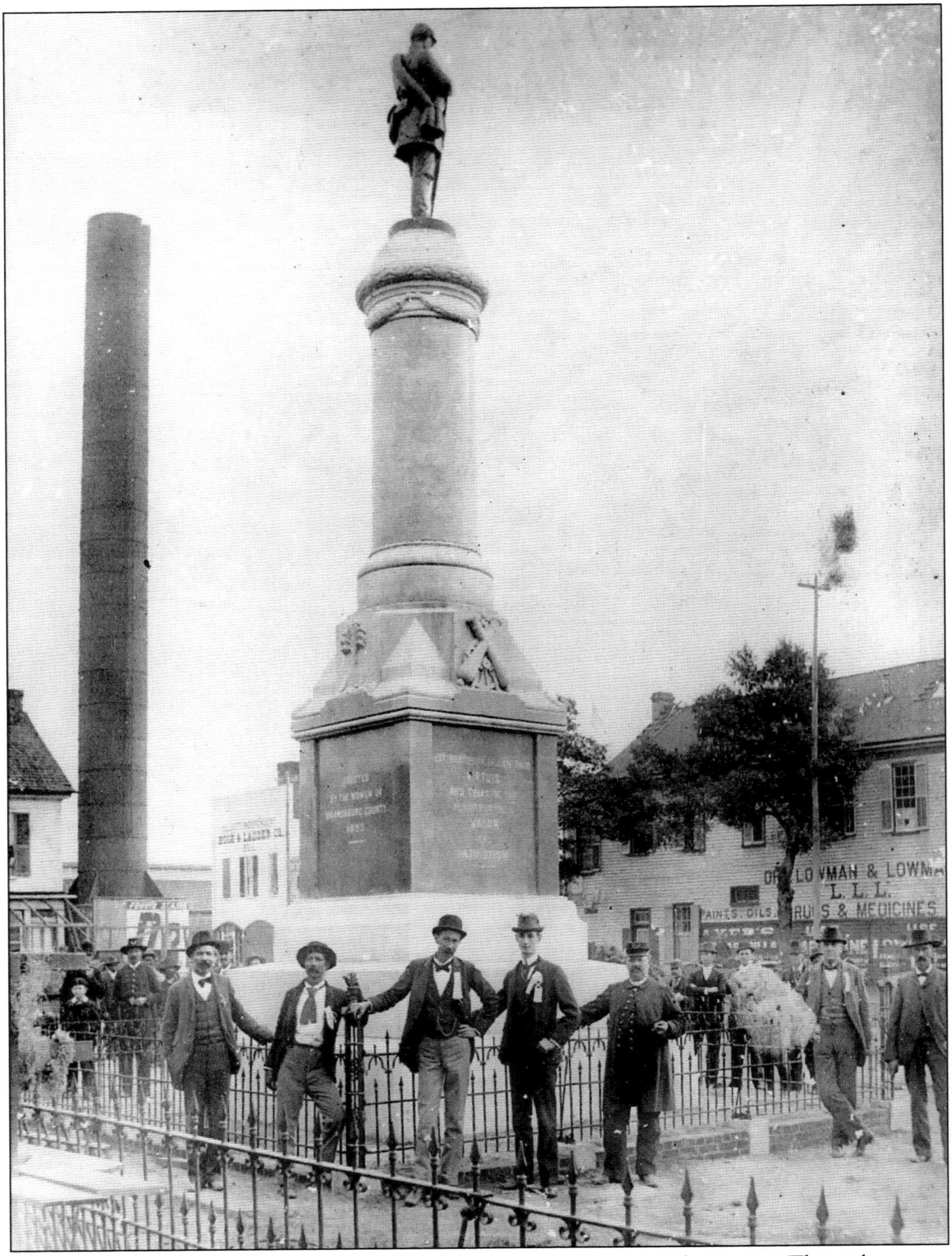

COURTHOUSE SQUARE, c. 1905. Several local citizens pose here on the square. The only person identified is Police Chief Augustus S. Fischer, in uniform. Among the others are Jim Kelley (a city policeman) and Virgil Dibble. The building on the far left was the station house for the Young America Steam Fire Engine Co., a volunteer fire department. One of the standpipes for the city water system is beside the fire station. Lowman's Drug Store, which is located on the right, was at the corner of Russell and Middleton Streets. (Courtesy Orangeburg County Historical Society.)

IMAGES
of America

ORANGEBURG

Dr. Gene Atkinson

ARCADIA
PUBLISHING

ISBN 978-0-7385-1410-9

Published by Arcadia Publishing
Charleston, South Carolina

Printed in the United States of America

Library of Congress Catalog Card Number: 2001096944

For all general information contact Arcadia Publishing at:
Telephone 843-853-2070
Fax 843-853-0044
E-Mail sales@arcadiapublishing.com
For customer service and orders:
Toll-Free 1-888-313-2665

Visit us on the Internet at www.arcadiapublishing.com

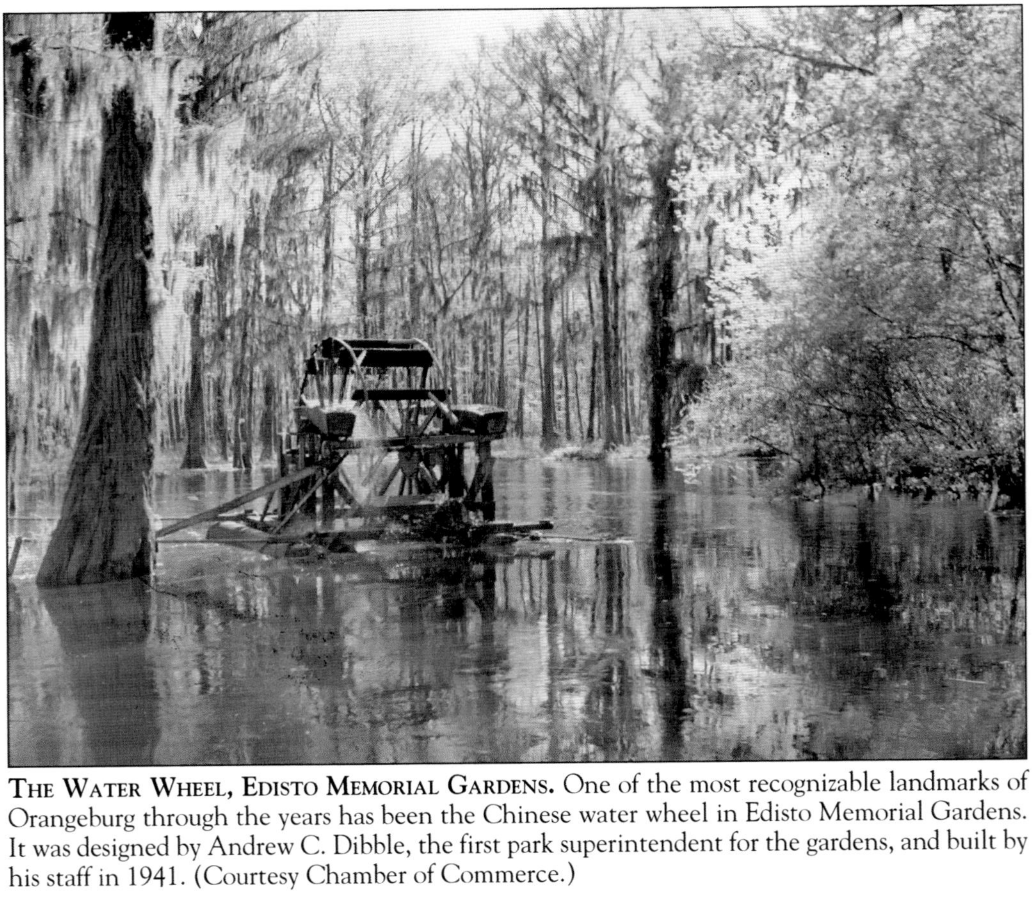

The Water Wheel, Edisto Memorial Gardens. One of the most recognizable landmarks of Orangeburg through the years has been the Chinese water wheel in Edisto Memorial Gardens. It was designed by Andrew C. Dibble, the first park superintendent for the gardens, and built by his staff in 1941. (Courtesy Chamber of Commerce.)

Contents

Acknowledgments		6
Introduction		7
1.	Around the Town	9
2.	Schools	49
3.	Churches	67
4.	County Fair	77
5.	Police and Fire Departments	81
6.	Businesses	87
7.	Hospital	105
8.	Hawthorne and The Methodist Home	111
9.	Recreation	115
10.	Edisto Memorial Gardens	121

ACKNOWLEDGMENTS

For years I had been fascinated by my family's collection of old photographs from various events from the early part of this century. As my historical interest grew over time, the advent of modern computer technology helped make possible copying these old faded pictures. With these new methods, old brownish faded pictures with various imperfections could not only be copied, but restored to their original dignity.

Over time I began to amass a small collection of old photographs of activities from Orangeburg's past. As word spread of my interest, others began to let me copy some of their old pictures, which I had restored by this new technology. Thus my collection began to grow.

After purchasing several books in Arcadia Publishing's *Images of America* series featuring old photographs of Columbia and Charleston, my interest had swelled to where I knew I wanted to produce a book like that about my hometown of Orangeburg.

Thus was born the idea for this treasure trove of informative old photographs featuring Orangeburg's rich history.

I am truly appreciative for the outpouring of support from the community for all the historical photographs of Orangeburg's past that were brought to me for this book. Altogether the citizens of Orangeburg were wonderful with this spirit of cooperation.

Assembling together over 225 old photographs required many citizens and organizations to come forth with their treasured old pictures. I am truly thankful to those who contributed the majority of the images for this cause. Among them are the Orangeburg County Historical Society, the Orangeburg County Chamber of Commerce, the Russell Wolfe family, Cleveland Dempsey, Dr. Clemmie Webber, Anna Lou Wolfe, Sylvia and Louis Boone, Harry Wannamaker III, Al and Edna Fischer, Taylor Garick, the Regional Medical Center, the City of Orangeburg, the Orangeburg County Fair Association, the Department of Public Utilities, and W.C. Ziegler Sr. There were many others who also contributed photographs, and everyone is given credit under each specific image in this book.

During the conceptual stage of planning this collection, Dr. Lawton Salley and J. West Summers Jr. were most helpful. Both also proofed my descriptive captions as well as authenticated their historical accuracy. Mrs. Evelyn Weathersbee and the volunteers at the Orangeburg County Historical Society were invaluable with their assistance in locating many treasured old photographs. My friend and colleague in photography, Cecil Williams, did a masterful job scanning and restoring some of the images for this collection. Sam Fogle kept me thoroughly educated and entertained with his anecdotal history of Orangeburg that proved to be very useful in writing the captions.

In summary it is hoped that the citizens of Orangeburg will not only enjoy perusing through this book but also learn much about the history of our fair city through the informative descriptive captions with each picture.

Dr. Gene Atkinson

INTRODUCTION

Prior to the state legislature encouraging settlements in the interior of Carolina in 1730, only a few scattered traders lived in this area in addition to a small number of Native Americans. Orangeburgh was one of eleven townships created by the governing body in Charles Towne. Most of these new areas were located near rivers so that water was available for consumption, cooking, and cleaning.

Orangeburgh was given its name by Lt. Gov. Thomas Broughton, being named in honor of William IV, Prince of Orange, who was the husband of Princess Anne, the daughter of King George II of England.

The first group of settlers arriving in 1735 were of German-Swiss origin. The township was 20,000 acres in size, and each family head received a lot in town and 50 acres for each family member further out in the township. Everyone was given enough provisions for one year upon leaving Charles Towne for this new life in the frontier.

Early on most of the settlers were Lutheran, but when Reverend Gissendanner's nephew John returned to Orangeburgh in 1750, he had just been ordained in the Church of England, so the settlers followed suit by switching over.

By the time the American Revolution came about, there were many people on both sides—Patriots and Tories. However, most of the Tories eventually left. Many of the locals participated in some of the militias during the Revolutionary War.

During the early years of Orangeburgh, the center of town known as the Public Square was bounded by today's streets of Broughton, Waring, Middleton, and Bull. The stream bisecting this area today was also present in that day. The old town graveyard is still located there, now known as Pioneer Graveyard.

In the aftermath of the War between the States, Orangeburgh, like most other Southern towns, had been destroyed by General Sherman's troops. While in Orangeburgh, Sherman made his headquarters in the Judge Glover home, which is still standing today on Whitman Street. Mrs. Glover reminded Sherman that she had known him as a young lieutenant stationed at Fort Moultrie in Charleston, that he had conducted himself as a gentleman then, and that she expected no less from him now. Thus General Sherman ordered that her house be spared from being burned.

In 1869 the town of Orangeburgh officially dropped the "h" from its name to be known as Orangeburg, as it remains today.

Gradually Orangeburg climbed out of its post-war devastation during the rest of the 1800s.

Claflin University was established as an institution of higher learning for African Americans in 1869, and South Carolina State University opened its doors in 1896. A public graded school system was established in 1890 as two separate schools—one for females and one for males.

Orangeburg was incorporated as a city in 1883. One of our leading merchants, George Cornelson, built a water system downtown in 1887 and leased it to the city, which was too poor to build it outright. Electricity was introduced here in the 1890s.

After many years of a local fall festival, the Orangeburg County Fair Association continued this trend when it was established in 1911. It is still in existence today as the oldest continuous fair in South Carolina.

A hospital was established in 1919 after many years of pursuit, as well as a nursing school. The year of 1927 saw construction of a first class high-rise hotel called the Hotel Eutaw, as well as a new city hall, city auditorium, jail, and fire station.

Edisto Memorial Gardens began in 1926, and after a shaky first decade, it began to really progress upon the arrival of Andrew Dibble in 1937 as the first superintendent of parks to lead its development.

None of the banks in Orangeburg survived the Great Depression, but new ones opened in the 1930s to begin years of progressive service to our area.

During World War II a pilot training school, known as the Hawthorne School of Aeronautics, opened a few miles south of the city. Over 4,000 American pilots and 1,600 French pilots were certified there for the war effort. Today this same campus is the home for The Methodist Oaks, a religious affiliated retirement community.

Agriculture, especially cotton farming, was king in Orangeburg County until the late 1950s. By that time agriculture was beginning to dwindle and progressive efforts had to be made to attract new industries into the area to provide much needed jobs for citizens to pursue. Many industries have located in Orangeburg since then, but more are always needed to provide these jobs for our citizens.

Orangeburg has made many progressive efforts through the years to improve the quality of life for its citizens and will continue to do so to meet the needs of our community in the future.

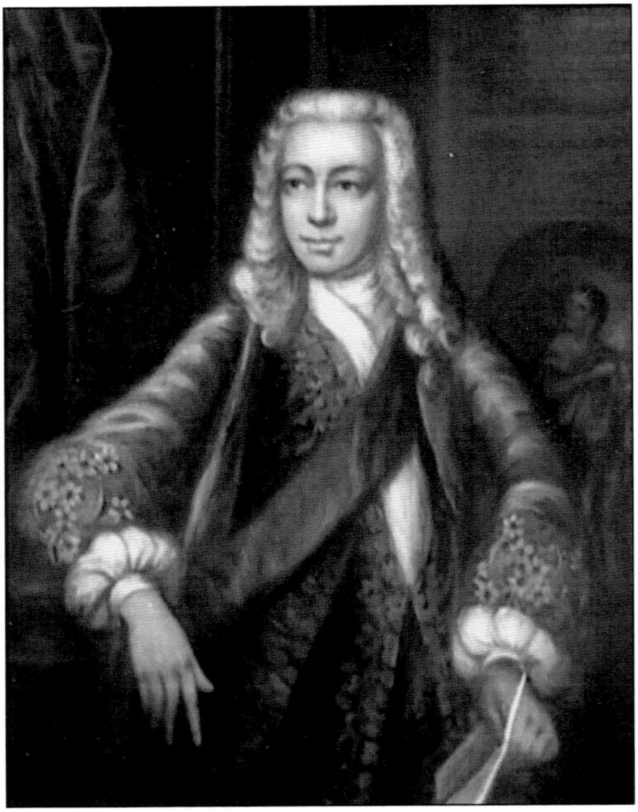

WILLIAM, PRINCE OF ORANGE. Orangeburg was first given its name by Lt. Gov. Thomas Broughton, who named our town after William IV, Prince of Orange. He was the husband of Princess Anne who was the daughter of King George II of England. In the beginning it was spelled Orangeburgh, with the "h" finally being dropped in 1869. (Courtesy Tom Langford.)

One

Around the Town

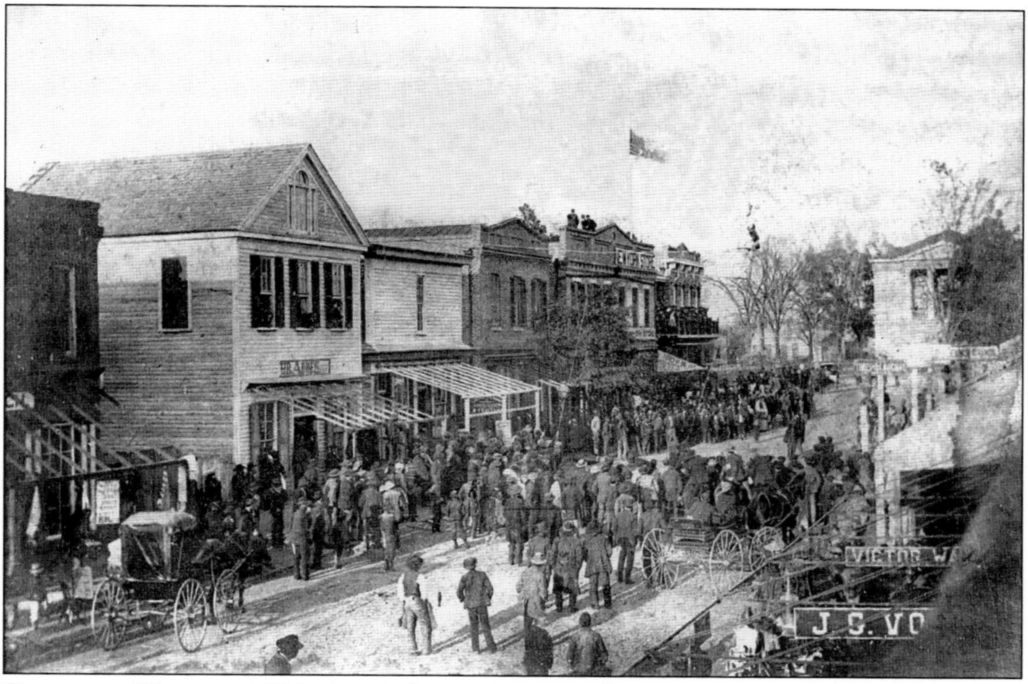

Tightrope Walker, 1886. A traveling tightrope walker came to Orangeburg to entertain the local citizens. This picture is faded to the point where only the acrobat's lower legs can be seen just to the right of the American flag. The building with the flag has been identified as that of the mercantile business of Fritz and Luther Adden. Next door to the right, with all the people standing on the balcony, was the business of William Lightfoot. His residence was the upstairs part of the building. The P.A. Lefvendahl novelty store was just to the left of the Adden's building. During this era most of the downtown buildings were wooden and considered fire hazards. Gradually brick buildings began replacing these wooden structures. (Courtesy Orangeburg County Historical Society.)

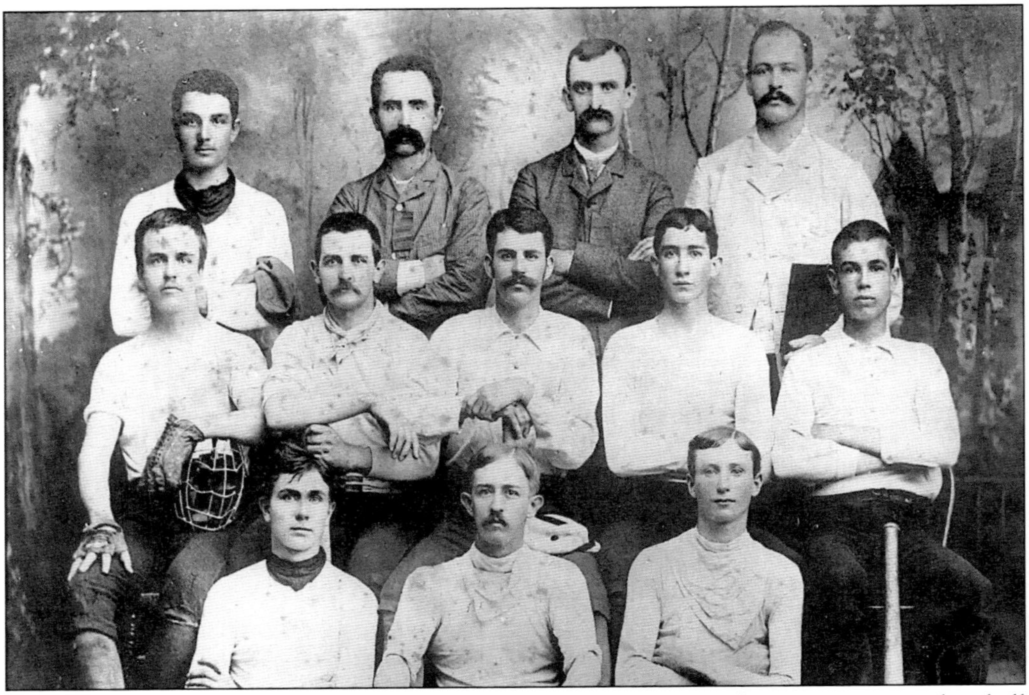

Orangeburg Diamonds, 1886–1887. The Orangeburg Diamonds was a semi-pro baseball team that represented our city in games against other towns. From left to right are (front row) Marion C. Raysor, Dr. T.A. Jeffords, and Dr. John H. Perreyclear; (middle row) Henry S. Holman, Julian A. Salley, John A. Zeigler, J.W. (Willie) Smoak, and Joe (or Tom?) Taylor; (back row) W. Hampton Dukes, B. Frank Slater, A.C. Lindstedt, and Norman Bull. (Courtesy Orangeburg County Historical Society.)

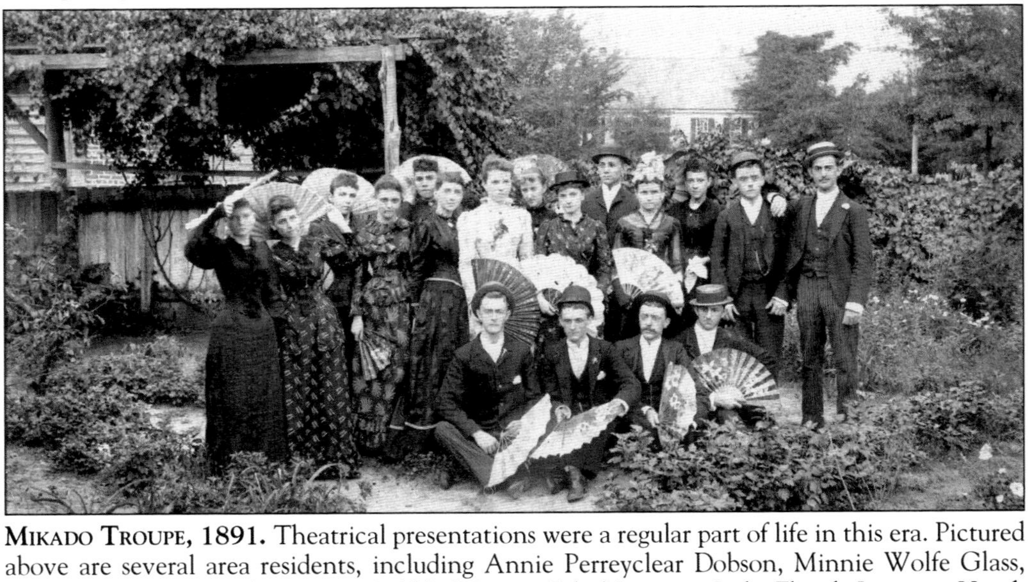

Mikado Troupe, 1891. Theatrical presentations were a regular part of life in this era. Pictured above are several area residents, including Annie Perreyclear Dobson, Minnie Wolfe Glass, Edith Mellichamp Andrews, Mae Dibble Watson, Ethel Lowman Lide, Floride Lowman Hood, Jessie Vince Moseley, Delores Stevens Holt, W.W. "Will" Wannamaker Sr., Flossie Willcox, Nina Oliveros, Otto Spahr, Marchie Bull, Russell Zemp, W. McMichael, and Alex Salley. (Courtesy Orangeburg County Historical Society.)

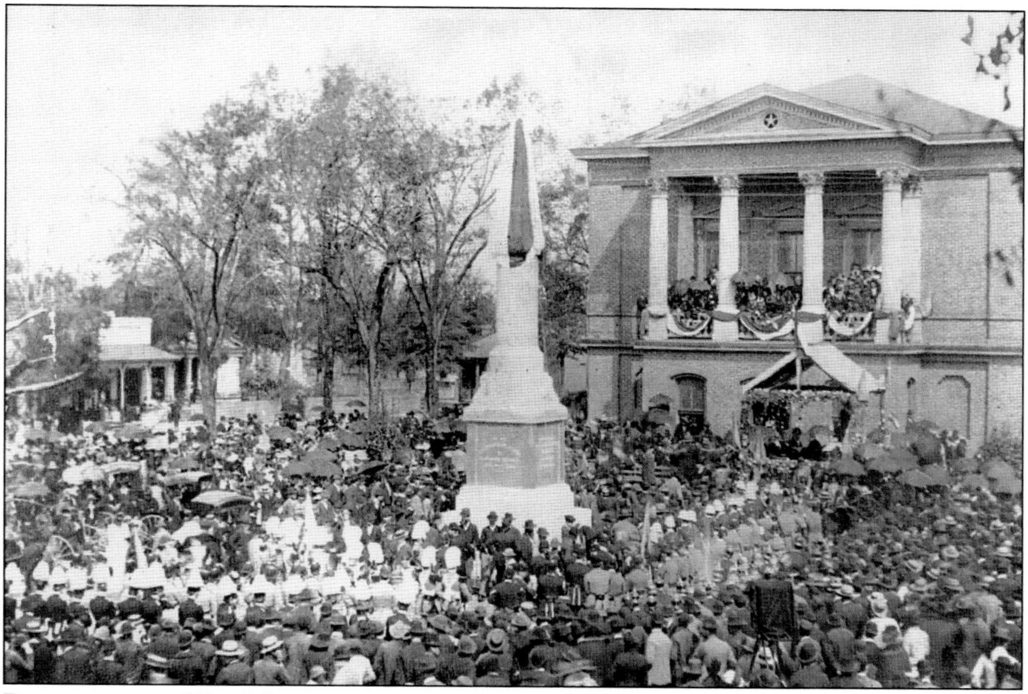

Dedication of War Monument, 1893. On October 18, 1893, the war memorial for those who died in the Civil War was dedicated on Courthouse Square with an impressive ceremony. The ladies of the county led a fund-raising drive for seven years to raise the $7,000 needed. The monument was designed by Theo Markwalter from Augusta and cast in Massachusetts. The model for the soldier was Capt. John S. Palmer who, at that time in the 1890s, had the "shape and bearing of a man from the 1860s." (Courtesy Orangeburg County Historical Society.)

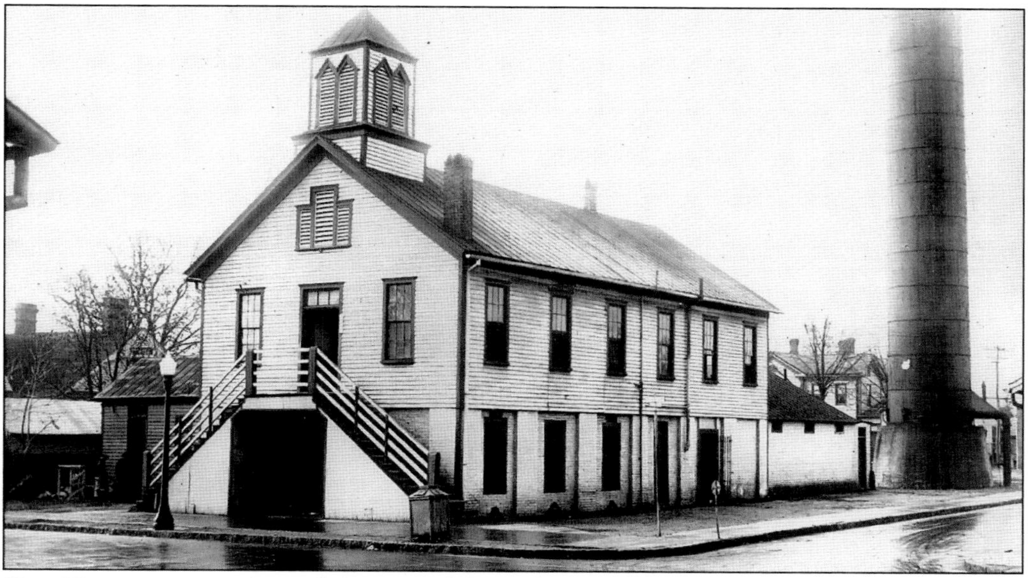

City Hall, c. 1900. Around the turn of the 20th century, Orangeburg's city hall was located in the same place it is today on Middleton Street. In 1926 it was torn down so that the new city hall and auditorium/theatre could be constructed. The tower in the rear was a water storage tank for the city's water system. (Courtesy Orangeburg Historical Society.)

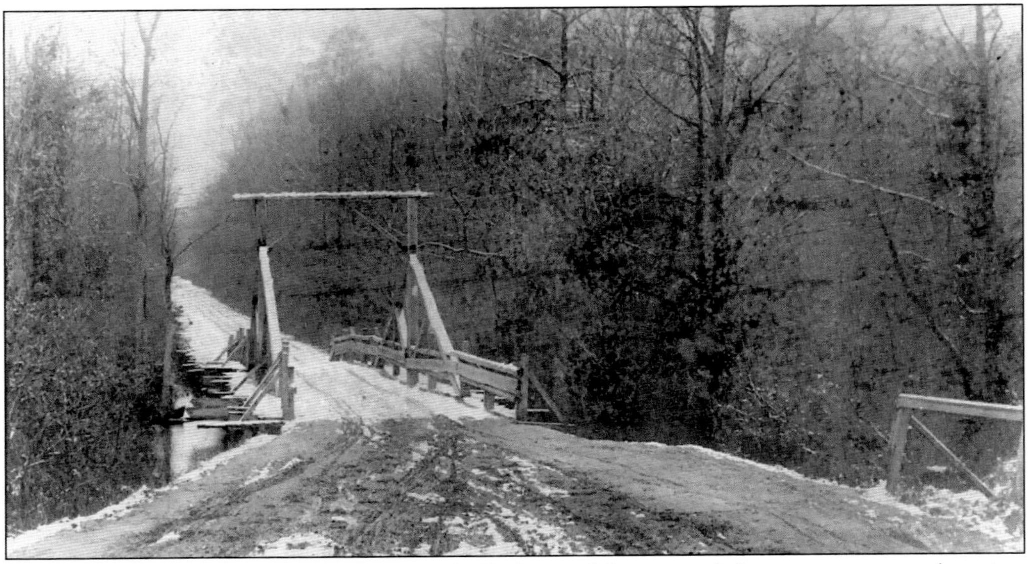

Bridge Across the Edisto River, c. 1905. Around the turn of the century a new location for the bridge across the Edisto River was determined, and the above bridge was built. This is the same location as today's bridge on John C. Calhoun Drive. The original entrance bridge to Orangeburg was located where the footbridge is today at the Orangeburg Fine Arts Center. (Courtesy Orangeburg County Historical Society.)

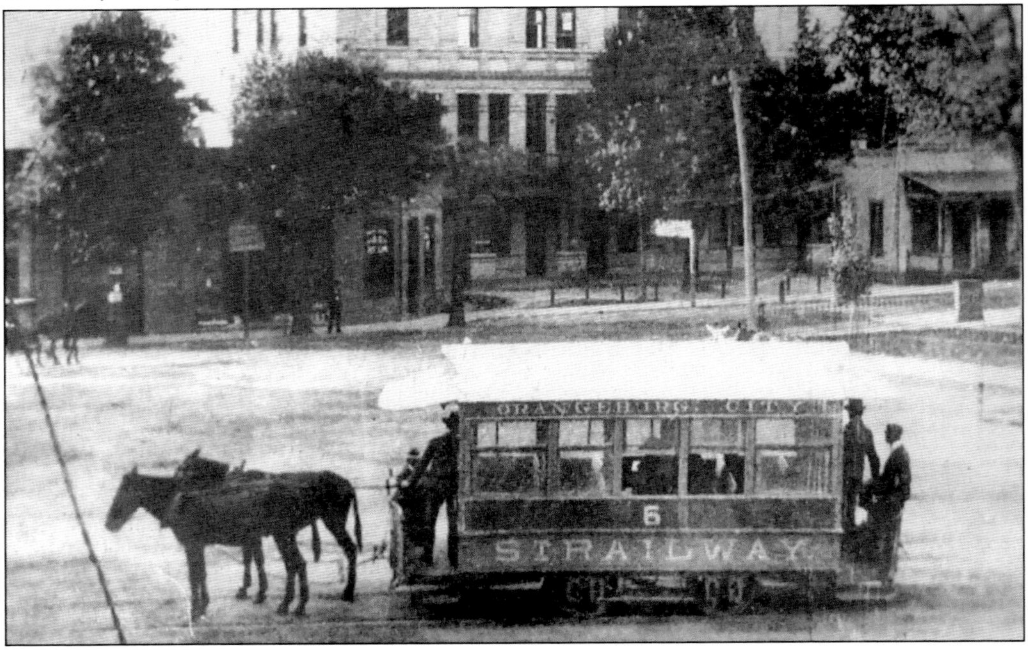

Orangeburg Street Railway, c. 1905. A street trolley system was constructed in 1888 that eventually ran from the Atlantic Coast Line Railroad station on Broughton Street through downtown to the Southern Railway station on Railroad Avenue, which is now the junction of Boulevard, Russell Street, and Magnolia Street. During the day it operated as a mule-drawn passenger trolley. At night a small steam locomotive would be used to haul freight to various downtown businesses on these same tracks. This trolley system was discontinued in 1908. (Courtesy Orangeburg County Historical Society.)

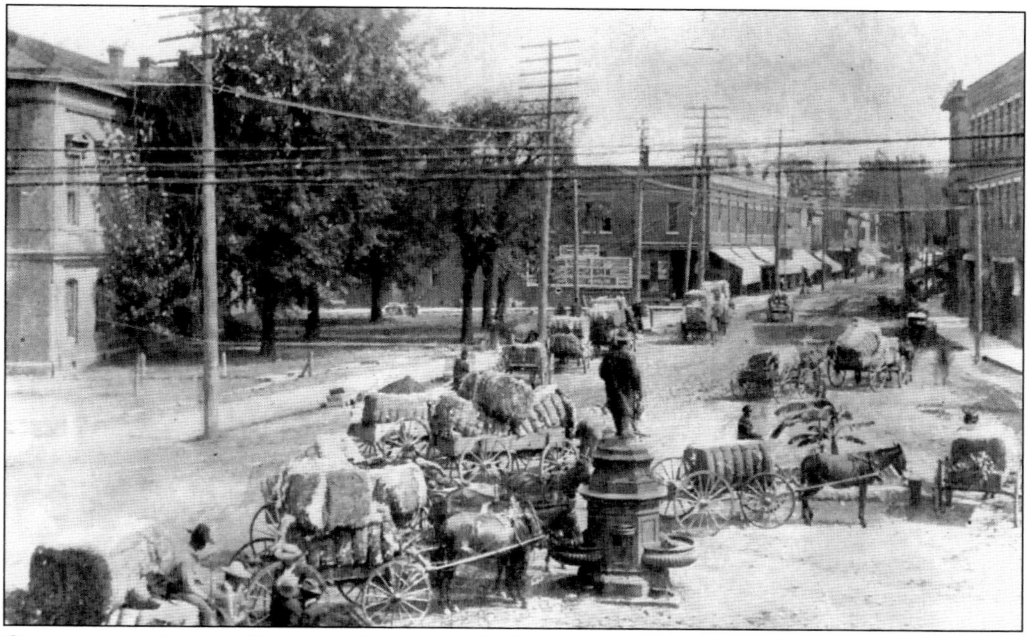

COURTHOUSE SQUARE LOOKING EAST, c. 1908. Cotton was coming to market in this scene on the town square. The fireman's statue that was so prominent on the square for many years also served as a public drinking fountain. Horses and mules used the large troughs on each side, while dogs had four "dog laps" just above ground level. Humans used two higher level fountains. Inside the statue base was room for 500 pounds of ice which, when melted, provided the cool water for all of the fountains. The fountain cost $700 and was financed by the Young Men's Business League, a forerunner of today's chamber of commerce, with proceeds from a carnival as well as a city council appropriation. (Courtesy Orangeburg County Historical Society.)

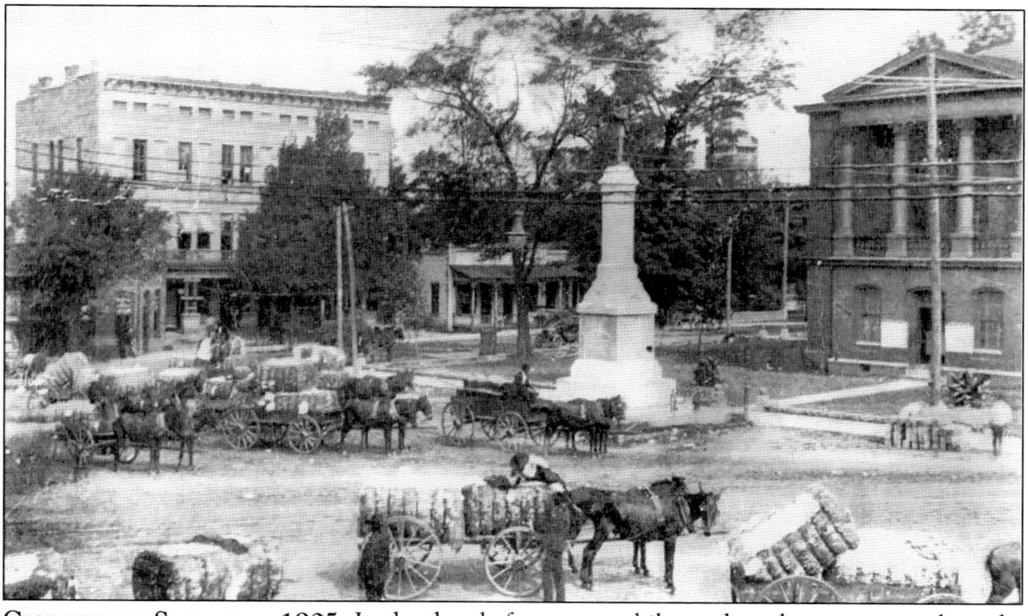

COURTHOUSE SQUARE, c. 1905. In the days before automobiles and trucks, cotton was brought to market on wagons pulled by mules. The building on the left housed the local Elk's Club. (Courtesy Orangeburg County Historical Society.)

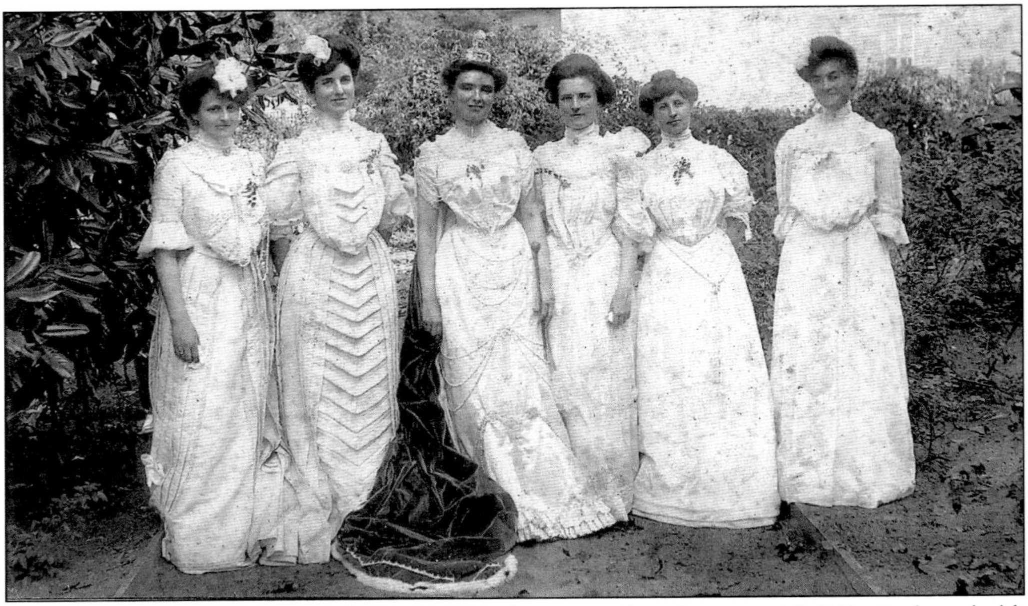

FALL FESTIVAL, 1902. For many years prior to the county fair, the annual Fall Festival was held. Here is the 1902 queen and her court dressed in the finest gowns of the day. They are, from left to right, Gertie Roessler (later Weeks), Ida Kohn, Queen Ray Slater (later Lining), Ada Doyle, Pearl Cannon, and Pena Sorentrue. The queen, Ray Slater, later married Mr. W.S. Lining, a prominent cotton broker in town. The home they built on Russell Street was later used by Dukes-Harley Funeral Home for over 60 years. (Courtesy Gene Atkinson.)

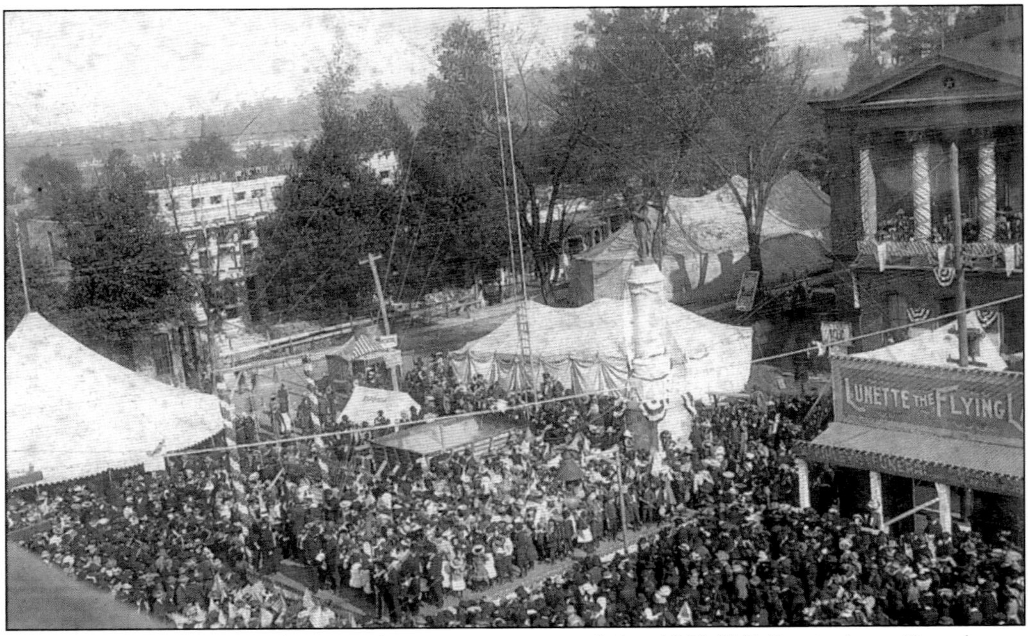

FALL FESTIVAL, 1902. This was the opening scene of the 1902 Fall Festival on Courthouse Square with over 500 school children singing patriotic airs. Some carnival-like entertainment was used at these festivals as evidenced by the high dive act set up here, as well as Lunette the Flying Lady, who walked the tightrope seen in the foreground. The old courthouse is seen on the right. (Courtesy Gene Atkinson.)

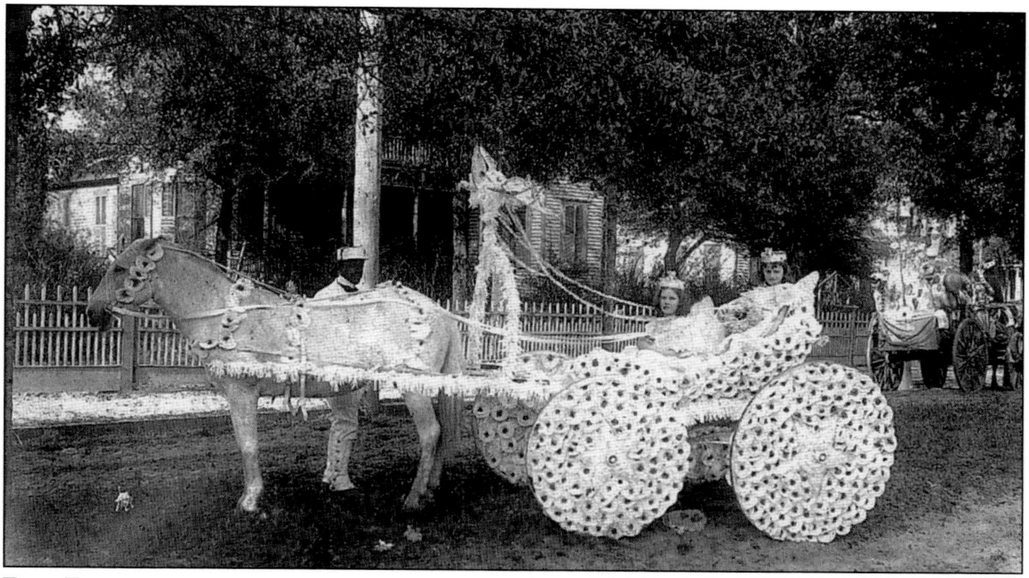

Fall Festival, 1902. The first prize for the best single team (one-horse buggy) in the floral parade at the 1902 Fall Festival was won by little Misses Winifred Doyle and Mignon Lowman. Their decorations were very elaborate as seen in this picture. (Courtesy Gene Atkinson.)

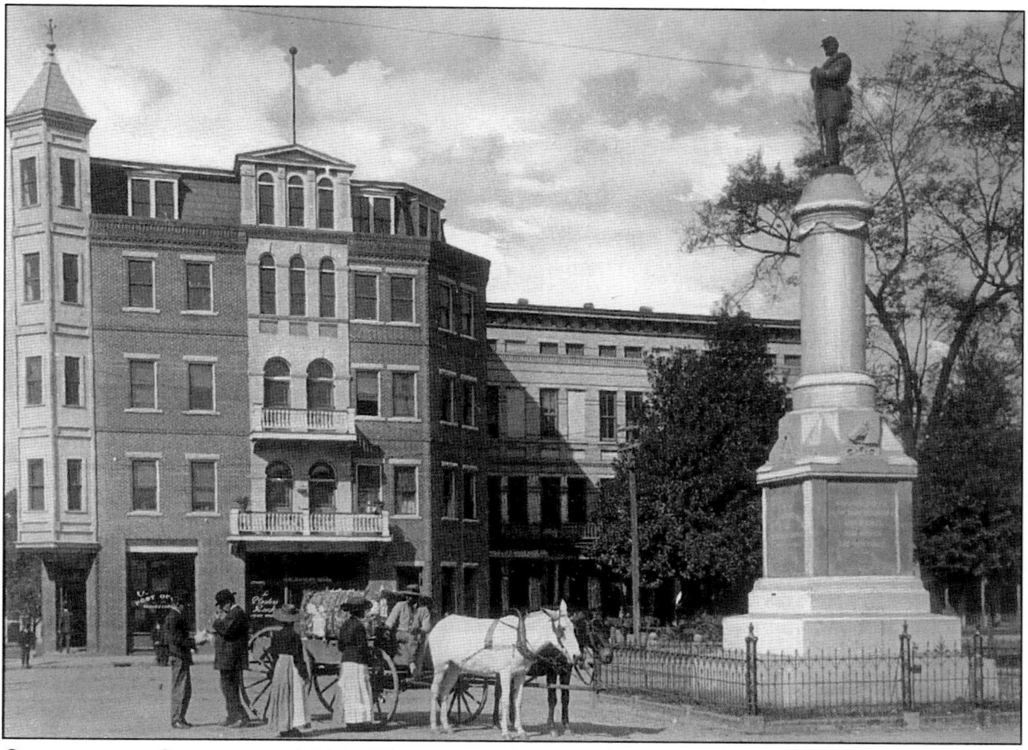

Courthouse Square, c. 1910. This tranquil scene shows a lone wagon of cotton coming to market at Courthouse Square. The Orangeburg Hotel is the large building on the left in the background. On the ground floor of the hotel is the Orangeburg Post Office and the Planters National Bank. The building to the right contained the Elks Club on an upper floor. (Courtesy E.J. Lackey.)

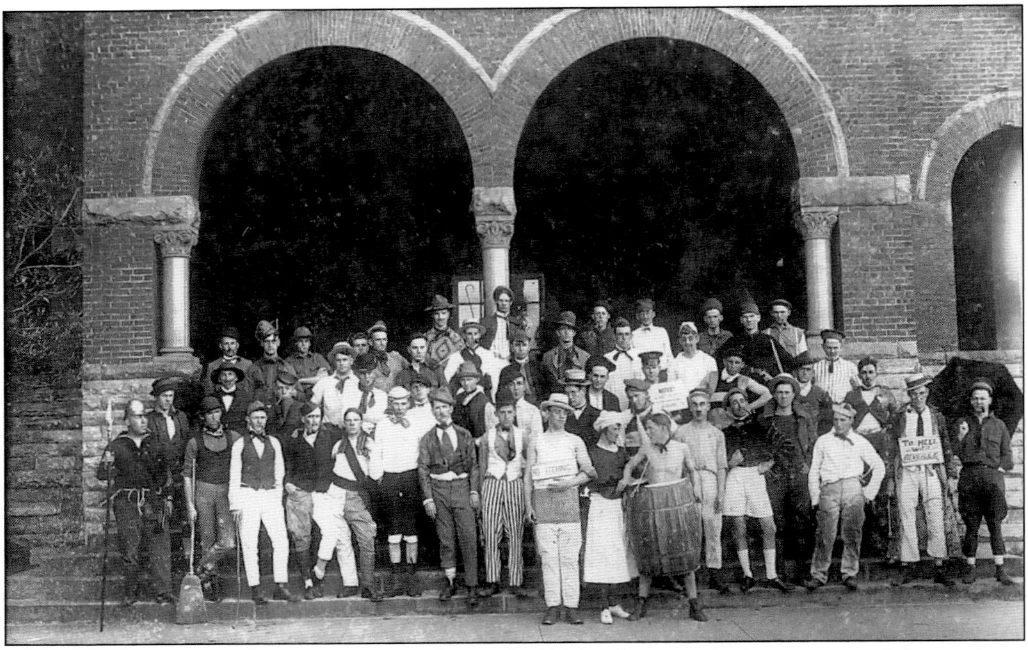

Orangeburg Collegiate Institute. This early 1900s photograph shows some of the students who had just given a comedic theatrical presentation. The Orangeburg Collegiate Institute was a Baptist-affiliated college located on Glover Street. (Courtesy Carolyn Mizzell.)

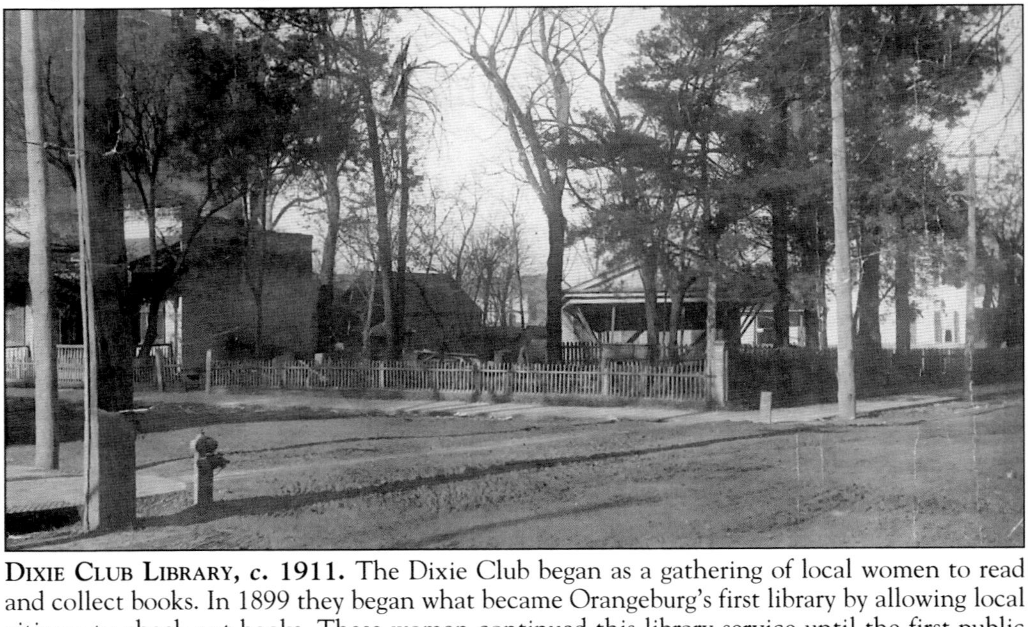

Dixie Club Library, c. 1911. The Dixie Club began as a gathering of local women to read and collect books. In 1899 they began what became Orangeburg's first library by allowing local citizens to check out books. These women continued this library service until the first public library was established in 1936. At that time the ladies of the Dixie Club donated over 25,000 books to the new public library. They continued to operate on a small scale for their members afterward. In 1911 the Dixie Club building was relocated to the rear of its lot on Courthouse Square to face Church Street so that Orangeburg's new post office could be built. In 1955 it was again relocated, this time to Pioneer Graveyard on Bull Street, the original center of town in the 1700s. (Courtesy Orangeburg County Historical Society.)

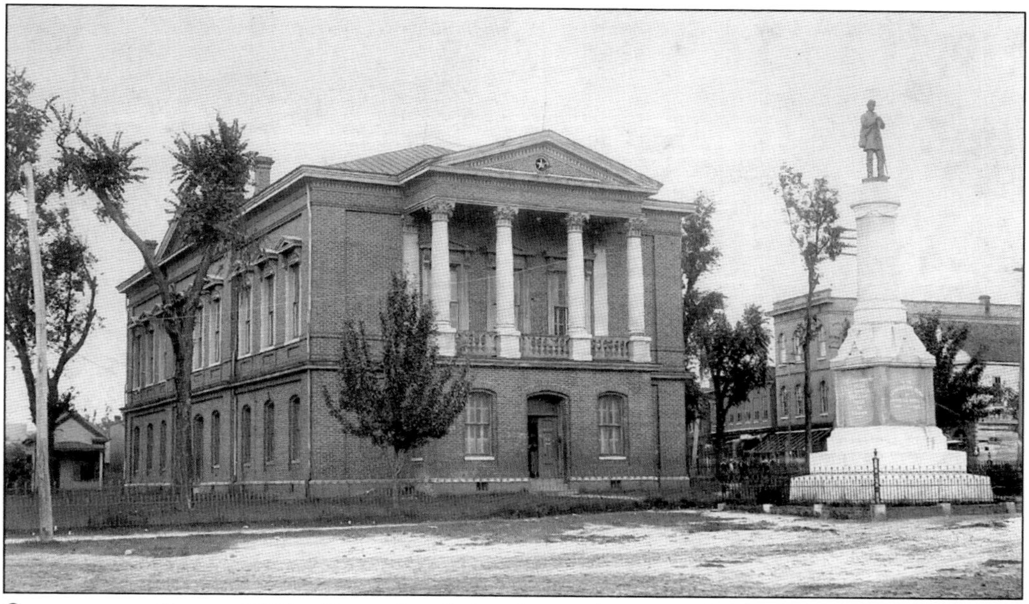

COURTHOUSE, EARLY 1900S. Orangeburg's fourth courthouse was built on the square in 1875 to replace the one that General Sherman destroyed. It was demolished in 1928 when our current courthouse was erected between Amelia and St. Paul Streets. (Courtesy Orangeburg County Historical Society.)

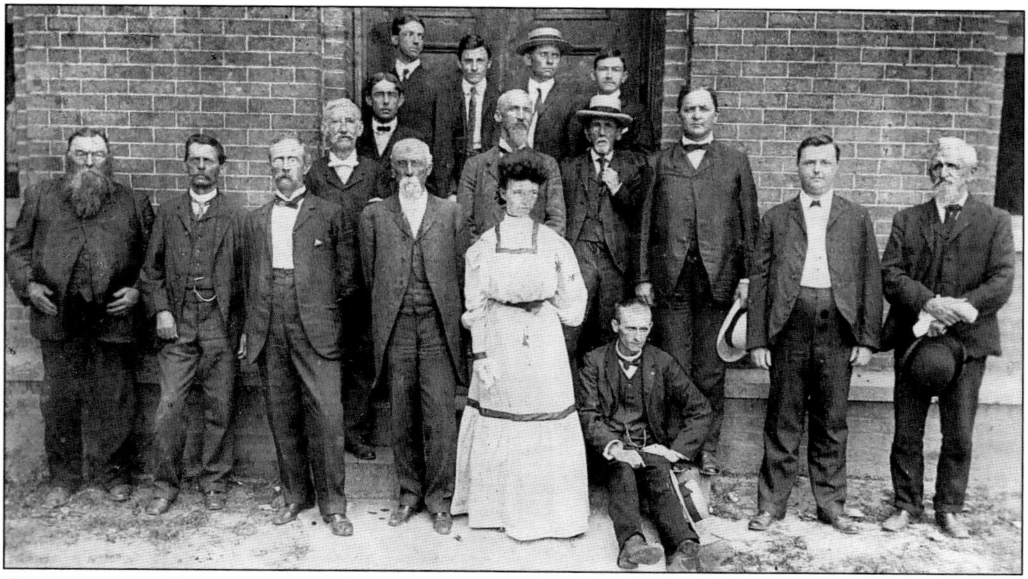

COURTHOUSE OFFICIALS AND EMPLOYEES, c. 1910. The Orangeburg County Courthouse, being located in the center of town on the square, was always a hub for activities. The courthouse officials and employees in this image, from left to right, are as follows: (front row) John Henry Dukes, Sheriff; ? Smith; G.L. Salley, Clerk of Court; Stiles R. Mellichamp, Superintendent of Education; Clementine Cummings; and (seated) Charles Brunson, Magistrate; (middle row) Robert Copes, Probate Judge; Tom Albergotti; Alex Tharin; Ab Fair, County Treasurer; ? Shirer; and P.T. Hildebrand, Solicitor; (back row) Marion F. Inabinet; Stokes Salley; John Bowman; ? Horner; and ? Dantzler. (Courtesy Orangeburg County Historical Society.)

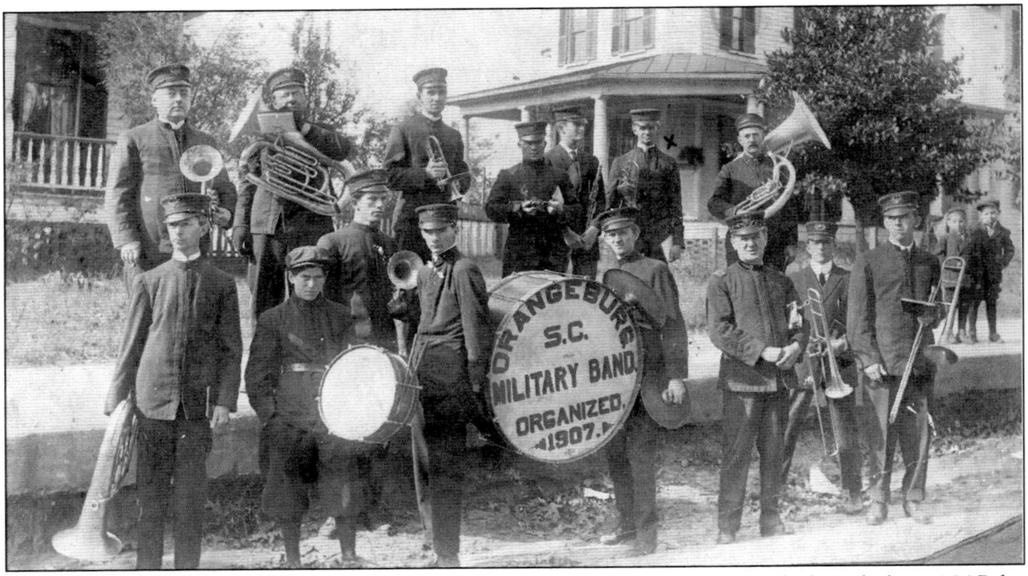

ORANGEBURG MILITARY BAND, 1907. The Orangeburg Military Band, founded in 1907 by O.K. Wilson, was composed of local citizens who provided our city with public concerts. Some of the inaugural members, from left to right, included (front row) Richard McMichael, O.K. Wilson Jr., Walter O'Cain, John Salley, George Schiffley, O.K. Wilson Sr., Lenaire F. Wolfe, and Archie Jordan; (back row) Otto Spahr, ? Heggy, Barrett Wilson, T.A. Jeffords Jr., Russell S. Wolfe, L. Bennett, and unidentified. (Courtesy Orangeburg County Historical Society.)

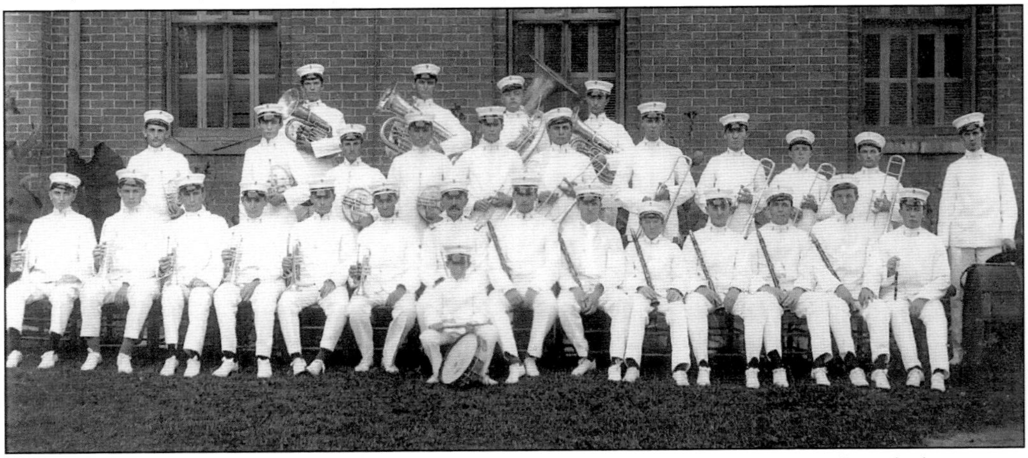

ORANGEBURG MILITARY BAND, 1908. Many summer Sunday afternoons found this group entertaining Orangeburg's citizens with free concerts from the bandstand on the courthouse grounds. More formal concerts were given in indoor auditoriums. Pictured from left to right are (first row) Orville Wilson, snare drum; (second row) Clarence Davis; Elliott Salley; Edward Inabinet and William Bryant, second and third cornets; Jim McMichael, Leonard Bennett, and O.K. Wilson, solo cornets; William L. Glover and Russell S. Wolfe, solo clarinets; Theodore A. Jeffords Jr. and Bob Bruner, first or second clarinets; Bob Arant and Adonis Avinger, second clarinets; and J.M. O'Dowd, piccolo; (third row) Frederick Schiffley and J.C. Day, second and third alto horns; Cecil Culler and Ashley Wannamaker, solo alto horns; Jerome McMichael, Marvin Arant, Pascal Albergotti, Lenaire F. Wolfe, and Rush Westbury, trombones; and George Schiffley, bass drum; (fourth row) Walter O'Cain, baritone; Mike Salley and Otto Spahr, basses; and Richard McMichael, baritone. (Courtesy Russell Wolfe family.)

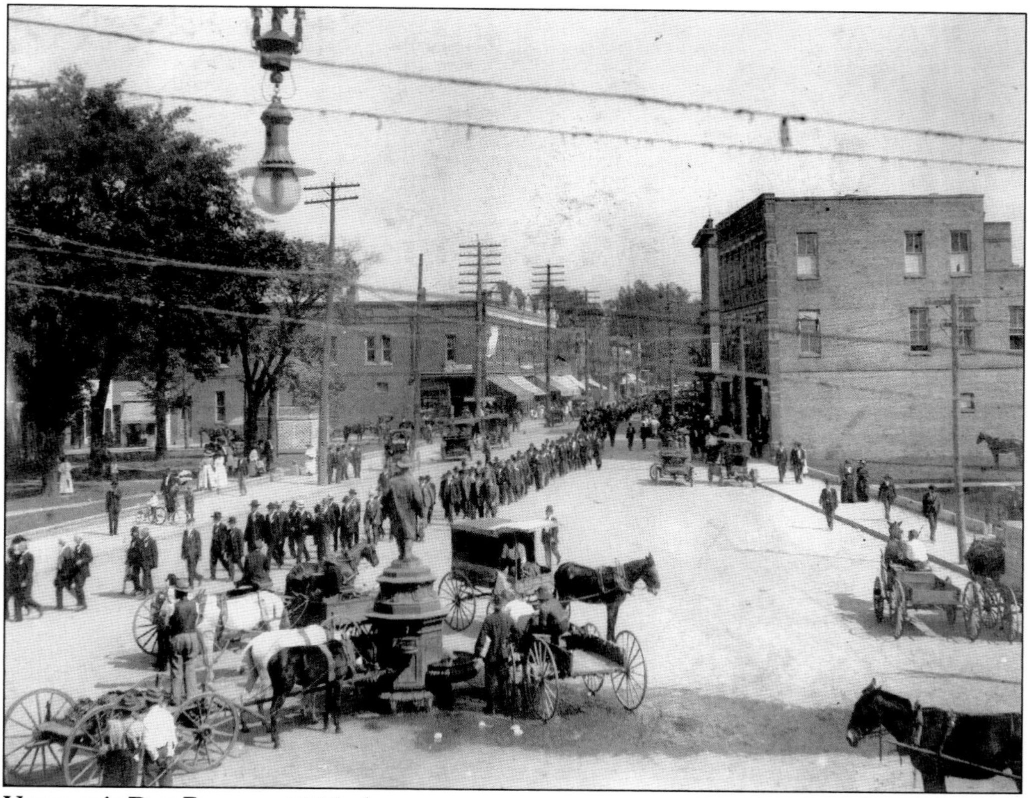

Veteran's Day Parade, 1910. Area Confederate veterans from the Civil War are shown during a veterans' recognition parade on the square in 1910. Approximately 240 veterans were able to participate in this parade. Note the public bandstand at the corner of the courthouse grounds where many Sunday afternoon concerts were given by the Orangeburg Military Band and other groups through the years. The bandstand was also a focal point for political speeches and public ceremonies. (Courtesy Orangeburg County Historical Society.)

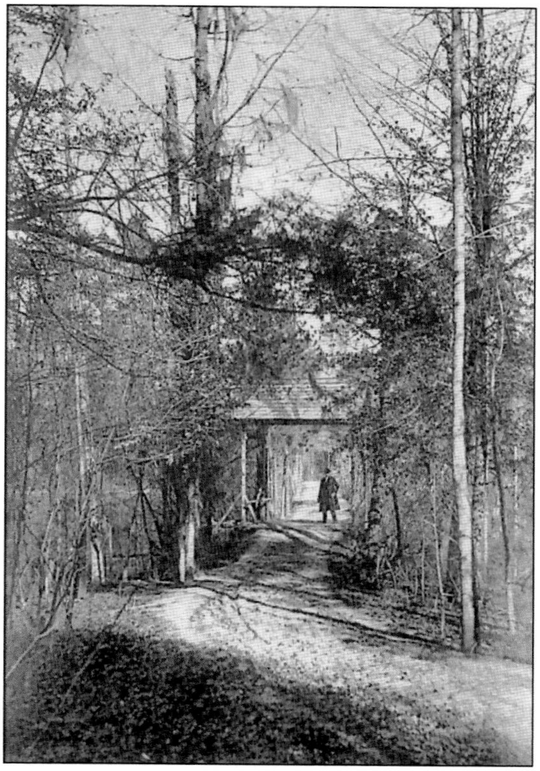

Dukes' Fishery, 1909. Dukes' Fishery was a commercial fish hatchery in the early part of the century. It consisted of a series of ponds located just off Caw Caw Creek where the western portion of the present Prince of Orange Mall now stands. (Courtesy of Anna Lou Wolfe.)

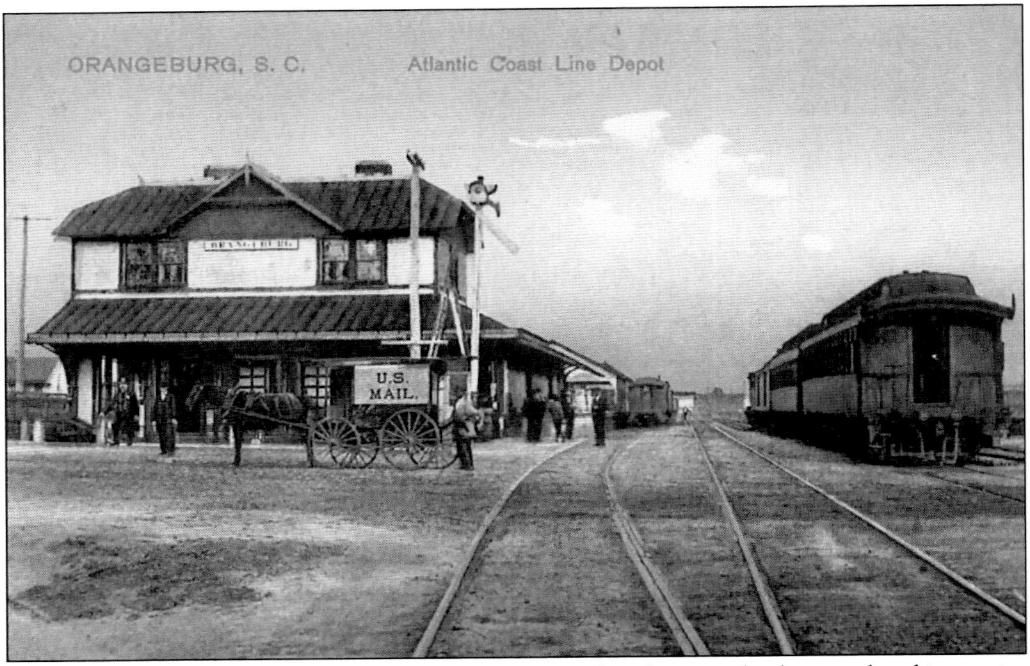

Atlantic Coast Line Railroad Depot, 1909. Railroads were the key mode of inter-city transportation before automobiles and good roads appeared. Railroad stations were indeed a hub of activity in those days. The ACL depot was located where the train tracks intersected Broughton Street. The last passenger train service through Orangeburg was discontinued in the 1960s when automobiles and airplanes became the chief modes of transportation. (Courtesy Anna Lou Wolfe.)

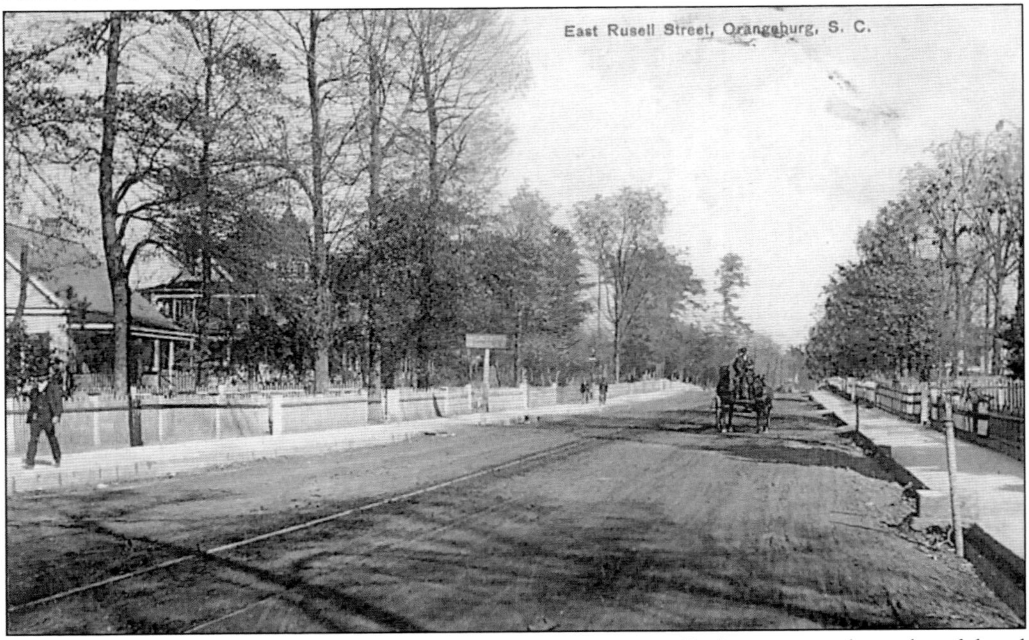

East Russell Street, 1909. Horses and buggies were still the principal mode of local transportation in this era. Note the trend by many residents in that day to have white picket fences surrounding their yards and homes. (Courtesy Anna Lou Wolfe.)

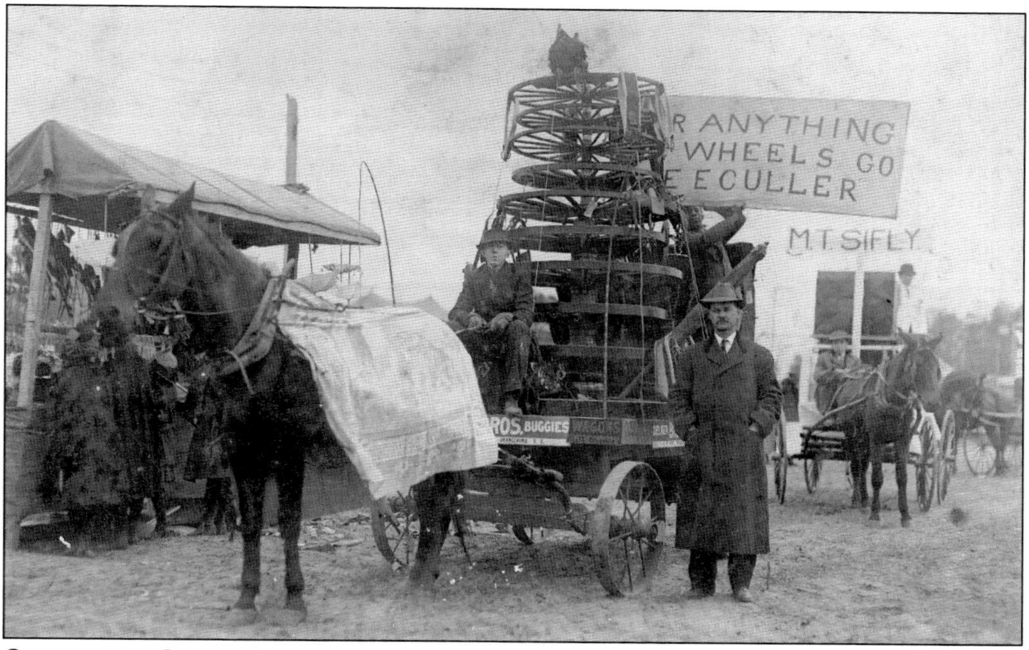

ORANGEBURG COUNTY FAIR PARADE, 1911. During the early years of the Orangeburg County Fair, a parade was held during fair week. It would feature the king and queen of the fair and their court, as well as local merchants displaying their products and other goods. The Orangeburg County Fair was organized in 1911, and this photograph shows part of the first fair parade with E.E. Culler and an elaborate display of his wagon wheels, as well as the M.T. Sifly mercantile display. (Courtesy Orangeburg County Historical Society.)

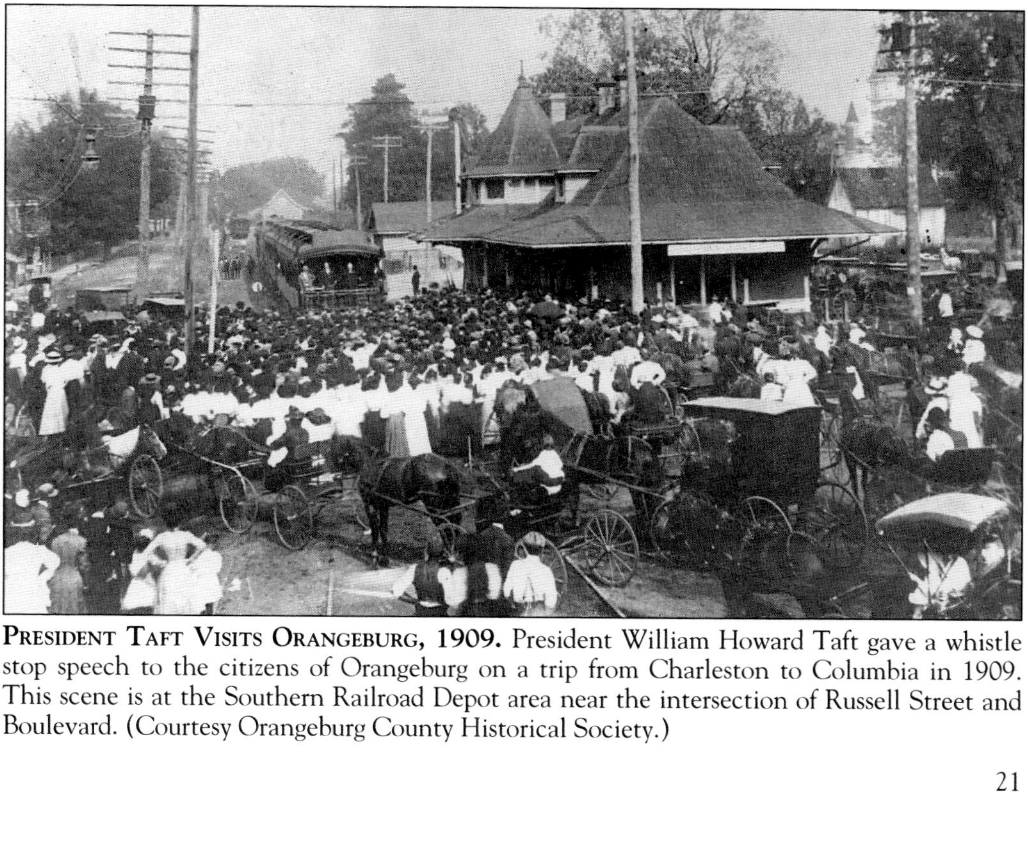

PRESIDENT TAFT VISITS ORANGEBURG, 1909. President William Howard Taft gave a whistle stop speech to the citizens of Orangeburg on a trip from Charleston to Columbia in 1909. This scene is at the Southern Railroad Depot area near the intersection of Russell Street and Boulevard. (Courtesy Orangeburg County Historical Society.)

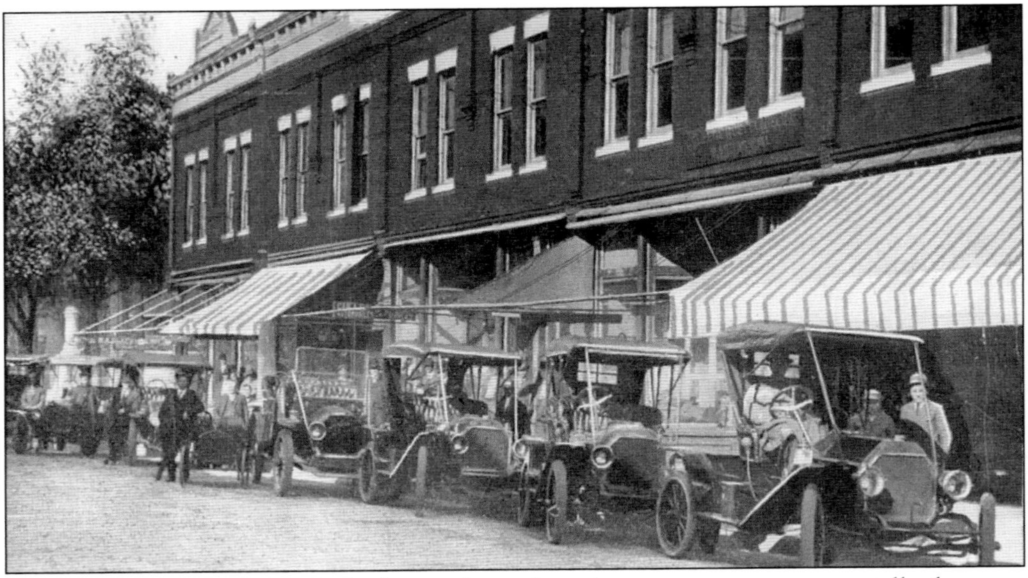

BULL BLOCK, 1910. In 1910 the quality of roads was very poor, especially between towns. Because automobiles were now being used more, a group of concerned local car owners gathered together to form the Orangeburg Auto Club. The mission of the group was to seek improvement of roads in the county between towns so cars would not bounce around or get stuck in potholes and low muddy areas. (Courtesy Orangeburg County Historical Society.)

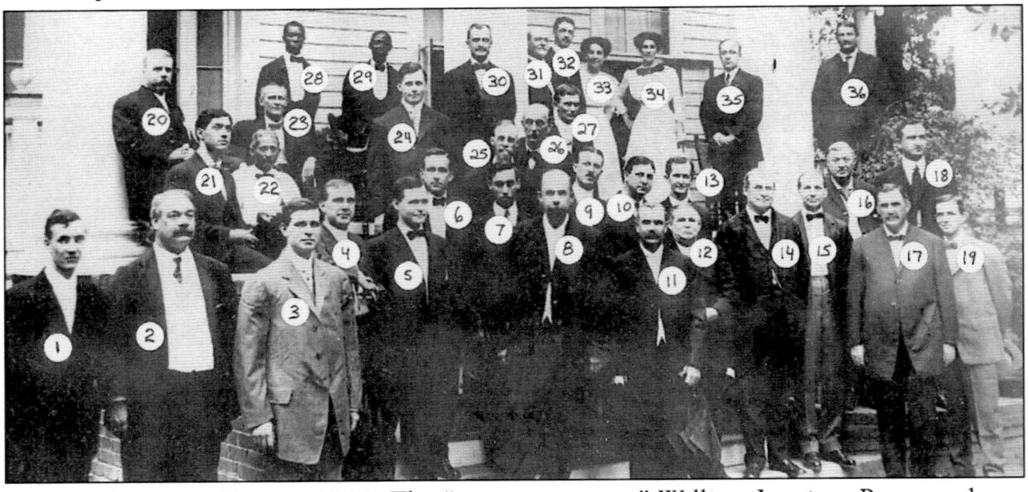

WILLIAM JENNINGS BRYAN, 1911. The "great commoner," William Jennings Bryan, a three-time presidential candidate, came to Orangeburg to speak to the local bar association. While in town, he was the guest of his friend, Thomas F. Brantley, a prominent local attorney. Pictured and identified by number are 1) C.C. Berry, 2) Dr. L.K. Sturkie, 3) J.A. Berry, 4) M.E. Zeigler, 5) James M. Brailsford, 6) John Henry Hydrick, 7) Simon Rich, 8) William L. Glaze, 9) Atticus H. Marchant, 10) Fred Wannamaker, 11) A.W. Summers (with umbrella), 12) James L. Sims, 13) B. Hart Moss, 14) William Jennings Bryan, 15) Thomas F. Brantley, 16) J.W.H. Dukes II, 17) I.W. Bowman, 18) A.J. Hydrick, 19) Adam Moss, 20) William L. Izlar, 21) Leroy Dukes, 22) H.O. Dawson, 23) C.P. Brunson, 24) John S. Bowman, 25) Andrew C. Dibble, 26) Abiel Lathrop, 27) S.B. Martin, 28) unidentified, 29) unidentified, 30) Thomas M. Raysor, 31) unidentified, 32) J. Stokes Salley, 33) Mrs. Lucile Paulling, 34) Mrs. Thomas F. Brantley, 35) W.L. Moseley, and 36) F.J.D. Felder. (Courtesy Orangeburg County Historical Society.)

Downtown Fire, c. 1910s. Smoke can be seen rising downtown from a fire at Slater's Stables in this picture from the 1910s. The stables were in a building that had its entrance on St. John Street, about where the back part of Palmetto Office Supply is located today. (Courtesy Orangeburg County Historical Society.)

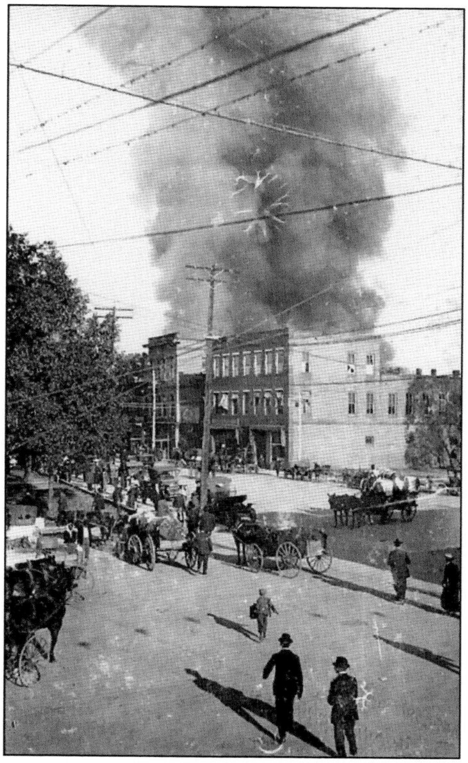

New Downtown Post Office, 1912. The new post office for Orangeburg on Courthouse Square is shown nearing completion in 1912. After being occupied on January 1, 1913, it served our city until a larger location was needed in the 1960s. (Courtesy Orangeburg County Historical Society.)

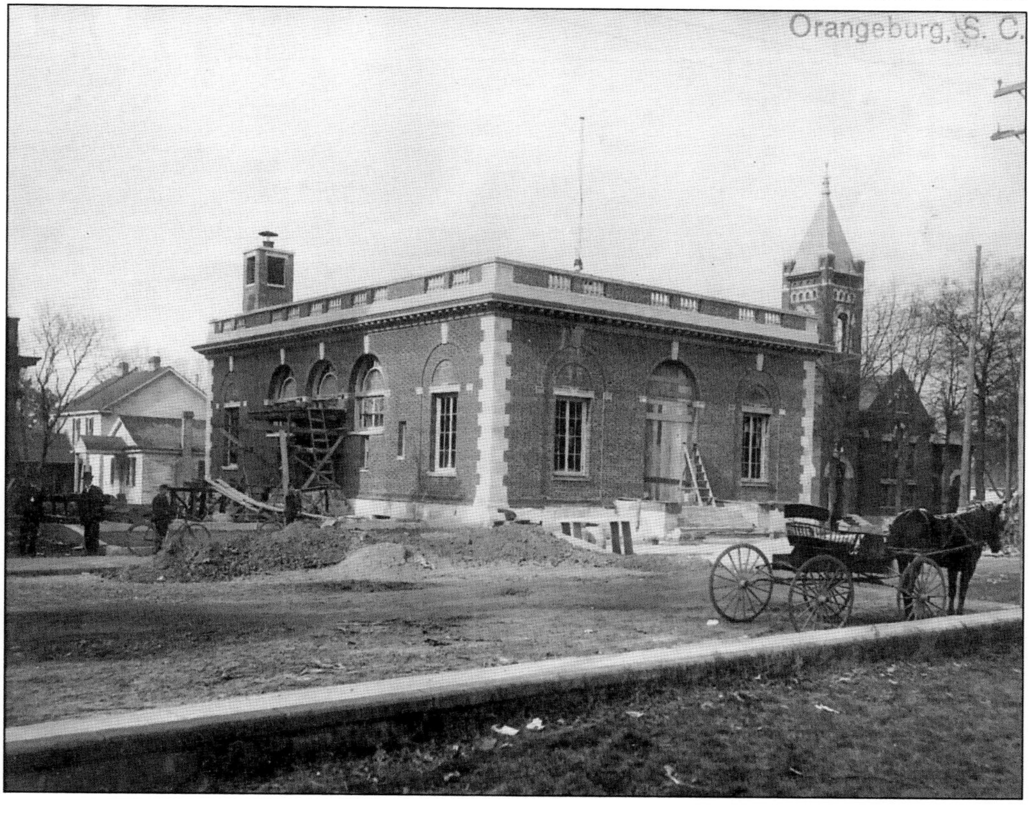

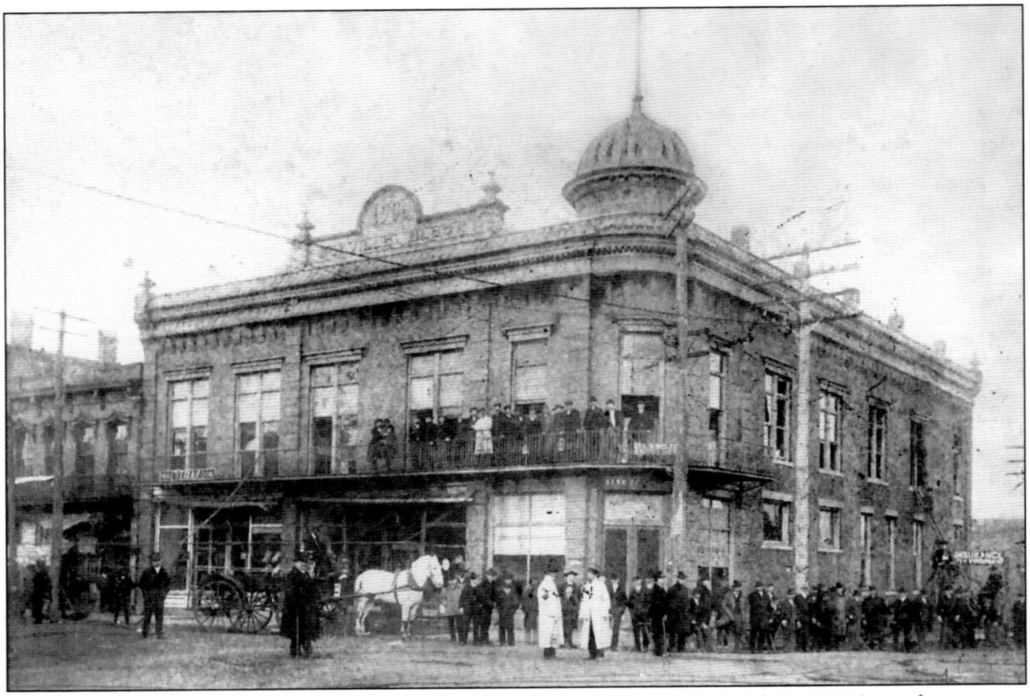

Scoville Building, 1916. The Scoville Building was constructed in 1906 at the corner of Russell and Middleton Streets. The ladder on the right side was used in extinguishing a fire here in 1916. The volunteer fire department's horse-drawn steam pumper is in the foreground. Today the beautifully landscaped Downtown Orangeburg Revitalization Association's (DORA) park occupies the location of this grand old building. (Courtesy Orangeburg County Historical Society.)

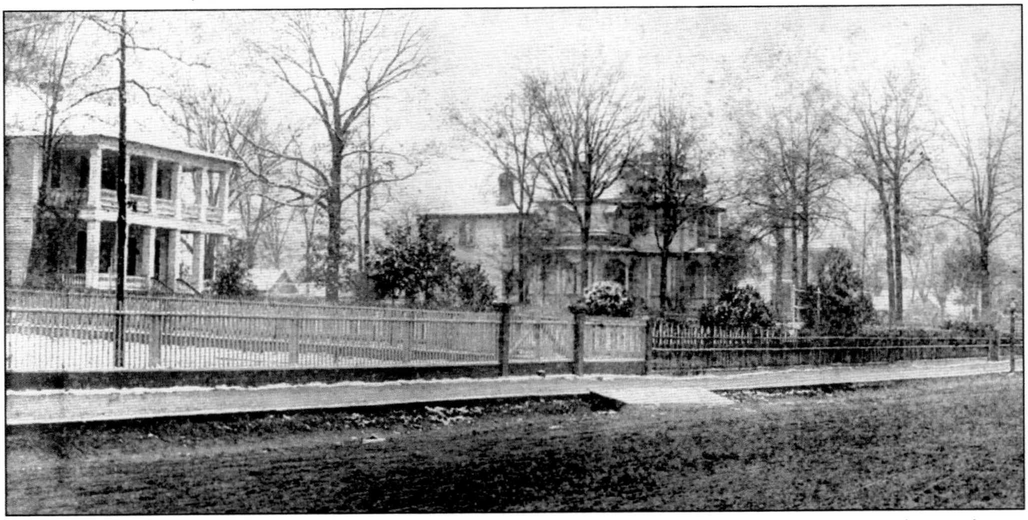

Berry and Dibble Homes, Early 1900s. Two notable downtown residences are shown here: the Berry home on the left and the Samuel Dibble home on the right. The Berry family home was run as a guest home for transient tourists for many years before the popularity of hotels and motels emerged. Today the popular Orangeburg fast food restaurant the Dairy-O is located there. The Dibble home area is now occupied by the recently vacated Winn-Dixie grocery store. (Courtesy Orangeburg County Historical Society.)

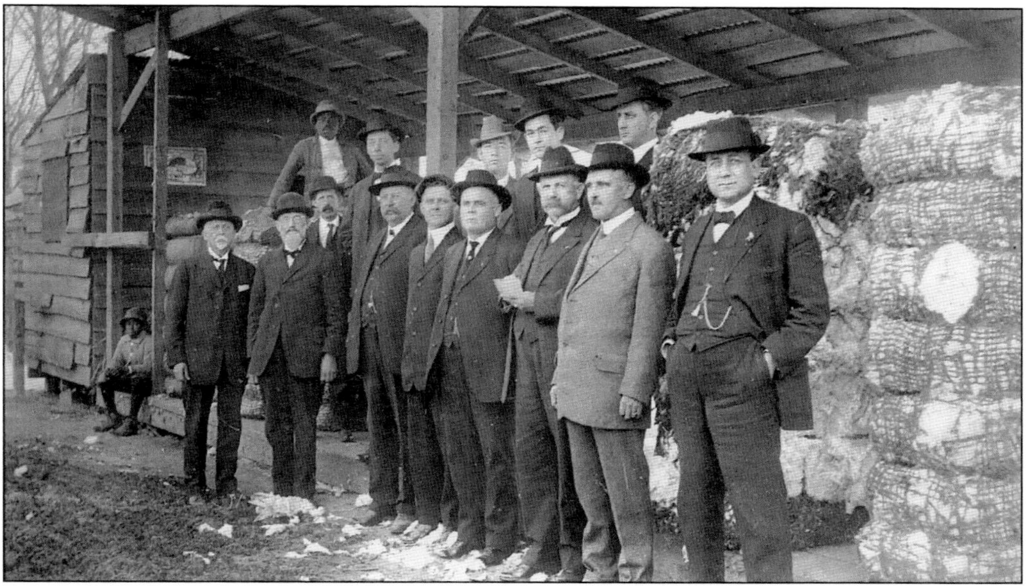

COTTON BROKERS, 1914. In this era the entire economy of the area was driven by the success, or lack thereof, of the cotton crop. Some of Orangeburg's leading cotton brokers, as well as prominent citizens, are shown in this 1914 scene at the cotton sales platform located behind the county jail (later known as the "Pink Palace"). They are, from left to right, (front row) John F. Mewborne, George H. Cornelson, Julius Ahrens, Albert C. Watson, J.H. Exum, W.G. Smith, John Cart, and W.W. Wannamaker; (middle row) Milton K. Jeffords, W. Eugene Atkinson, James M. Albergotti, George M. Seignious, and R.S. Stewart; (back row) Arthur Scott, employee. (Courtesy John F. Shuler.)

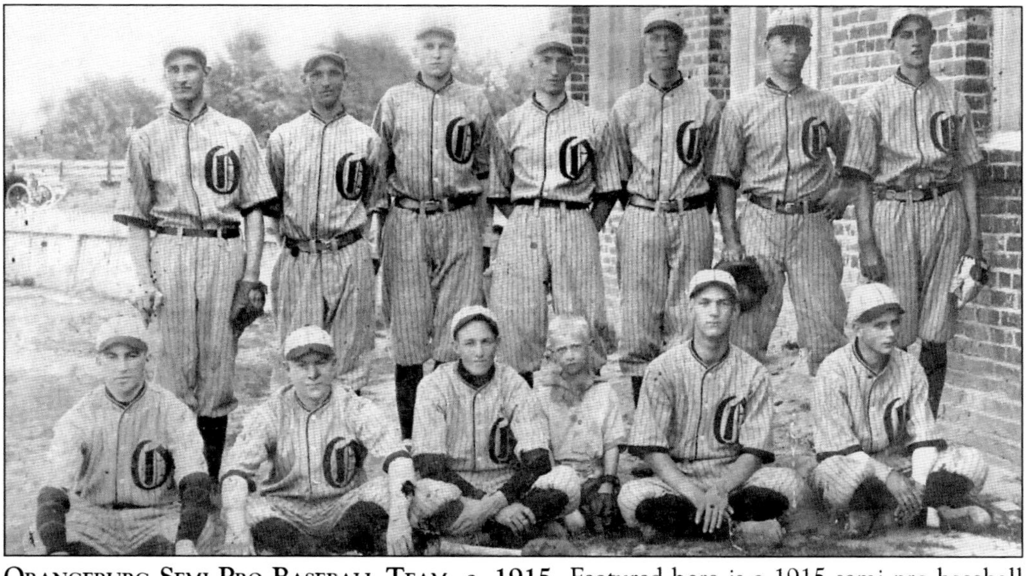

ORANGEBURG SEMI-PRO BASEBALL TEAM, c. 1915. Featured here is a 1915 semi-pro baseball team representing Orangeburg that played teams from other towns and cities. They are, from left to right, (front row) Bernardo Seignious, Doc Jeffords, Wesley Farnum, Wallace Jeffords (mascot), Ingram Lowman, and Johnnie Scoville; (back row) Roger Fairey, Oliver Farnum, Lawrence Thackston, Oscar Lowman, Joe Brunson, William Glaze, and Hyde Smith. (Courtesy Orangeburg County Historical Society.)

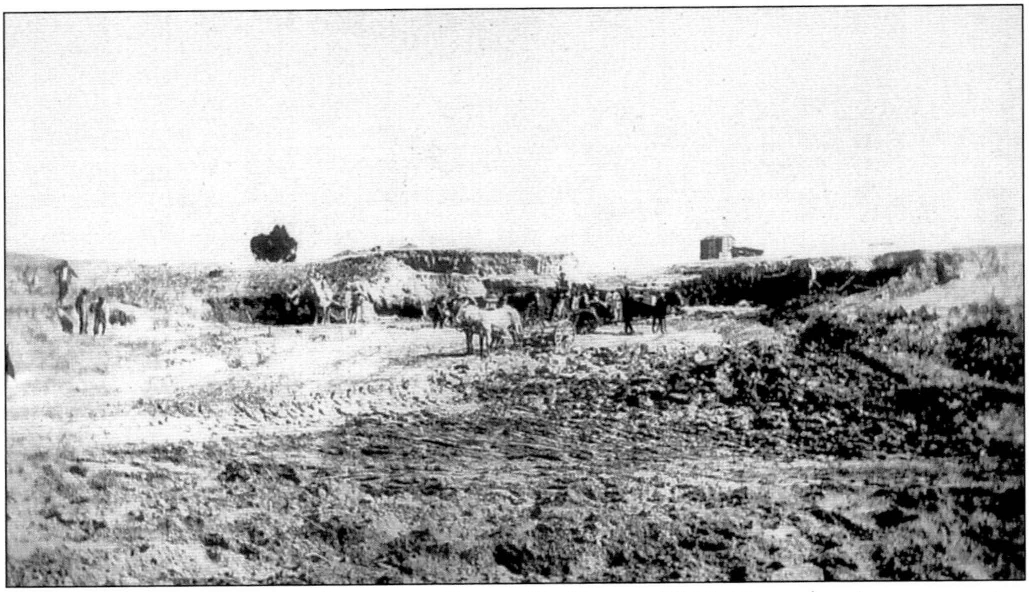

New Orangeburg Electric Light and Power Co. Plant, 1916. Orangeburg's new emerging need of electricity forced the construction of a larger power plant in 1916 to provide more of this popular new technology. The site was prepared by using dynamite under the supervision of Russell Wolfe to blast away stumps and part of the hill for this new facility by the Edisto River. The plant was located next to today's water plant where a holding reservoir now stands. (Courtesy Russell Wolfe family.)

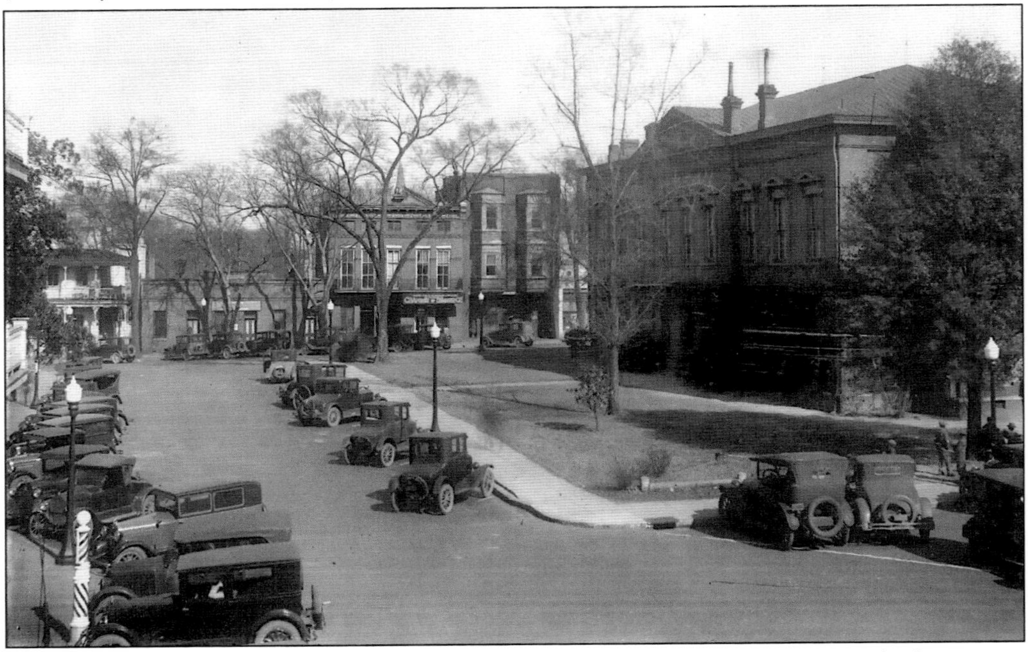

Courthouse Square, c. 1928. This view shows the Courthouse Square looking east. Middleton Street runs from left to right just below the lower border of this photograph. Two-way automobile traffic went around the square back then. The Chamber of Commerce building is seen in the center background and the courthouse is on the right. (Courtesy Dr. Clemmie Webber.)

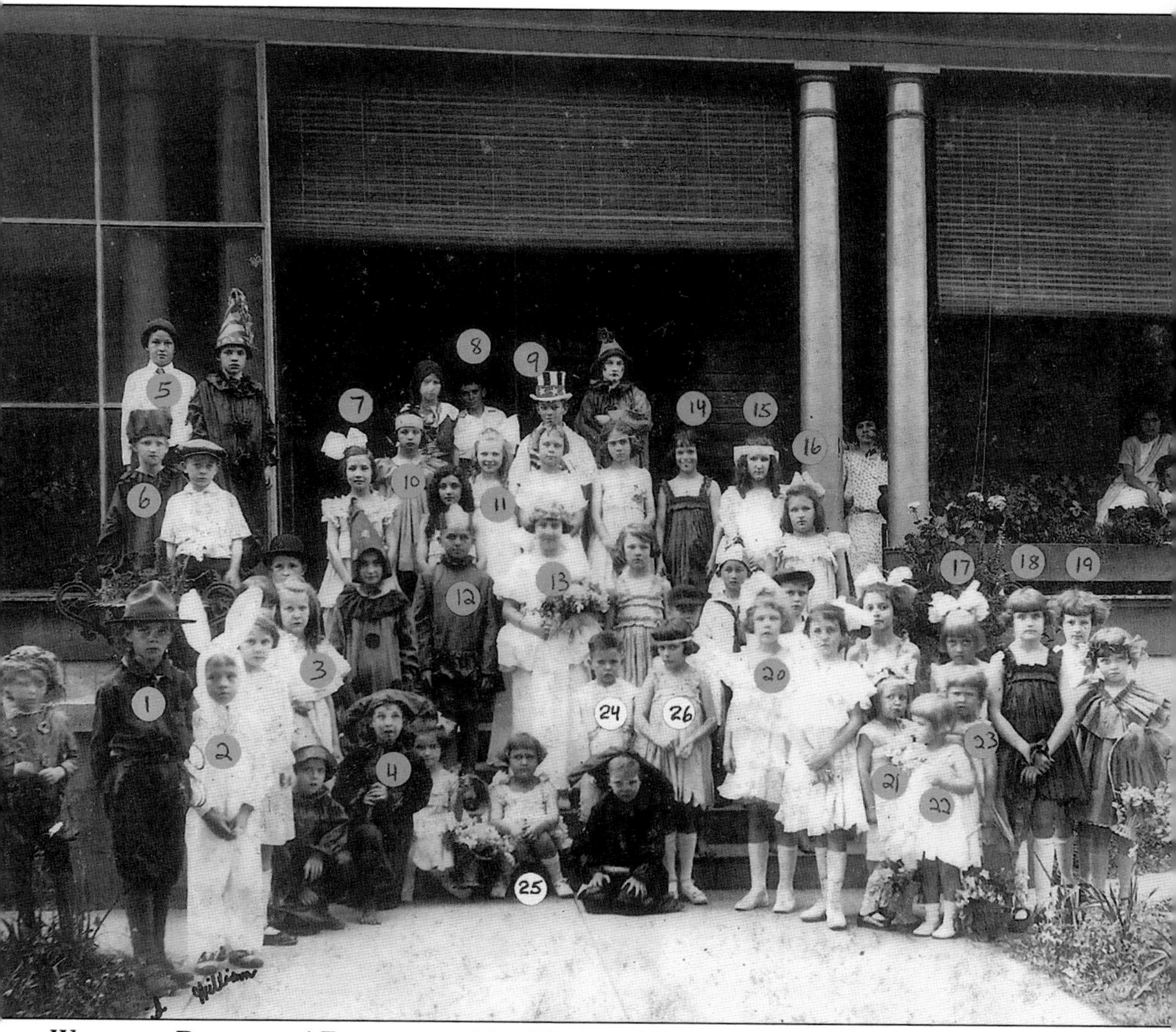

WINTHROP DAUGHTERS' FESTIVAL, c.1921. The Winthrop Daughters' Festival was an annual event in town for children, who would dress up in costume for the festive occasion. Pictured and identified by number are 1) David Atkinson, 2) Bill Atkinson, 3) Sybil Houck Riley, 4) Ed Mann, 5) Robert Owens, 6) Harry Dawson, 7) Louise Hill, 8) Lester Finkelstein, 9) Wilkes Atkinson, 10) Virginia Salley, 11) Love Bregeau?, 12) Jimmy Brailsford, king, 13) Rose Henri Kahnweiler, queen, 14) Elizabeth Limehouse, 15) Agnes Moss, 16) Margaret Arant, 17) Mary Schiffley Fairey, 18) Angie Ray Bryant Wannamaker, 19) Marie Bryant, 20) Ruth Sprinkle, 21) Elizabeth Schiffley, 22) Betty Richardson McCants, 23) Eleanora Richardson, 24) Sumter Williams, 25) Lucia Wannamaker, and 26) Mamie Bryant Walter Terry. (Courtesy Gene Atkinson.)

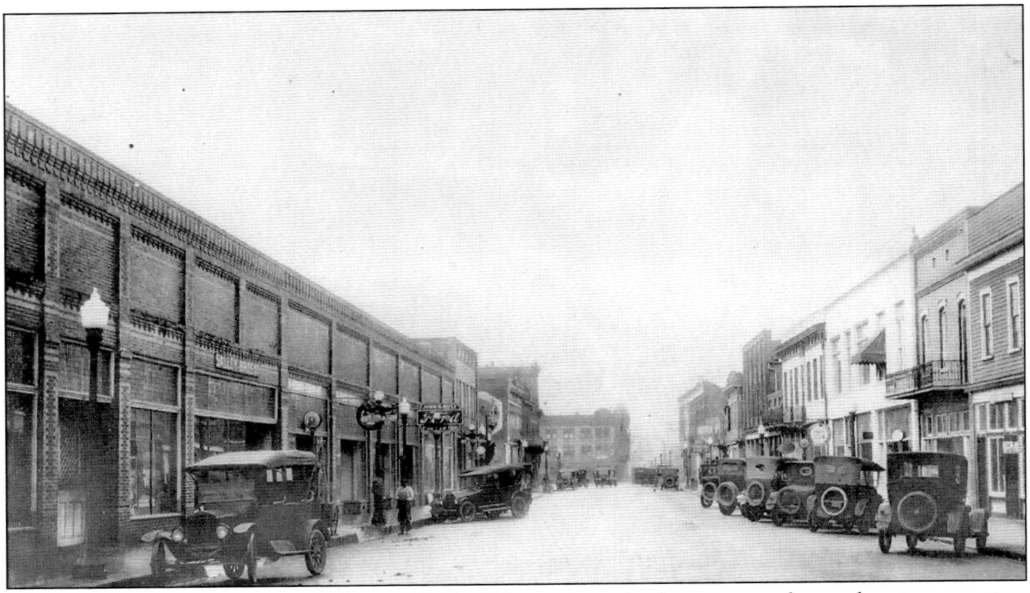

Russell Street Looking West, 1922. This view, looking west from the intersection of Russell and Doyle Streets, shows part of the downtown business district. The new novalux ornamental street lights had just been installed by the forerunner of today's Department of Public Utilities. Note the angle parking in that era downtown. (Courtesy Department of Public Utilities.)

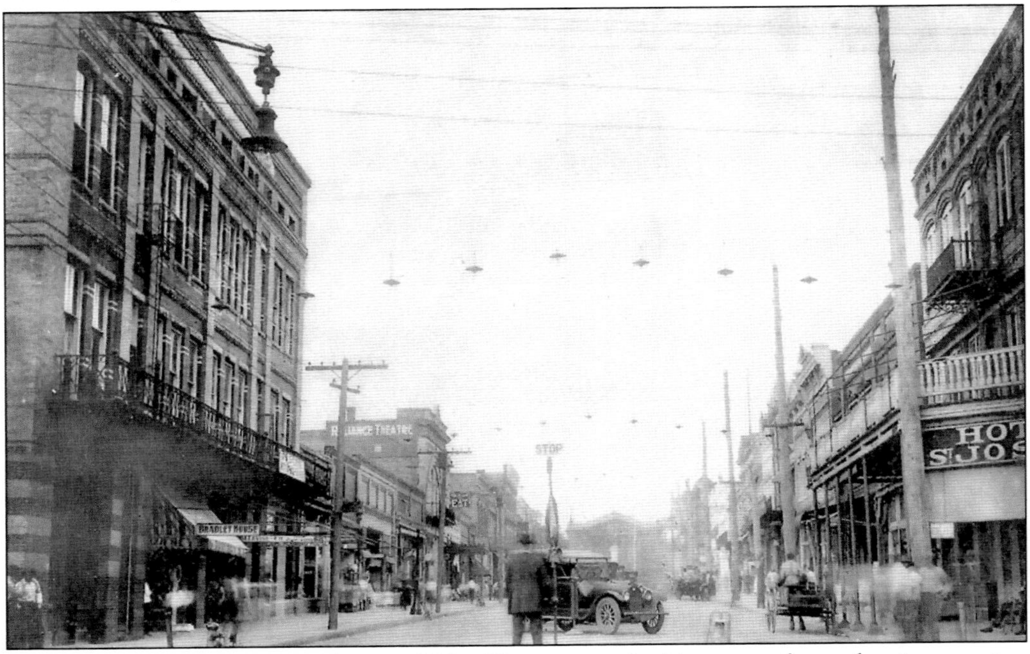

Russell Street Looking East, 1922. This scene, looking east from the intersection of Russell and Broughton Streets, shows an unusual middle-of-the-street parking pattern. Policemen were stationed as above to manually turn stop signs before the advent of stoplights. Note the Bradley Boarding House on the left. It operated out of the Riggs' house later on the northwest corner of Broughton and Russell Streets. (Courtesy of Department of Public Utilities.)

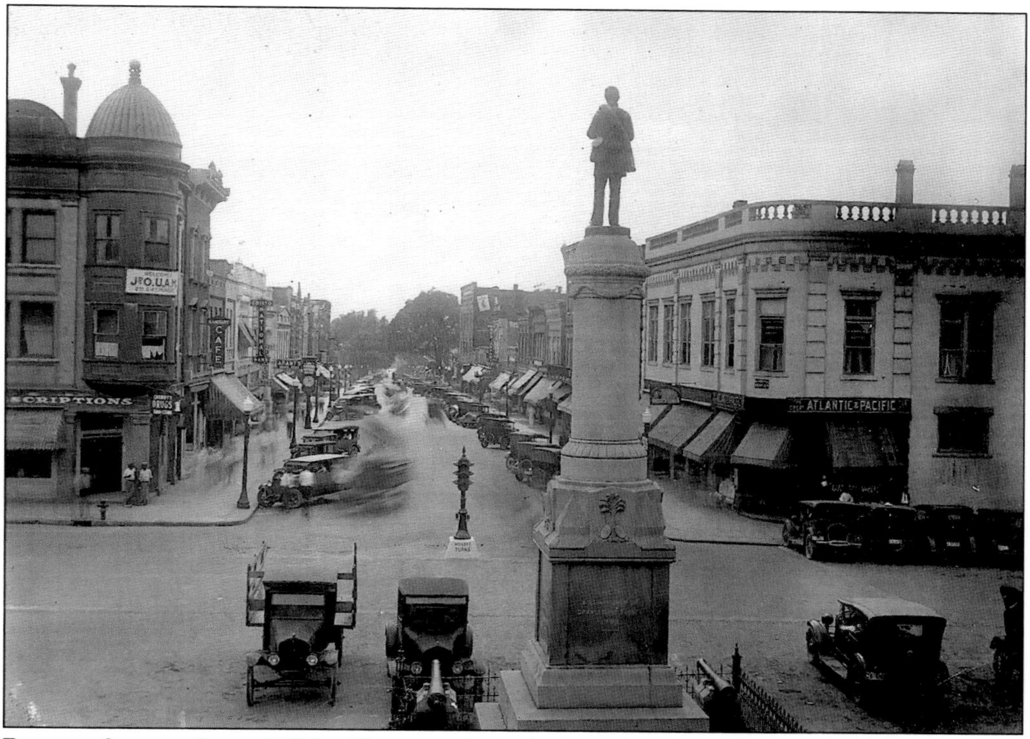

Russell Street, Late 1920s. This view from the courthouse on the square looking west on Russell Street shows the newly installed traffic stoplight in the middle of the intersection to help the orderly flow of vehicles through downtown. (Courtesy Cleveland Dempsey.)

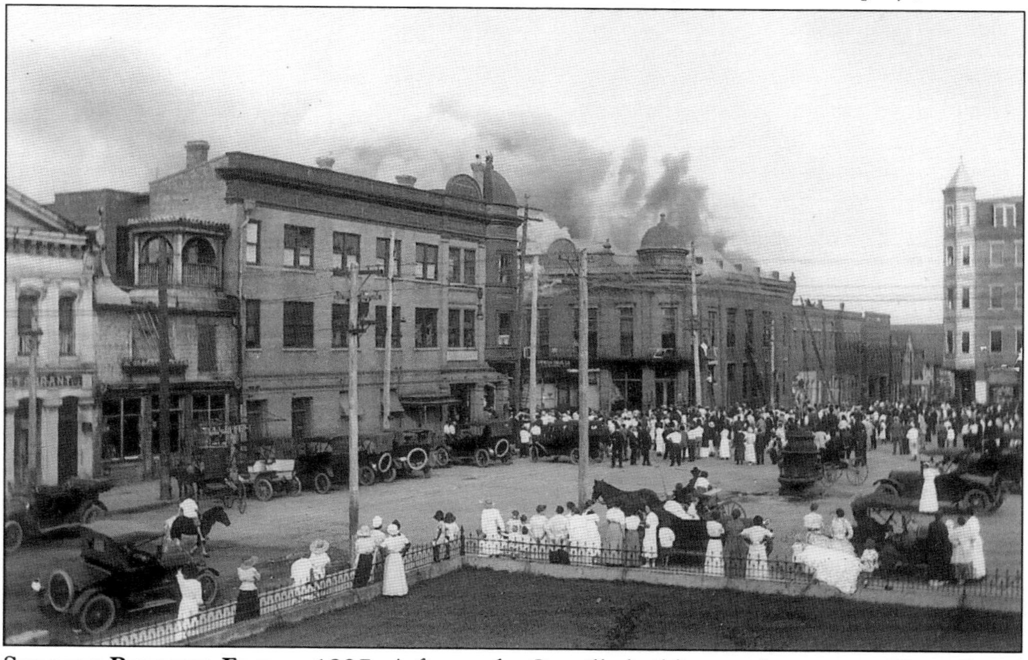

Scoville Building Fire, c. 1927. A fire at the Scoville building at the corner of Russell and Middleton Streets caused major damage, as shown in this c. 1927 photograph. A mixture of horses and buggies and automobiles was still prevalent in this era. (Courtesy E.J. Lackey.)

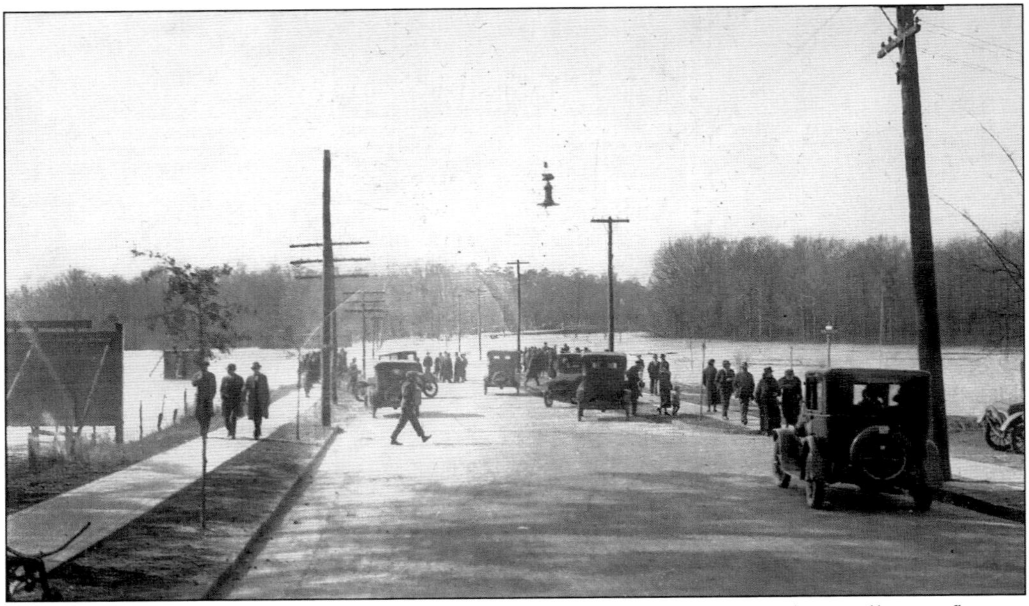

Edisto River Flood, 1928. Significant rain caused the Edisto River to drastically overflow its banks in 1928. The flood waters came all the way up to the intersection of Russell and Riverside Streets causing Edisto Gardens and the city playground, where today's rose garden is located, to be covered completely with water. (Courtesy Orangeburg County Historical Society.)

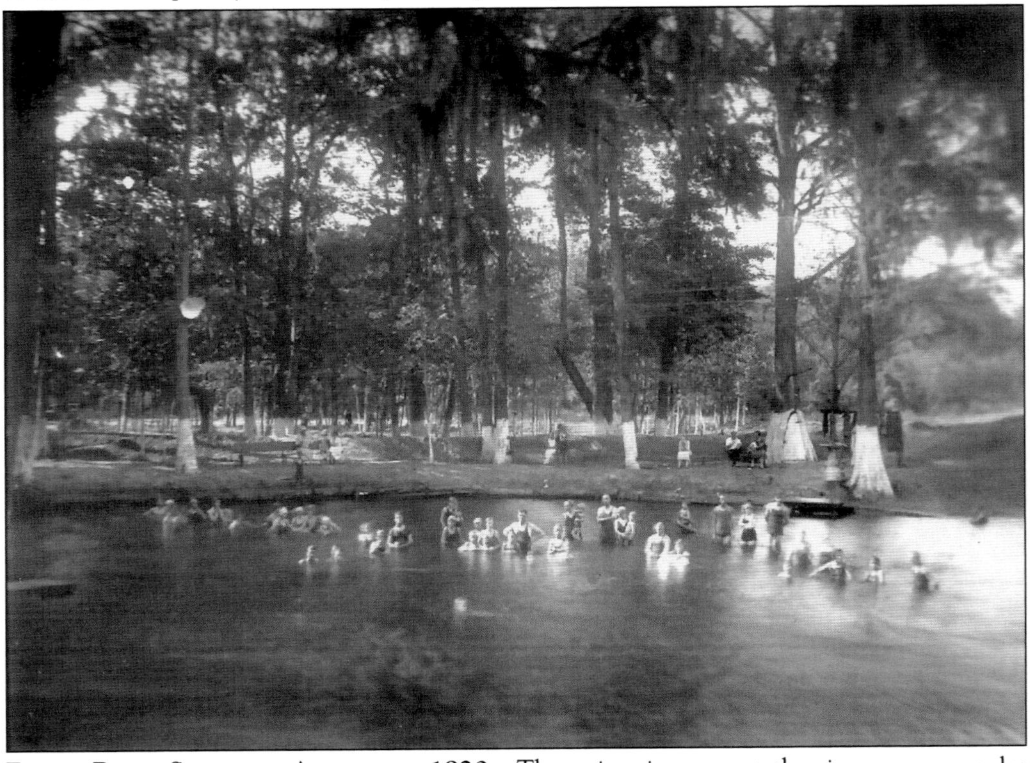

Edisto River Swimming Area, late 1920s. The swimming area at the river was a popular retreat from the heat of the summers in Orangeburg. Note the whitewashed trees, a practice many considered then to ward off insects causing tree damage. (Courtesy Taylor Garick.)

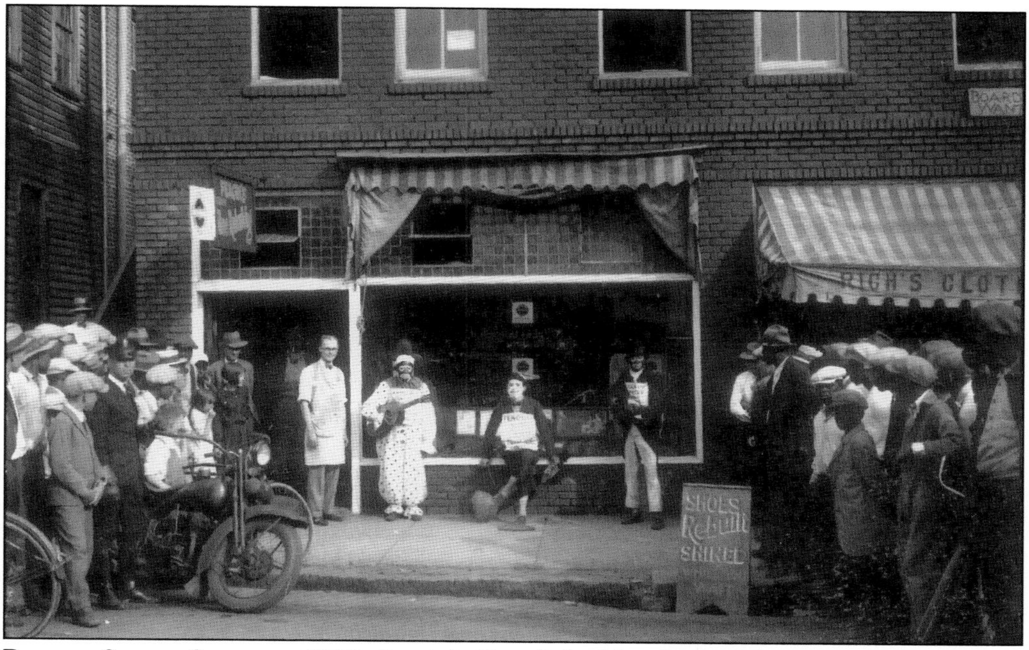

RUSSELL STREET SCENE, c. 1928. Feagin's Shoe Rebuilding had a "clown minstrel" show out front to attract business. William C. Feagin, the proprietor, is shown in front of the doorway. Lipman Rich's clothing store is on the right, while a sign upstairs indicates boarders were being sought to rent the rooms there. Today this very same building houses the Travel Center. (Courtesy Dr. Clemmie Webber.)

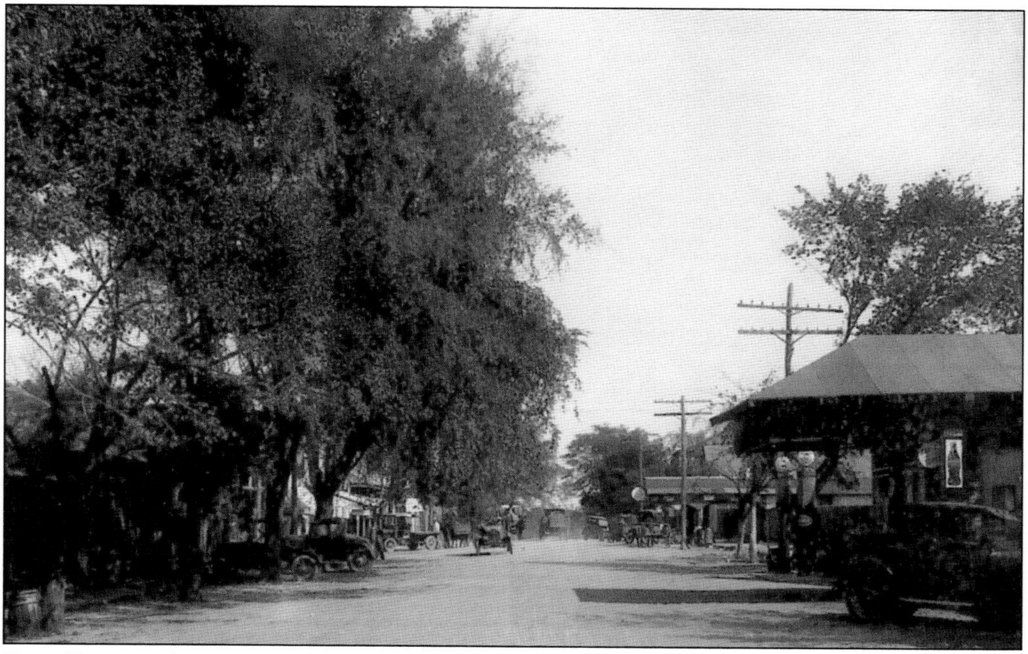

EAST RUSSELL STREET, c. 1929. Looking east on Russell Street shows Amaker's store on the right. Just beyond it was Ulmer's store, then the Five Chop Road (Highway 301), and then the store that would later become Wactor's store. Residential homes comprise all the buildings on the left side of the street. (Courtesy Dr. Clemmie Webber.)

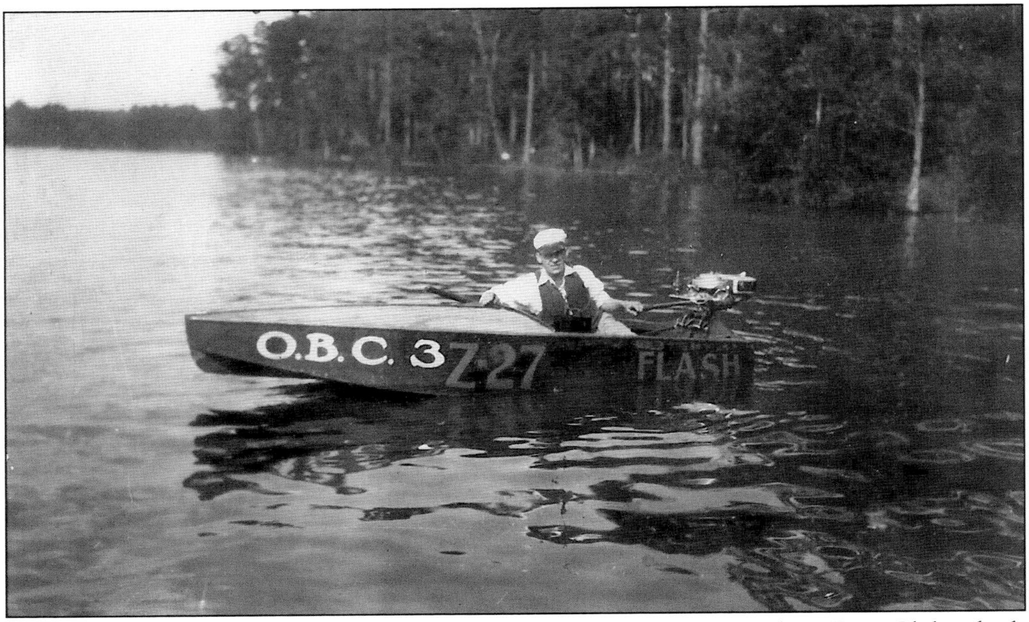

BOAT RACES, 1929. In 1928 a group of local men founded the Orangeburg Boat Club, which conducted boat races among its members in the newfound sport of motorboat racing. The first races were held at the swimming area on the Edisto River. By 1929 the club needed a larger area for these races and moved to Clear Pond between Bamberg and Ehrhardt. Shown here is Rudolph Culler, one of the founding members, in his racing boat at Clear Pond. (Courtesy Taylor Garick.)

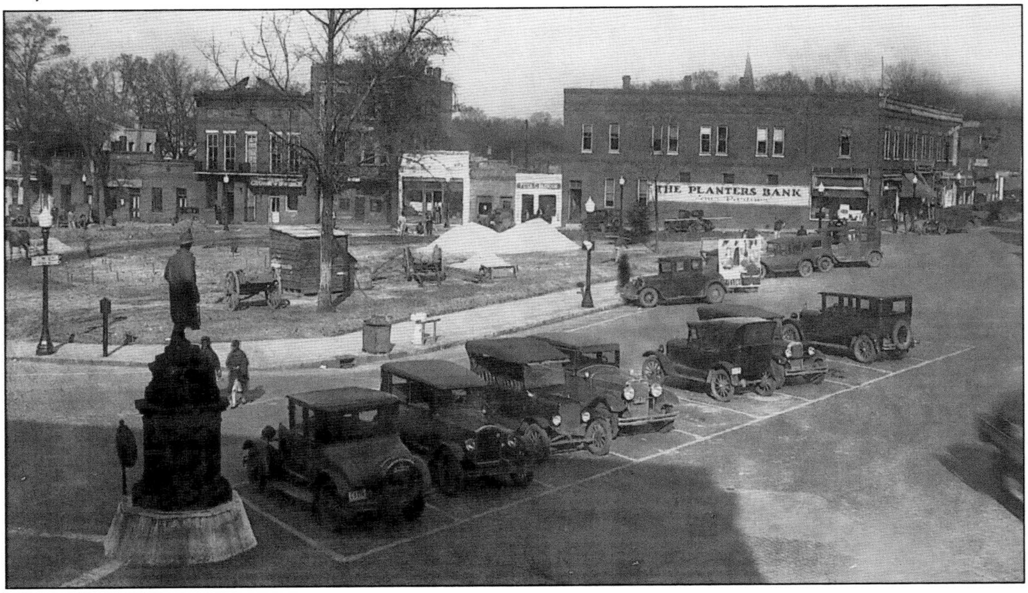

MEMORIAL PLAZA UNDER CONSTRUCTION, 1928–1929. For many years the Orangeburg County Courthouse occupied the square in downtown Orangeburg. In 1928 it relocated two blocks away, and the city of Orangeburg purchased this site for $35,000 to construct a downtown square. The old courthouse was razed and a fountain with scantily clad women, along with two goldfish pools on either side, was purchased to be placed in the middle of the square. Here is this new project under construction. (Courtesy Russell Wolfe family.)

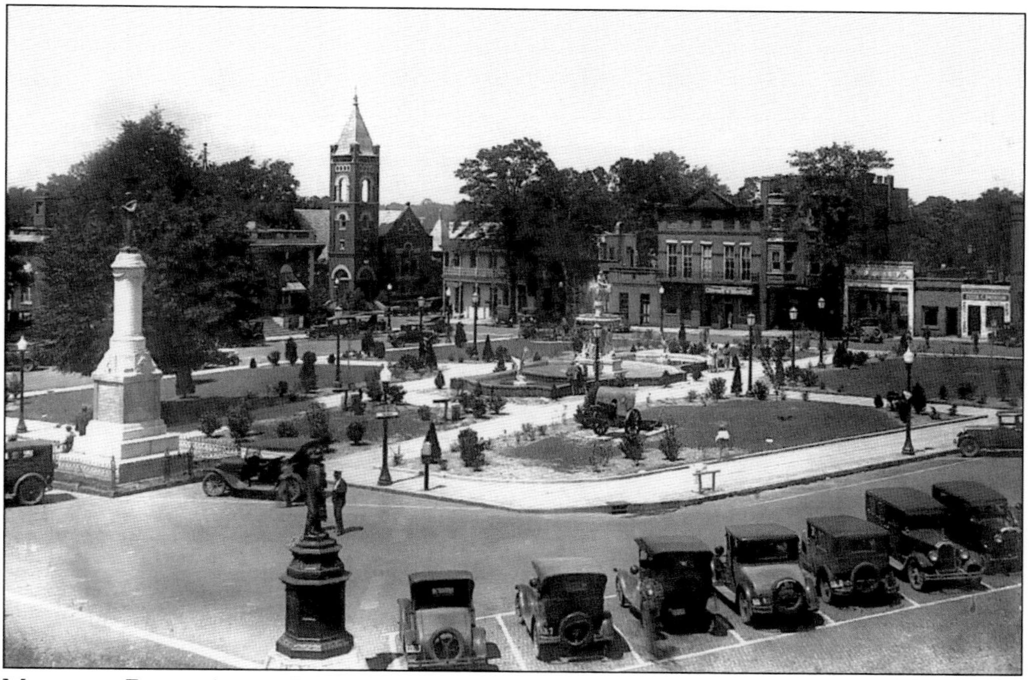

MEMORIAL PLAZA AFTER CONSTRUCTION, 1930. The town square began to take shape after much construction. The newly installed "ladies statue" had two adjacent pools where water would squirt upwards out of the mouths of two ornamental swans. By this time the streets had been paved with bricks around the center of town. (Courtesy Russell Wolfe family.)

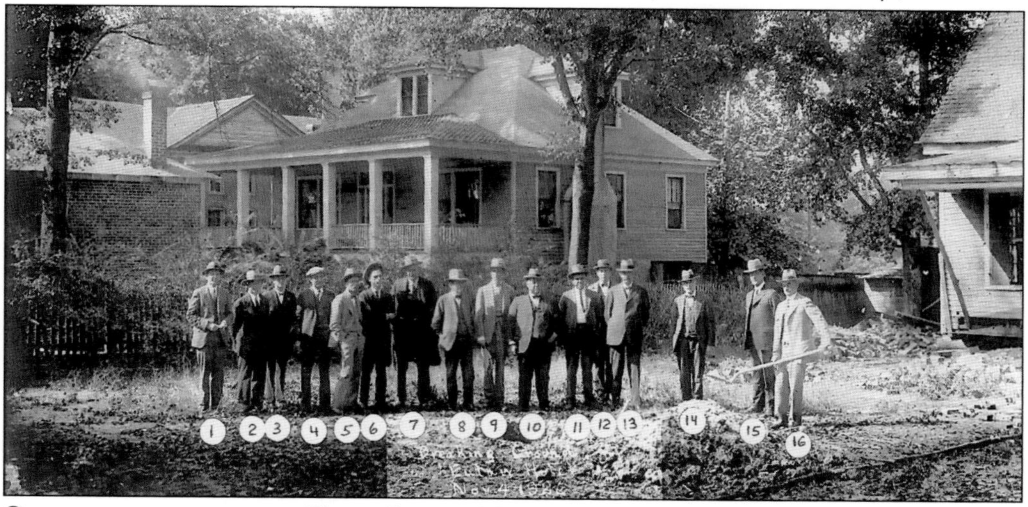

GROUNDBREAKING FOR THE HOTEL EUTAW, NOVEMBER 1926. The whole town came together buying shares to finance the new modern downtown hotel to be called the Eutaw Hotel in 1926. Shown above are some of the committee members for the groundbreaking at the corner of Russell and Centre Streets. They are, from left to right and also identified by number, as follows: 1) unidentified, 2) unidentified, 3) unidentified, 4) Cliff Berry, 5) Laurie S. Wolfe, 6) Herbert Pearce, 7) T. Elliott Salley, 8) Fred A. Adden, 9) Harry Wannamaker Jr., 10) J. Leroy Dukes, 11) unidentified, 12) unidentified, 13) Mayor Robert H. Jennings Sr., 14) Robert Lide, 15) John M. Sifly, city council, 16) Dr. George Walter, chairman of the Hotel Eutaw Committee. (Courtesy West Summers.)

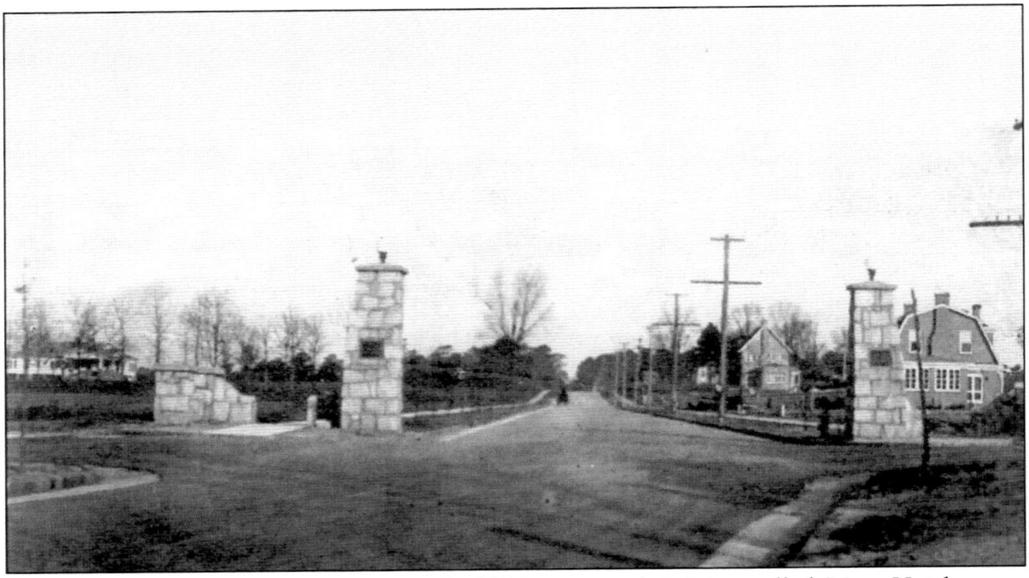

Entrance to Moss Heights, 1926. In 1922 a new subdivision called Moss Heights was opened up by Carroll and West Summers Sr. on the old Moss family farm. This view from the intersection of Broughton and Park Streets shows Rut Osborne's new home on the far right and Eddie Mirmow's home just beyond that. (Courtesy Harry Wannamaker III.)

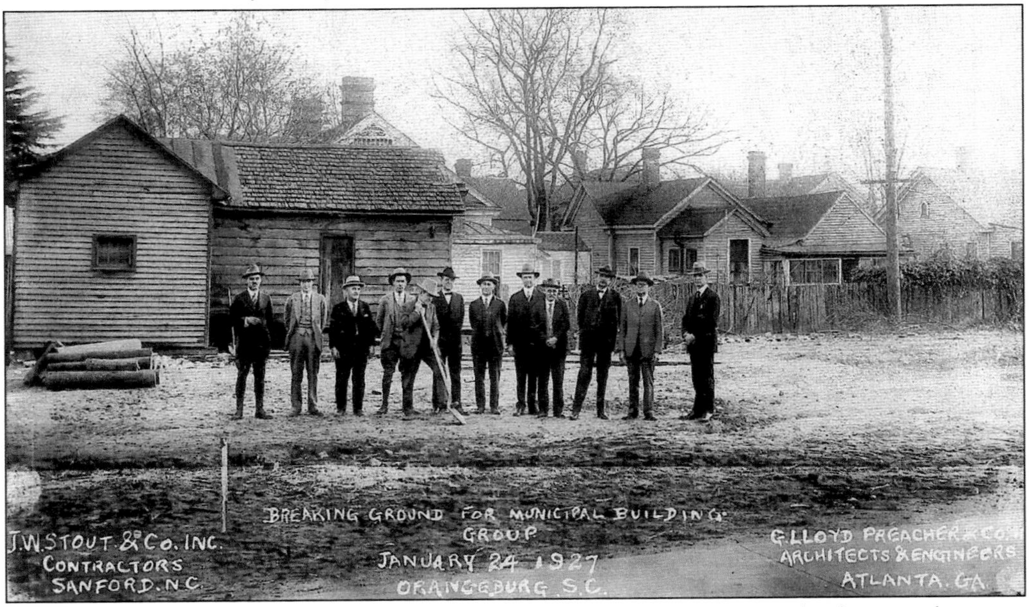

Municipal Group Buildings Groundbreaking, January 1927. City leaders are shown in this groundbreaking ceremony for the new city hall and auditorium, fire station, and city jail. The view is taken from the site of the city hall facing south. The men are standing on what is now the parking lot with the new fire station to be constructed a few feet behind them. The houses behind them are the back sides of the homes on Hampton Street, now Fischer Street. Pictured, from left to right, are unidentified; J. West Summers Sr.; Ed Hawes, city engineer; unidentified; Fred A. Adden; Adam Moss; John Pearson, DPU manager; unidentified; Sen. Robert Lide; Mayor Robert H. Jennings Sr.; councilman Albert C. Watson; and councilman John M. Sifly. (Courtesy Margaret Moss Watson Lundgren.)

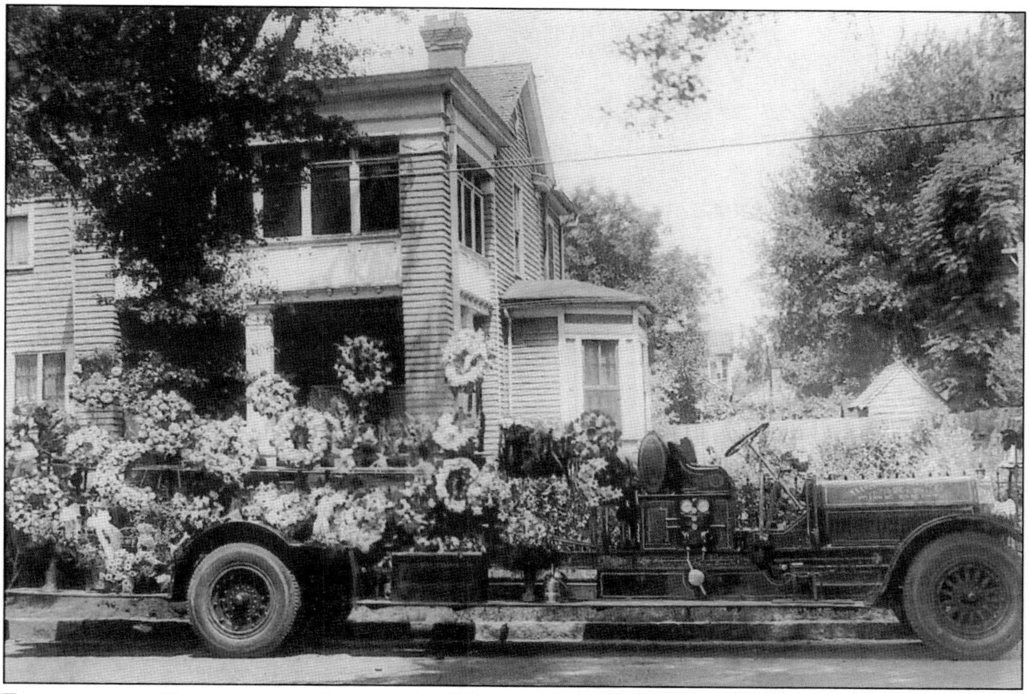

Funeral for Councilman Albert C. Watson, 1928. Popular city councilman Albert C. Watson's responsibilities included overseeing the city's fire department operations. At his death the funeral procession was led by the hook and ladder truck adorned with many floral offerings. The Watson house in the background was located on Calhoun Street, now John C. Calhoun Drive, next to the northeast corner of Calhoun and Broughton Streets. (Courtesy Margaret Moss Watson Lundgren.)

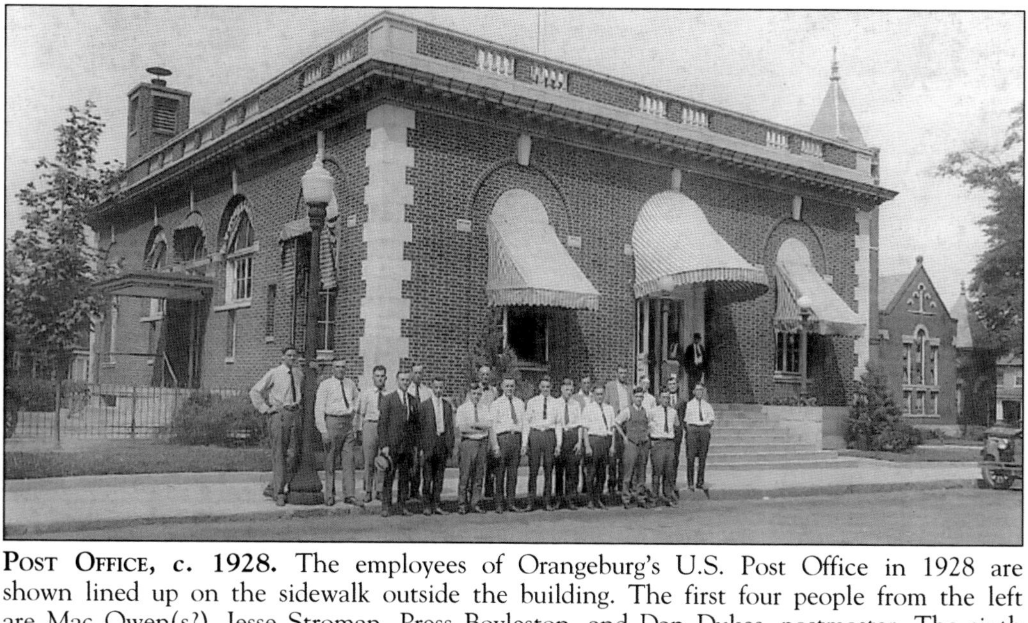

Post Office, c. 1928. The employees of Orangeburg's U.S. Post Office in 1928 are shown lined up on the sidewalk outside the building. The first four people from the left are Mac Owen(s?), Jesse Stroman, Press Boyleston, and Dan Dukes, postmaster. The sixth person is Clarence Wertz, and the person on the far right is Marvin Baldwin. (Courtesy Richard Stroman.)

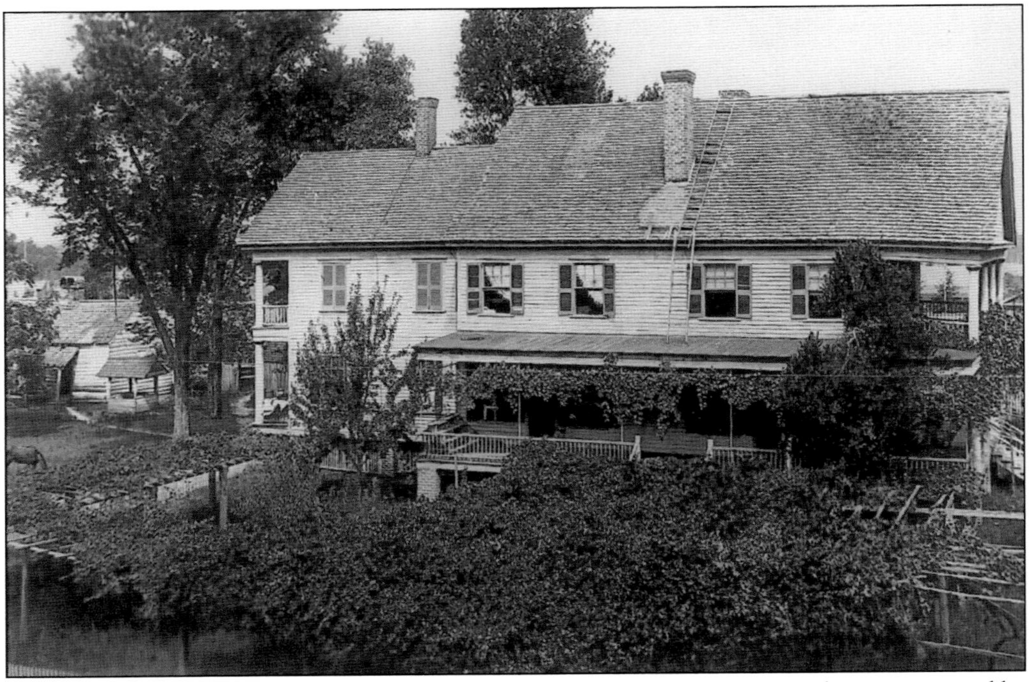

Riggs House, c. 1920s. Mr. Merritt Riggs built this home around 1840, and it was acquired by his brother Harpin Riggs a few years later. Harpin established numerous prosperous enterprises during his lifetime. He doubled the size of the home and lived there for over 50 years. Harpin's son, Walter Riggs, later became president of Clemson College. In the 1930s and 1940s the Riggs House was run by the Bradley family as the "Bradley Boarding House." Located on the northwest corner of Russell and Broughton Streets, it was finally torn down in the 1960s to make way for a new bank building. (Courtesy Orangeburg County Historical Society.)

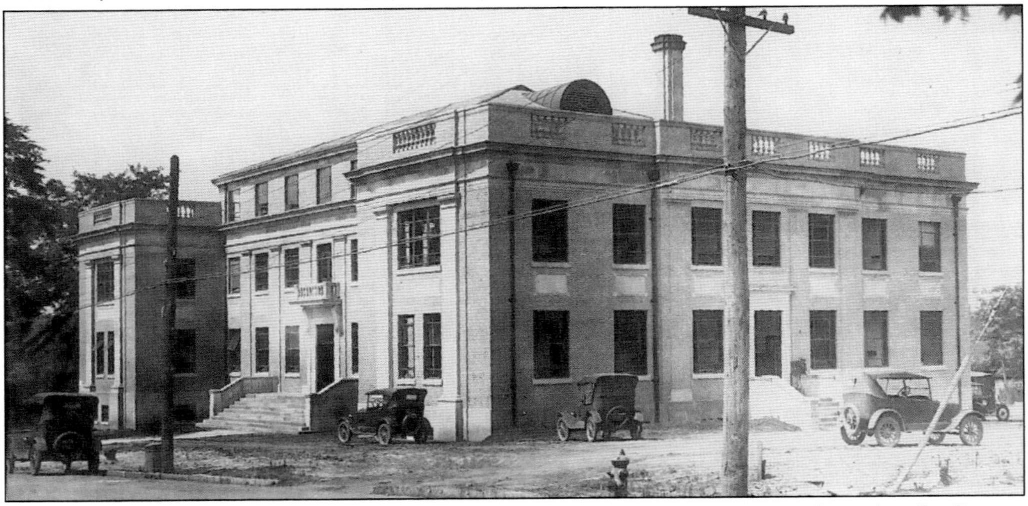

New Courthouse, c. 1928. Orangeburg's fifth courthouse was constructed on Amelia Street, adjacent to St. Paul's Methodist Church in 1927 and 1928. Previously this had been the location of Trinity Methodist Church, which had just moved to a new location on Boulevard across from what is now South Carolina State University. This 1928 picture shows the courthouse just after completion of construction but before any landscaping had been finished. (Courtesy Department of Public Utilities.)

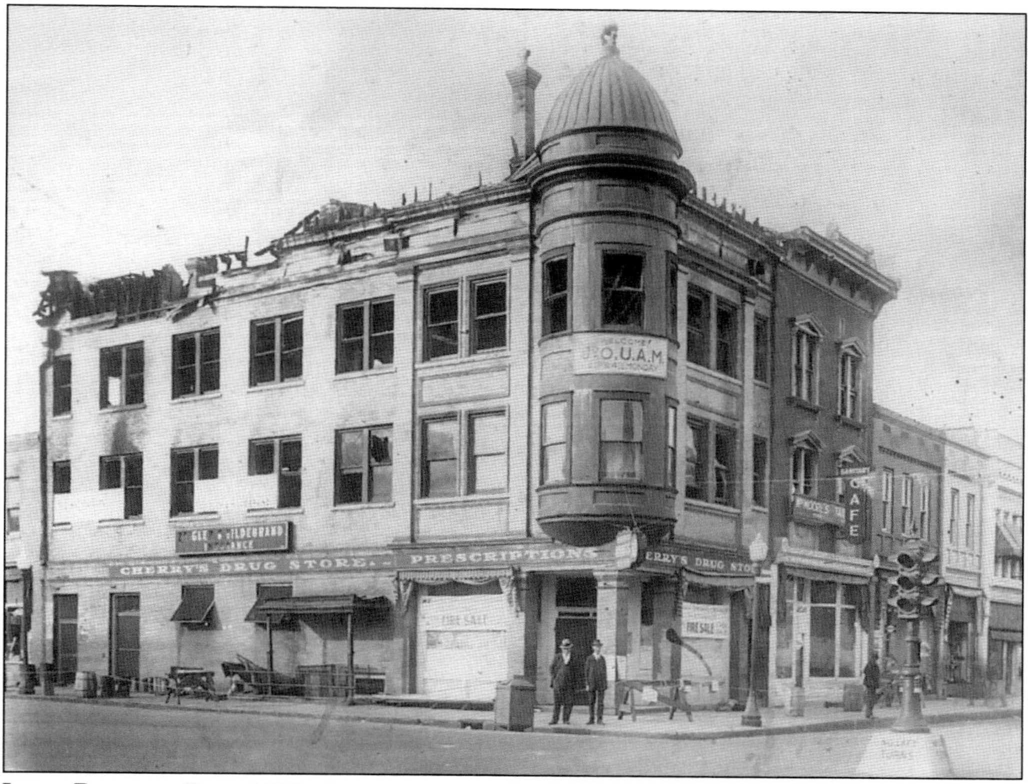

LOUIS BUILDING FIRE, 1927. A significant fire swept through the Louis Building, located at the southwest corner of Russell and Middleton Streets, in 1927. For many years the lower floor was occupied by the following stores, all of which were drugstores: Lowman's Drug Store, then Cherry's Drug Store as seen here, and later Fischer's Rexall Pharmacy. (Courtesy Orangeburg County Historical Society.)

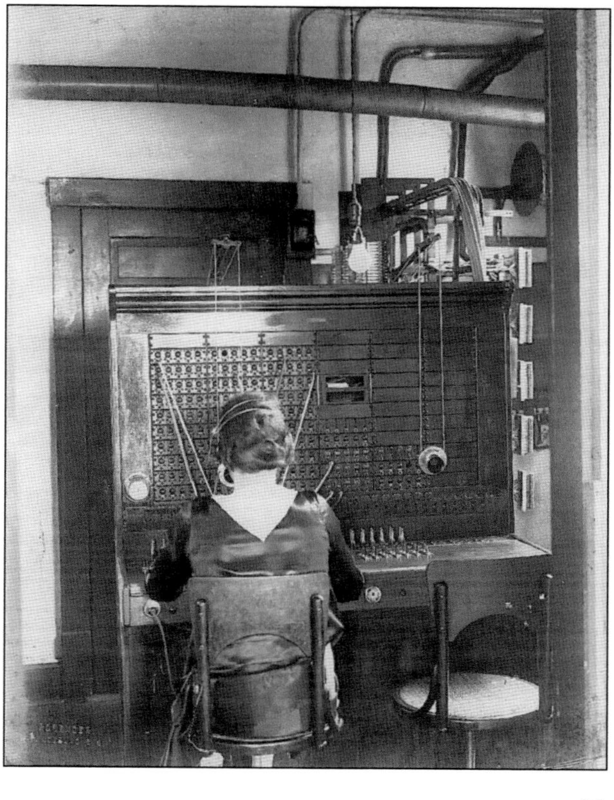

TELEPHONE OPERATOR, 1930S. Telephone communications began to rapidly evolve in the 1900s. Shown above is Mrs. Eva Mackay Ziegler at one of the old "plug-in" switchboards at Orangeburg's "Telephone Central." (Courtesy Russell Wolfe family.)

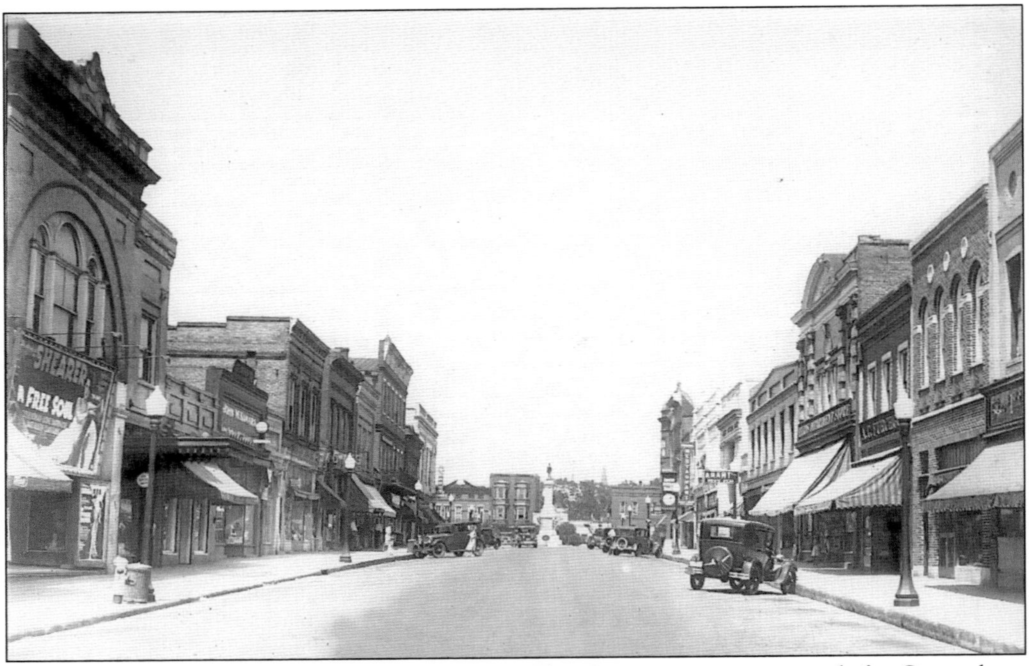

RUSSELL STREET LOOKING EAST, EARLY 1930S. The depression era was tough for Orangeburg and the whole country. This picture was taken during those challenging times. The Reliance Theatre is the building on the far left of this picture. (Courtesy Russell Wolfe family.)

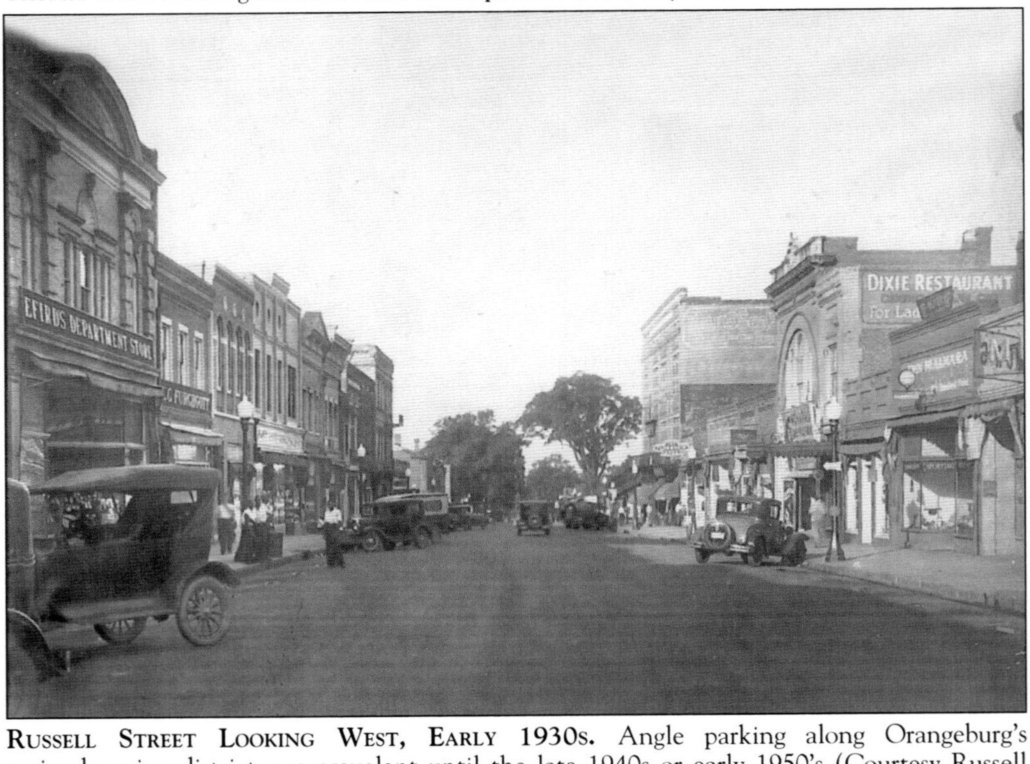

RUSSELL STREET LOOKING WEST, EARLY 1930S. Angle parking along Orangeburg's main shopping district was prevalent until the late 1940s or early 1950's (Courtesy Russell Wolfe family.)

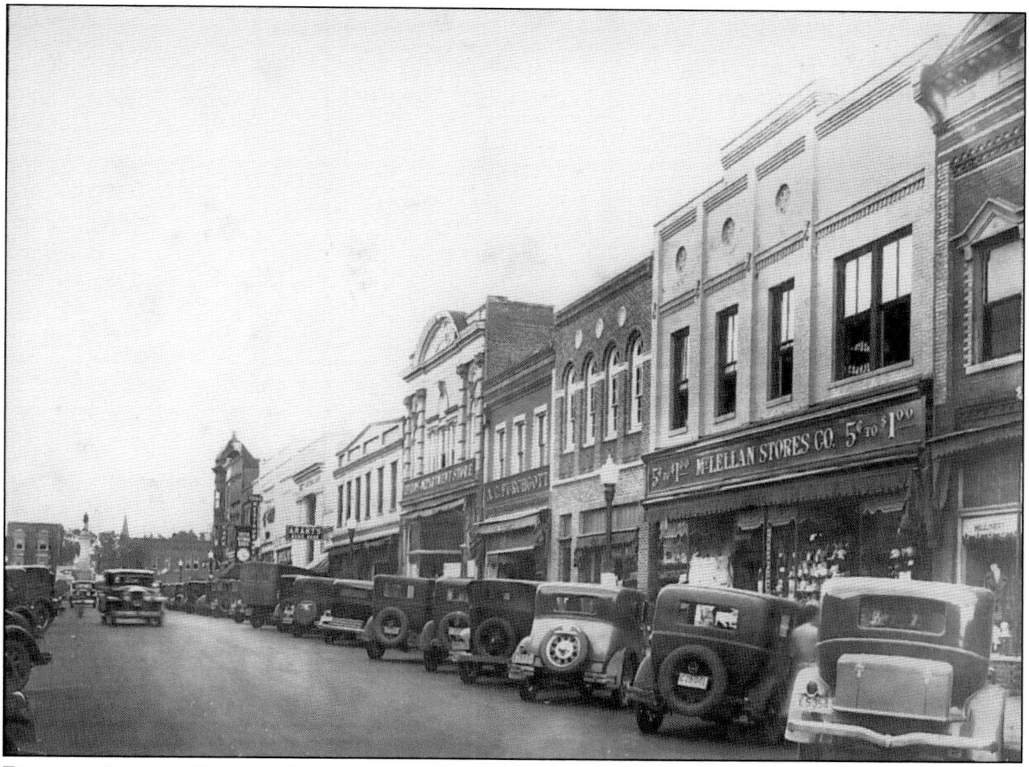

RUSSELL STREET, EARLY 1930S. Another view of Orangeburg's business district is shown here. This was an era when beautifully designed facades graced the buildings of downtown. (Courtesy Russell Wolfe family.)

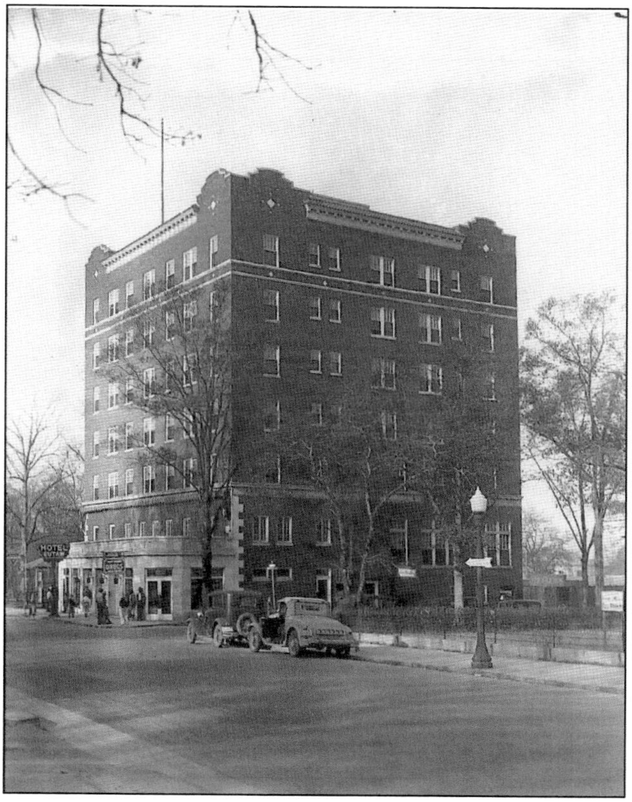

HOTEL EUTAW, EARLY 1930S. Orangeburg's new luxury high-rise hotel to attract tourists was completed in 1927. Many local social events and meetings were also held there during its heyday. (Courtesy Russell Wolfe family.)

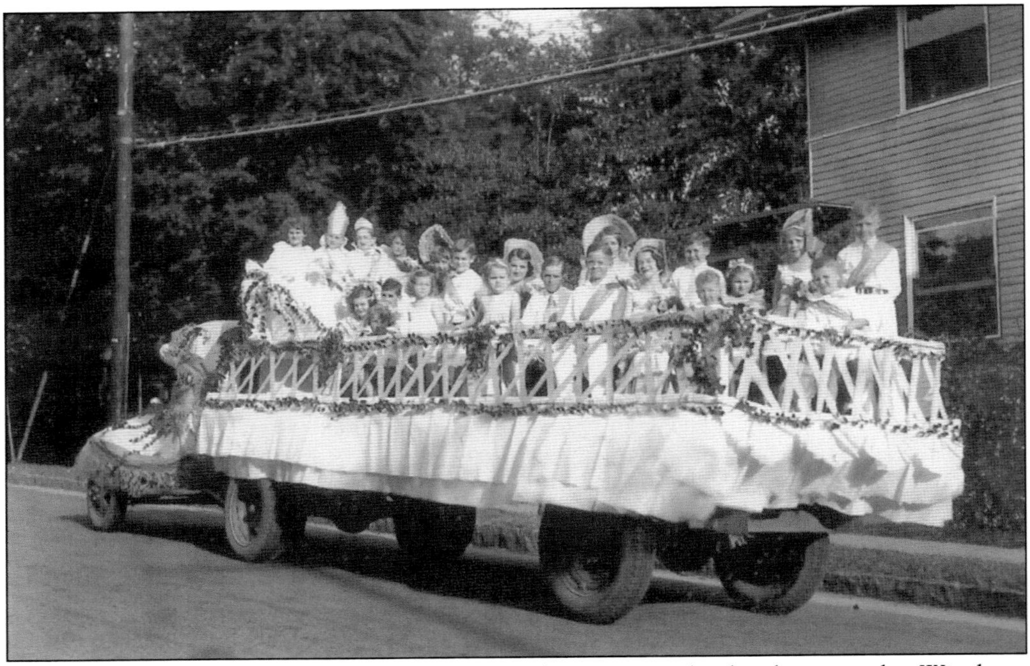

Winthrop Daughters' Festival, c. 1933. Always a popular local event, the Winthrop Daughters' Festival here features many local children all dressed up on a float for the parade. Two kings and queens were chosen, one each from Sheridan and Mellichamp elementary schools. Pictured, from left to right are (front of trailer) Helen Harley, queen, Andrew David Griffith, king, L.L. Hamilton, king, and Eloise Wise, queen; (rest of trailer) Lurline Livingston, Lally Green, Rut Osborne, Margaret Hoover, Lou Siebels Neely, Tommy Langford, Claire Smith, Nell Felder, Lawrence Hunter, Freddy Felder, Eunice Felder, Virginia Bozard, Bobby Adden, Ed Verdery, Deloris Shuler, Mary Elizabeth Avinger, Thomas Hughes, and Luther Adden. (Courtesy Mary Elizabeth Avinger.)

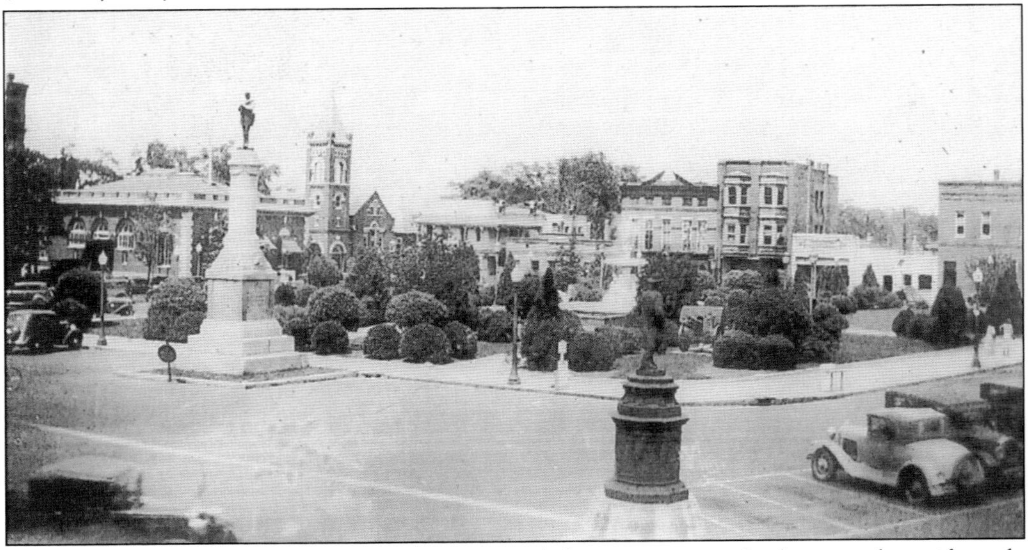

Memorial Plaza, c. 1933. Landscaping around the town square had matured significantly by the mid-1930s. The fireman's statue still stood prominently to the side. (Courtesy Gene Atkinson.)

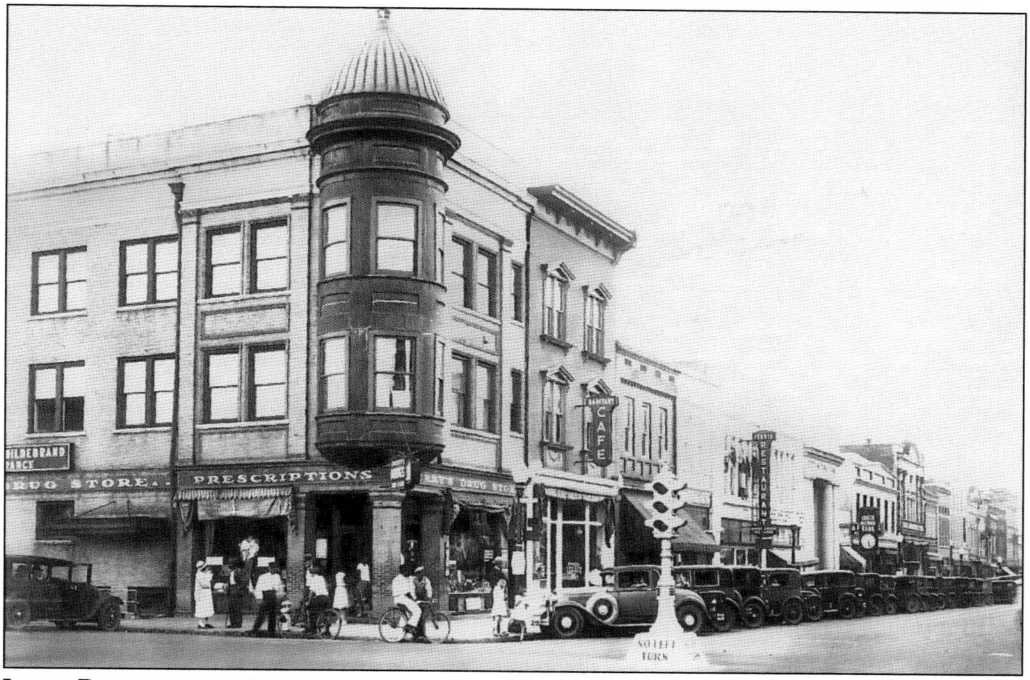

LOUIS BUILDING AND DOWNTOWN, c. 1933. The stoplight island was a familiar part of the downtown scene during the 1930s. The Sanitary Cafe and Ferris' Restaurant shown here were popular restaurants of the day. Bicycles were beginning to become more popular in this day and time. (Courtesy Department of Public Utilities.)

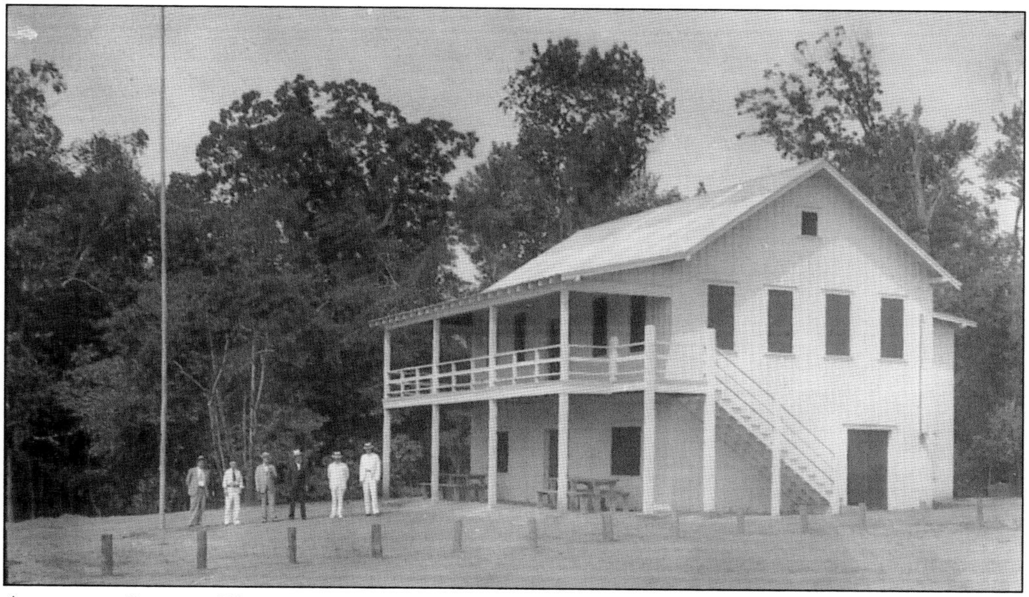

AMERICAN LEGION HUT, c. 1935. Many veterans volunteered to help build the American Legion Hut on Riverside in the early 1930s. This meeting place was used by both the American Legion and the V.F.W. for several years. It is said that in the early days there was a timer type coin operated electric meter, and when the lights went out someone would have to run downstairs and put another quarter in the box to get the electricity back on. (Courtesy Russell Wolfe family.)

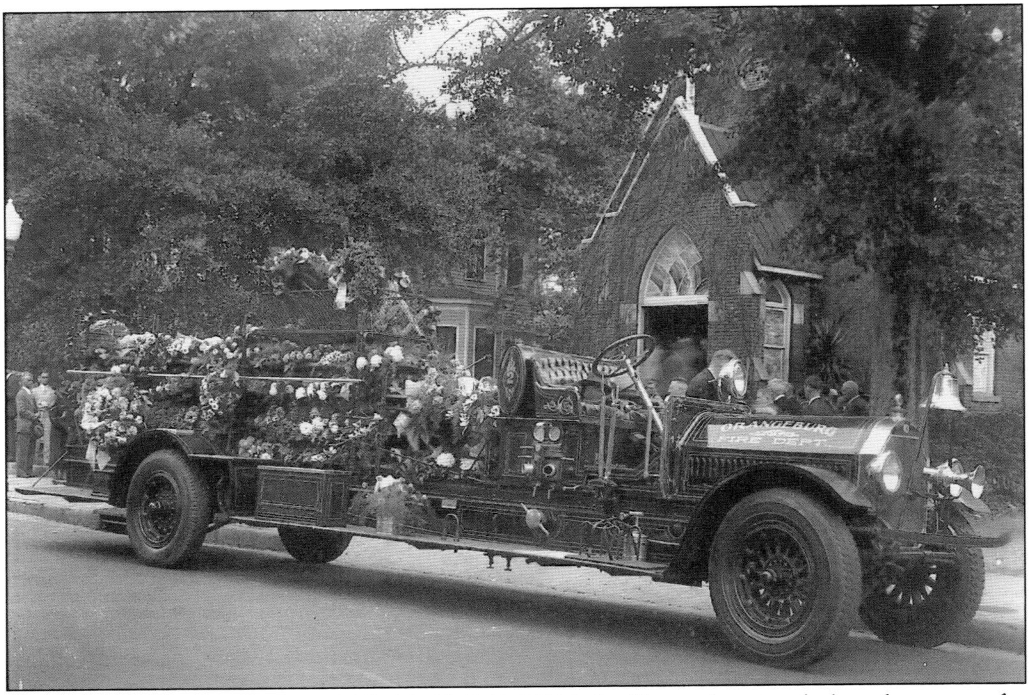

FUNERAL OF T.O.S. DIBBLE, 1935. Mr. T.O.S. Dibble had been the city clerk and treasurer for 22 years at his death in 1935. For 30 years he had been the Fire Chief for the Young America Steam Fire Engine Co., a volunteer firefighting organization before the city established its own fire department in 1920. Appropriately Orangeburg's hook and ladder fire truck was embellished with floral offerings as it carried the casket for his funeral at the Episcopal Church. (Courtesy Russell Wolfe family.)

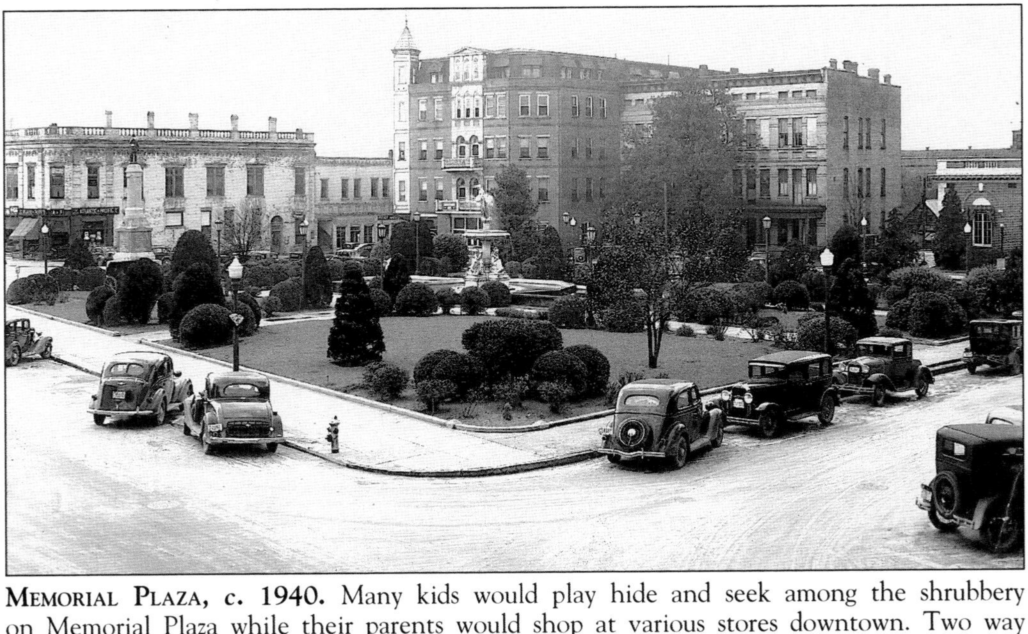

MEMORIAL PLAZA, c. 1940. Many kids would play hide and seek among the shrubbery on Memorial Plaza while their parents would shop at various stores downtown. Two way traffic was allowed on all sides of the square as noted here with the parking patterns. (Courtesy Cleveland Dempsey.)

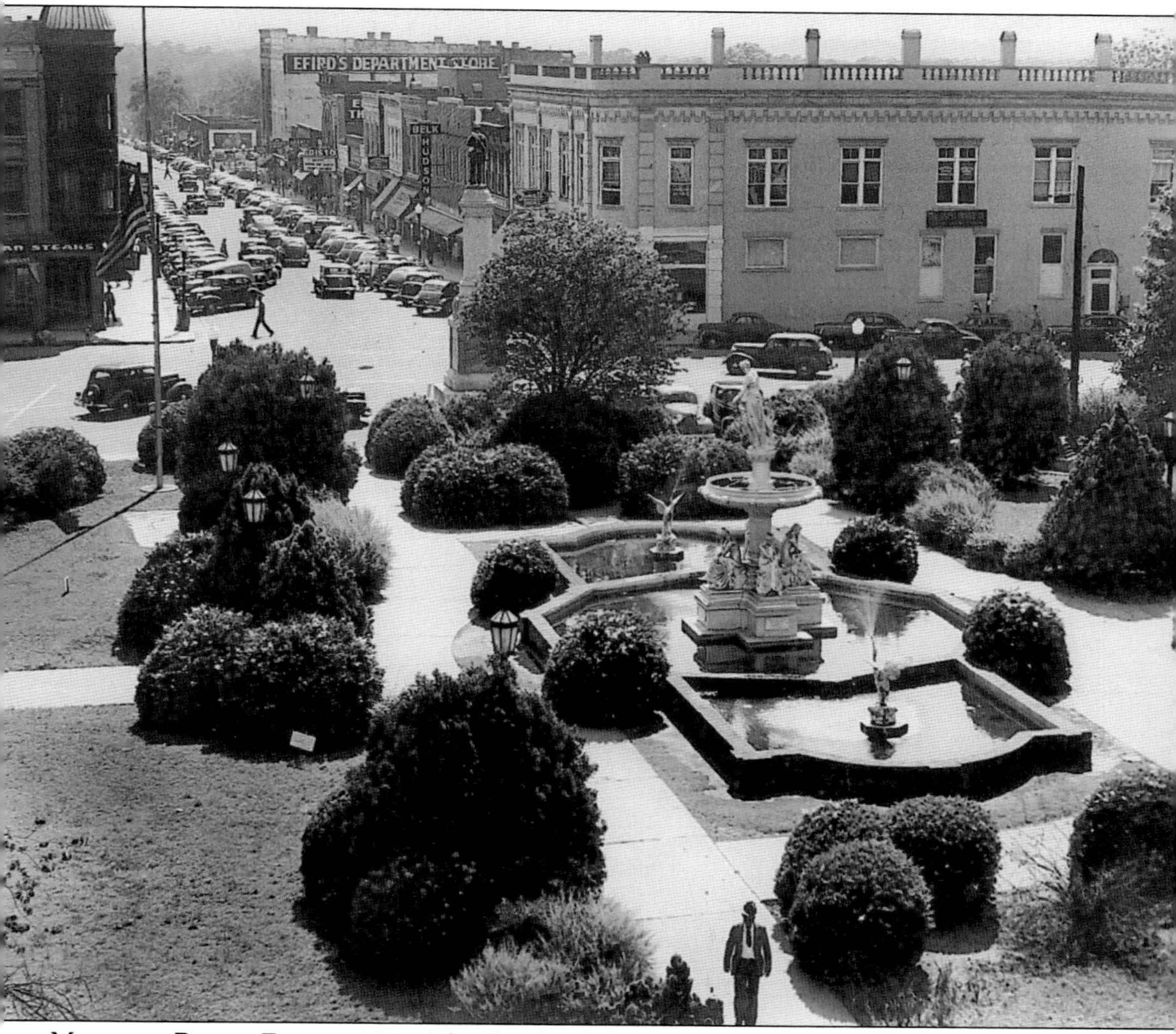

MEMORIAL PLAZA, EARLY 1940S. The details of the "Ladies' Fountain Statue" and goldfish pools are clearly shown here. This photograph appears to be taken from the World War II era, therefore the flag was probably at half staff due to some some significant event during the war. Legend has it that when the plans for the town square were being made upon the demolition of the courthouse, councilman John M. Sifly was sent up north to procure a suitable memorial statue for the square. This statue was what he purchased. Because these partly clothed women were difficult to accept by some, they were jokingly referred to as "Mr. Sifly's ladies," as Mr. Sifly was a lifelong bachelor. (Courtesy Louis Boone.)

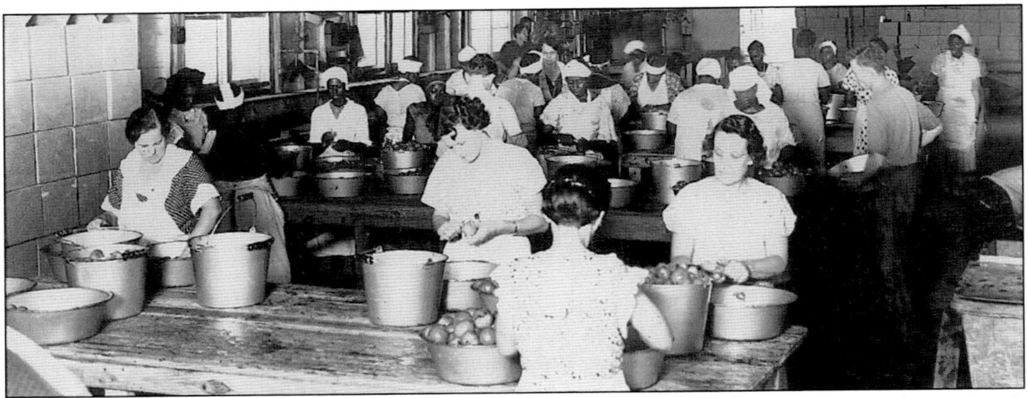

"The Cannery," c. 1940. In the days before widespread use of freezers to store frozen food, local citizens would take their summer vegetables to be canned at the cannery. This was a program supervised by the Clemson Extension Service at local school cafeterias where paid employees would cook and can these fresh vegetables. Citizens bringing the vegetables would participate in the process by shelling, peeling, or cutting up these products and the fees charged would cover the costs of the cooking and canning portion. (Courtesy Cleveland Dempsey.)

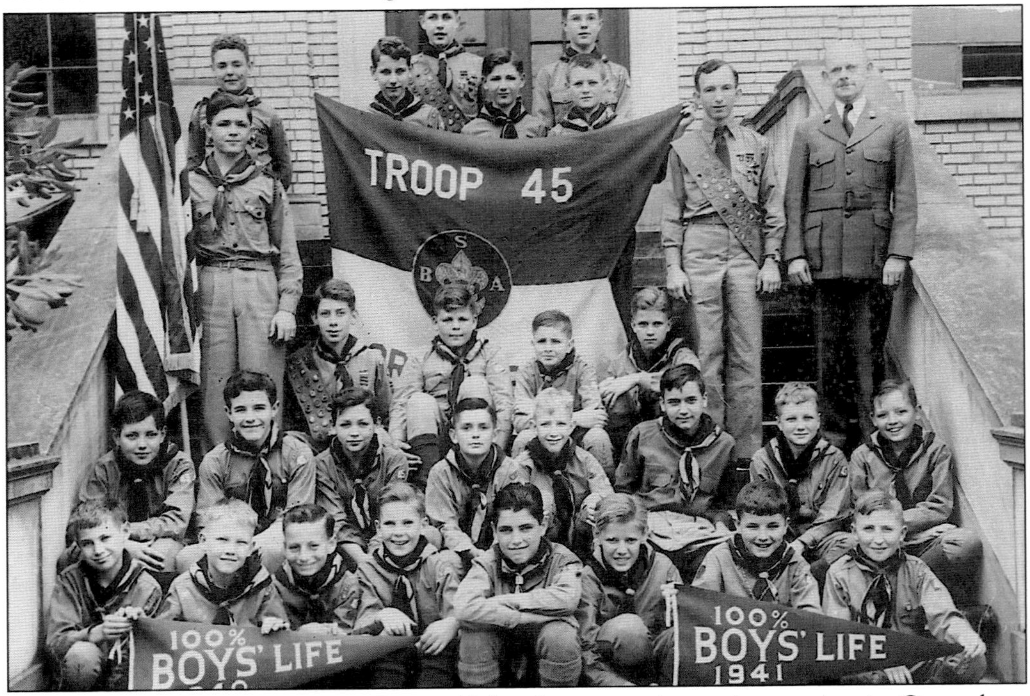

Boy Scouts, 1942. Boy Scout Troop 45 has been a mainstay in scouting in Orangeburg for many years, and it is still in existence today. This 1942 photograph shows all of the members with their scoutmaster. They are, from left to right (front row) George Mackay, Louis Deschamps, Conrad Martin, unidentified, Bobby Osborne, Alton Edwins, Bobby Blackwell, and Lewis Dibble; (second row) Jack Sims, Bobby Ayers, Walter Baxter, Donald Alexander, James Bradbury, Bobby Hayden, Harold Antley, and Ralph Antley, (third row) Lewis Hough, E.M. Funderburk, Haddon Holliday, and Billy Fairey; (fourth row) Thomas Antley, T.B. Jackson, Dr. Lewis M. Hough, Scoutmaster; (fifth row) Al Fischer, Joe Reed, Joe Harley, and Richard Hatchell; (sixth row) Marion Inabinet and Foster Theiling. (Courtesy Troop 45 Archives.)

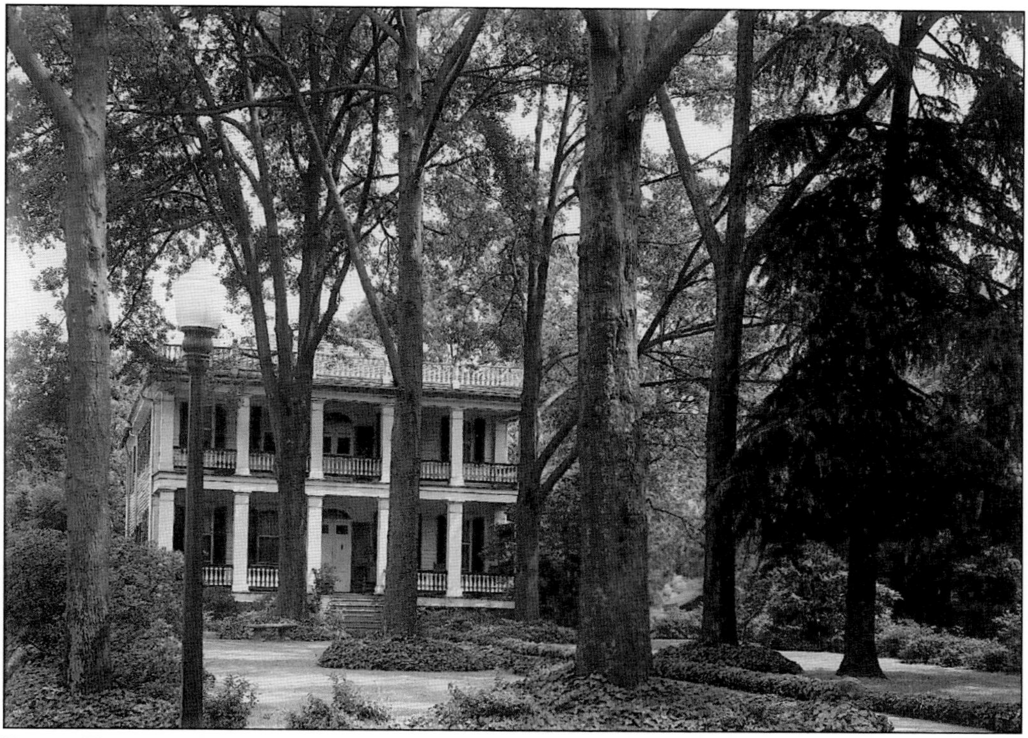

Berry Tourist Home, 1948. Sanders Glover built this beautiful home in 1828. Mr. Glover held the position of "ordinary" (now called probate judge) in Orangeburg County. In 1877 the house was sold to Mr. and Mrs. John Pike. For many years, from before the turn of the 20th century on, the Pike family and their descendants, the J.A. Berry family, rented rooms to tourists passing through our area. A popular local fast food restaurant, the Dairy O now occupies this site on Russell Street. (Courtesy Orangeburg County Historical Society.)

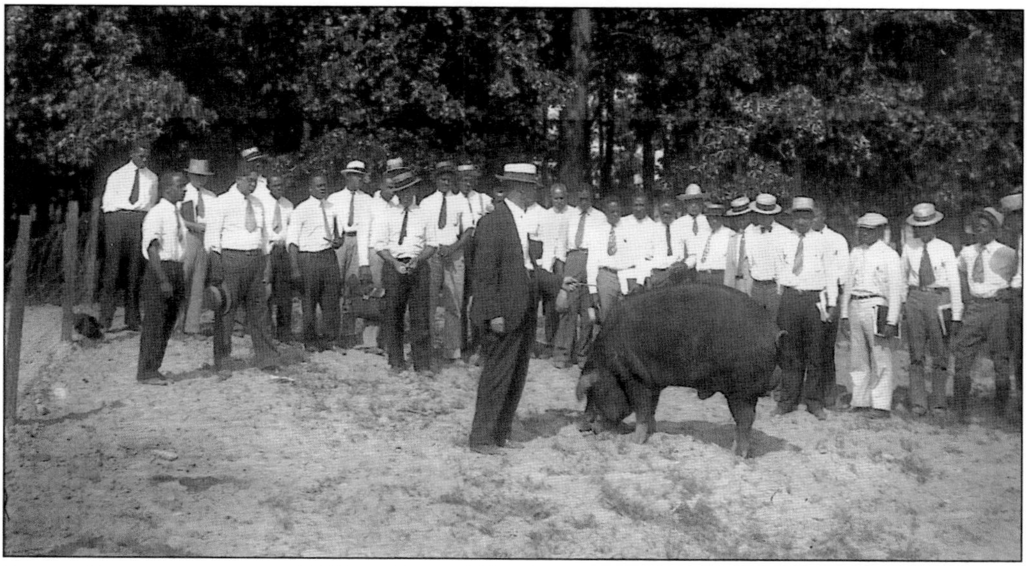

Swine Demonstration, 1940s. The 1890 Extension Service of South Carolina State University is shown here conducting a swine demonstration in the 1940s. (Courtesy Dr. Clemmie Webber.)

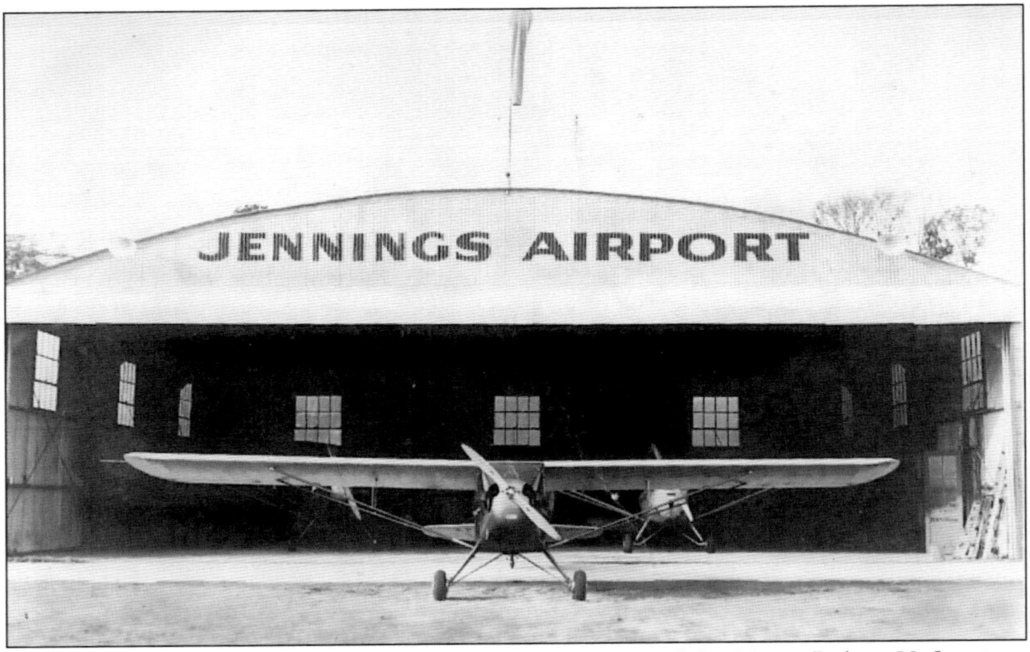

Jennings Airport, 1940s. Orangeburg's new airport, named for Mayor Robert H. Jennings Sr. opened in 1937 at a site a few miles south of town. Previously the airport was located near where Orangeburg Mall and Clark Middle School stand today. (Courtesy Sylvia Boone.)

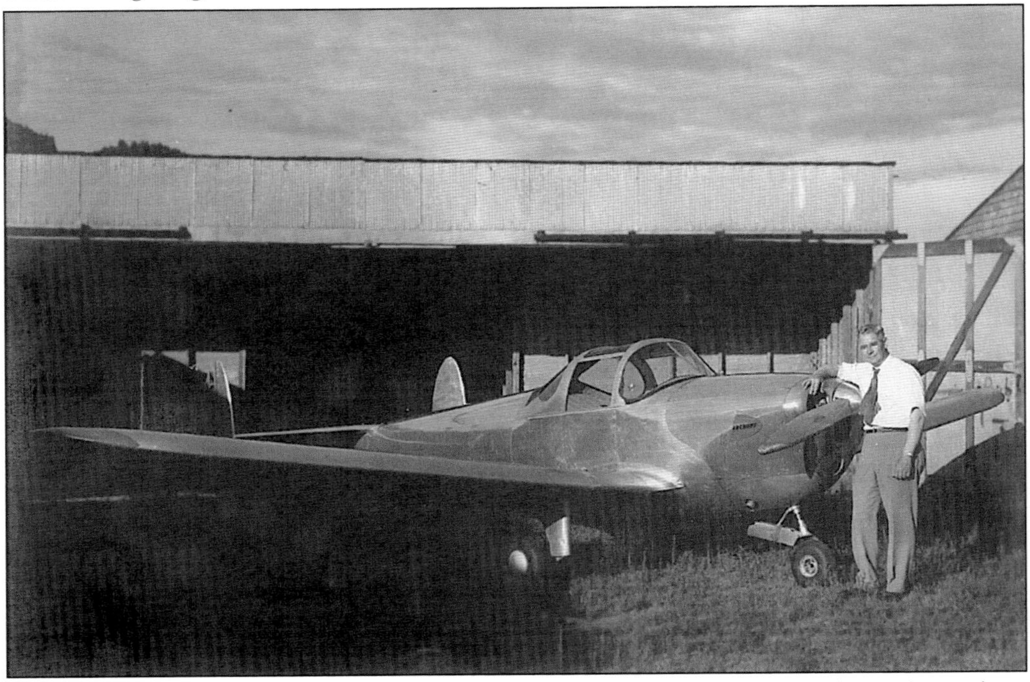

Tom Summers and Airplane, 1946. Tom Summers was a well-known jeweler in Orangeburg whose hobby was flying airplanes. He founded the "Breakfast Club" for pilots in South Carolina in the 1930s. Pilots from all over the state would have a "fly in" to a town's airport and meet for breakfast and fellowship. This was considered to be the first pilots' Breakfast Club in America and started a national trend. (Courtesy Sylvia Summers Boone.)

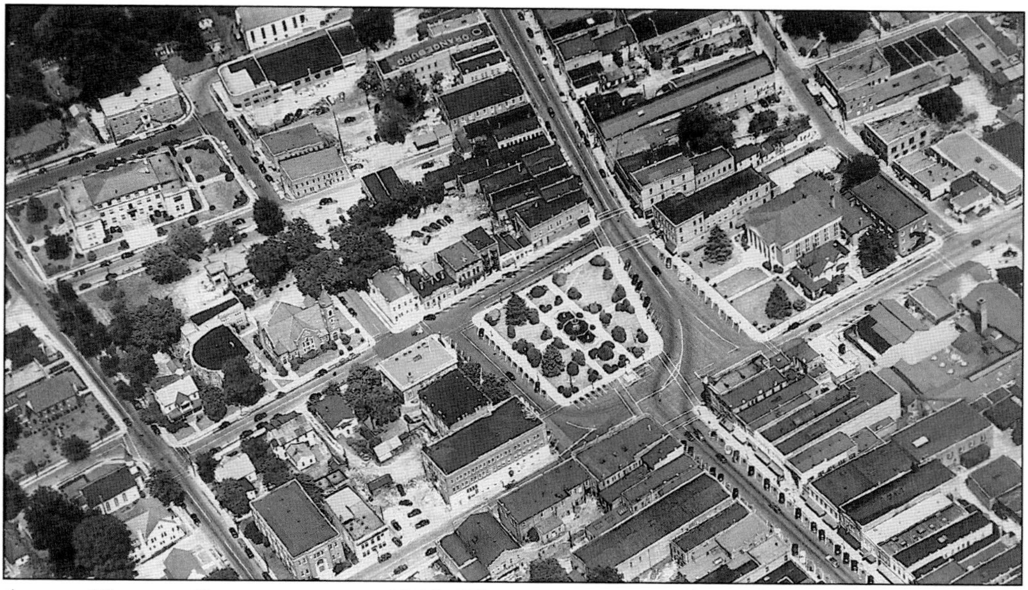

Aerial View of Orangeburg, c. 1949. The town square as shown here is the shape that it presented itself until 1951 when it first truly became an equal sided square. The old Lutheran Church is in the far left at the corner of Green and Amelia, while the previous First Presbyterian Church is on the top left beside Doyle Street. (Courtesy Chamber of Commerce.)

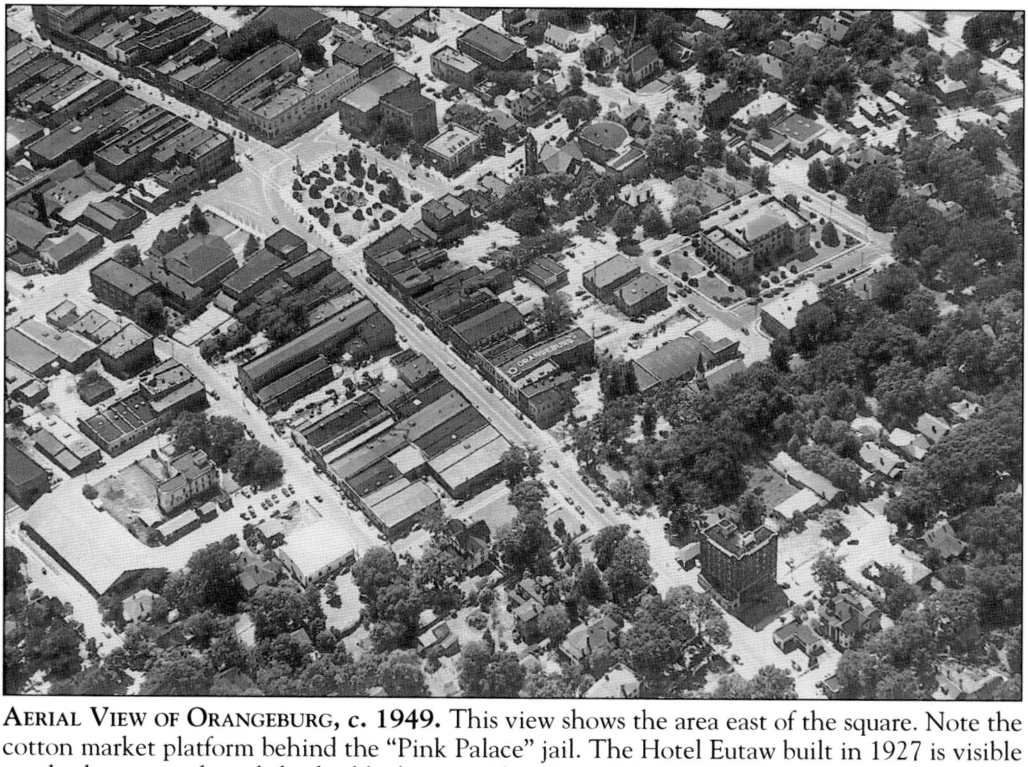

Aerial View of Orangeburg, c. 1949. This view shows the area east of the square. Note the cotton market platform behind the "Pink Palace" jail. The Hotel Eutaw built in 1927 is visible on the bottom right, while the block across the street still had residential homes. The name Orangeburg is painted on the roof of the Crum Brothers building, which later became Hub Covington, in the middle of the picture to help aviators. (Courtesy Chamber of Commerce.)

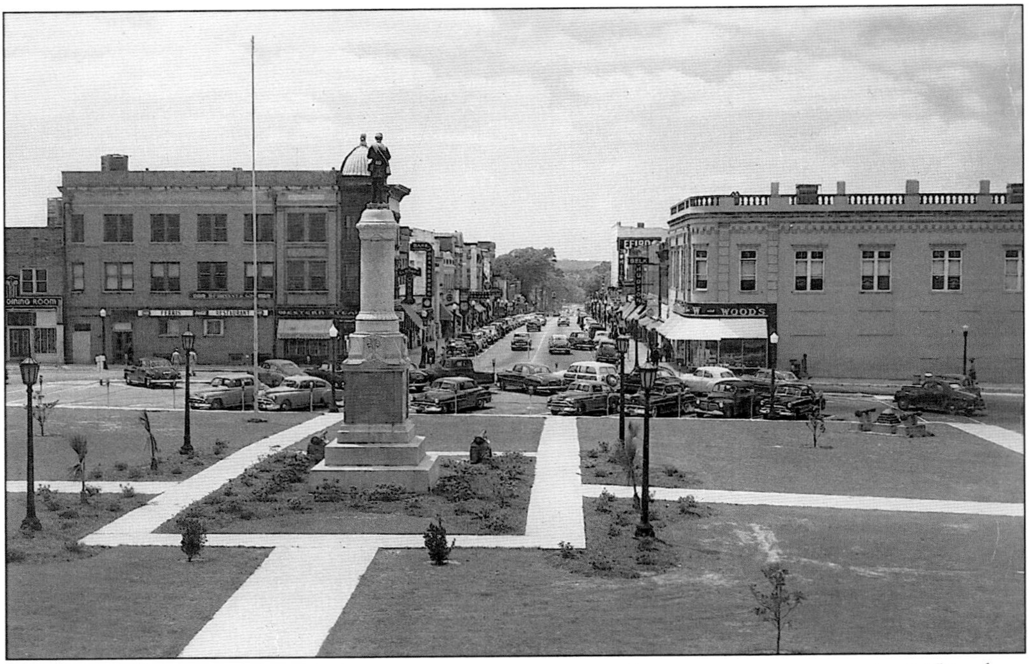

Memorial Plaza, c. 1952. Major renovations were made to our town square in 1951 when it actually became a "square" for the first time. The Ladies' Fountain was removed and later installed at the entrance of Edisto Memorial Gardens. The landscaping in this photograph had not had a chance to mature yet because of its recent planting after all the changes. (Courtesy Chamber of Commerce.)

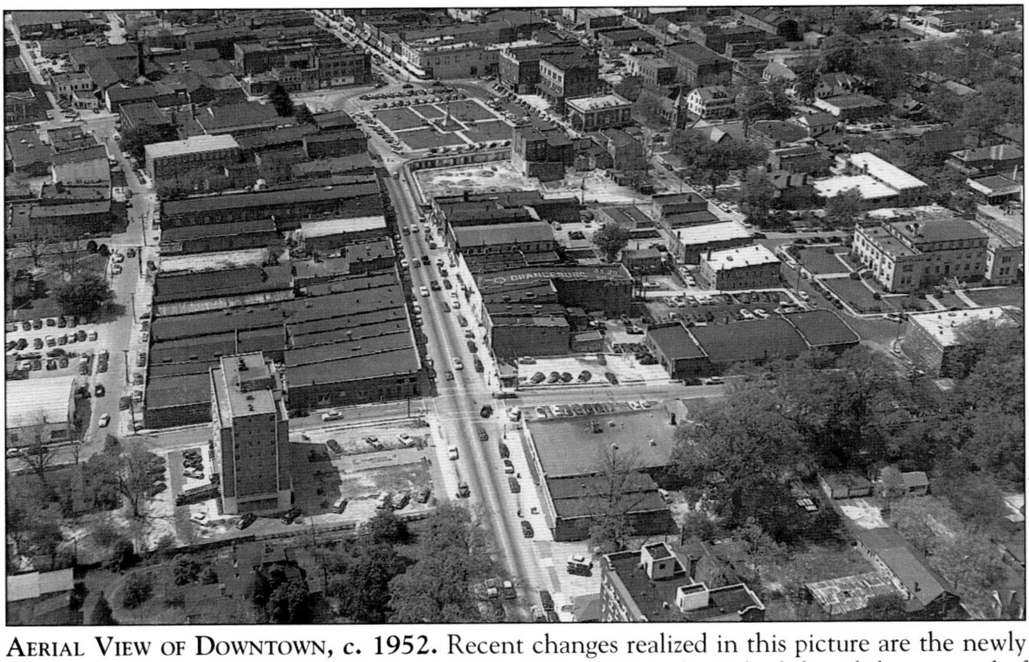

Aerial View of Downtown, c. 1952. Recent changes realized in this picture are the newly constructed high rise Glover Apartments (later Emory Towers) on the left and the removal of First Presbyterian Church and the Lutheran Church. Just below the square is the construction site of the new S.H. Kress five-and-dime variety store. (Courtesy Chamber of Commerce.)

Two

SCHOOLS

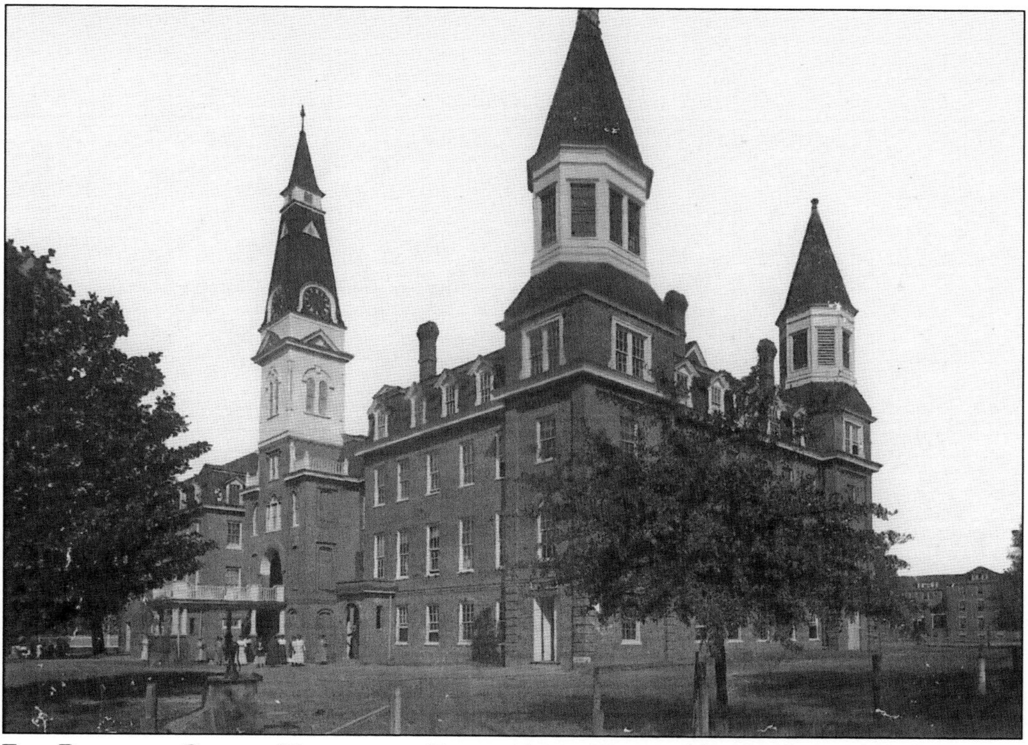

FISK BUILDING, CLAFLIN UNIVERSITY, EARLY 1900S. Designed by the first certified African-American architect in America, Robert Charles Bates, the Fisk building was the most prominent building at Claflin around the turn of the century. Through the years additional wings were constructed several times. (Courtesy Claflin University Archives.)

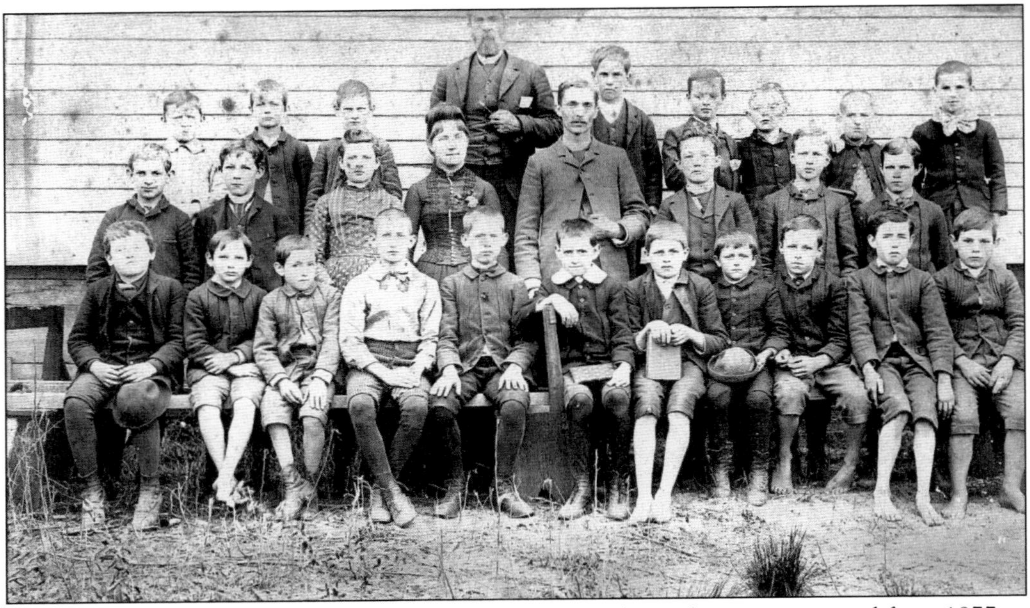

Sheridan Classical Institute, 1889. The Sheridan Classical Institute existed from 1877 to 1890 as a private school. Professor Hugo G. Sheridan established this school and was assisted by his son Hugo G. Sheridan Jr. and Miss Mary McMichael. Mr. Sheridan was chosen as one of the first two public school principals in 1890. The only people identified in this picture are Mr. Sheridan in the back center, Hugo Sheridan Jr. in the middle of the second row, and Marion F. "Buck" Inabinet on the first row, second from the right. (Courtesy Catherine Senn.)

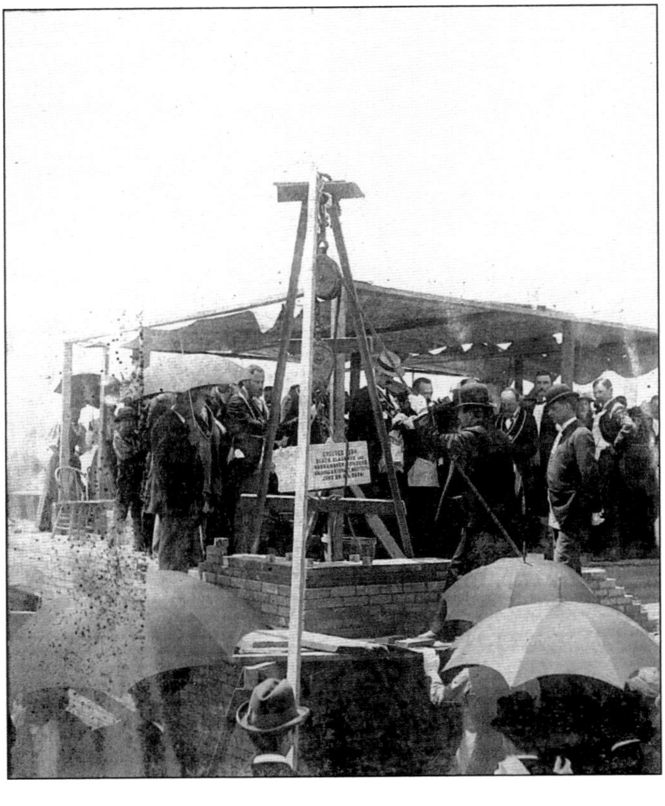

Old Mellichamp School, Cornerstone Laying, 1894. The first major school building construction after public schools were established was the old Mellichamp School on Sellers Avenue. The laying of the cornerstone in 1894 is shown here in a large public ceremony. One of the speakers was Hugo G. Sheridan, one of the two principals of the public school system at the time. This building was razed in 1961, but water leakage through the years had damaged the contents of the cornerstone when it was opened. (Courtesy Orangeburg County Historical Society.)

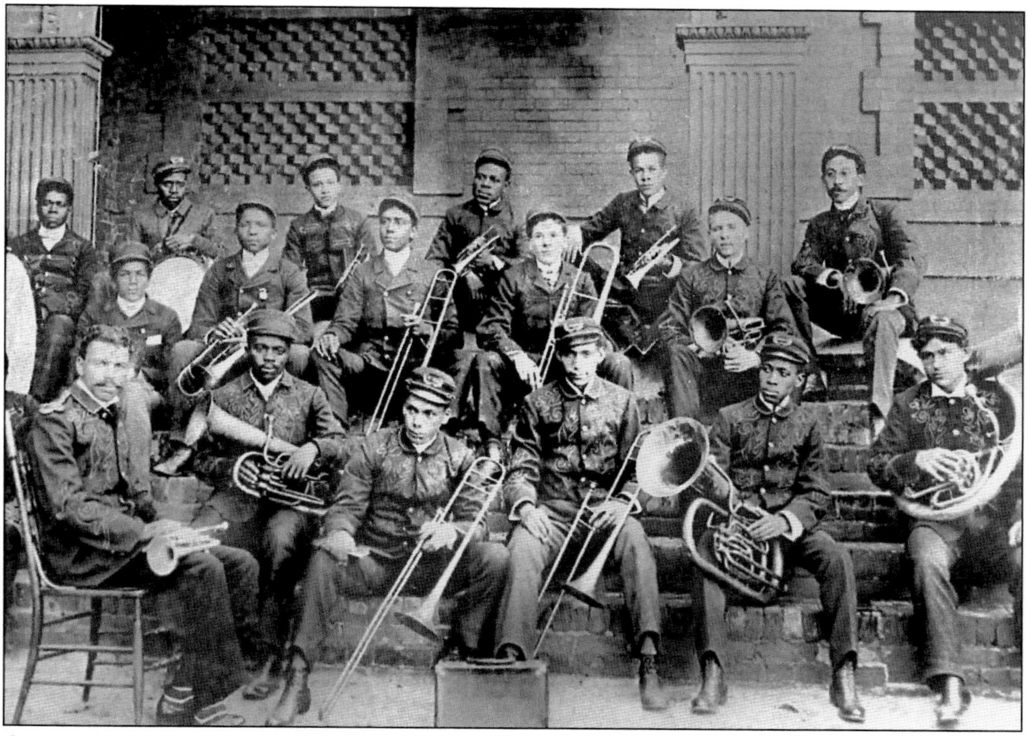

CLAFLIN BAND, 1901. During President Lewis M. Dunton's era at Claflin, musical appreciation and performances were an integral part of campus life. Pictured here is the 1901 Claflin University band. (Courtesy Claflin University Archives.)

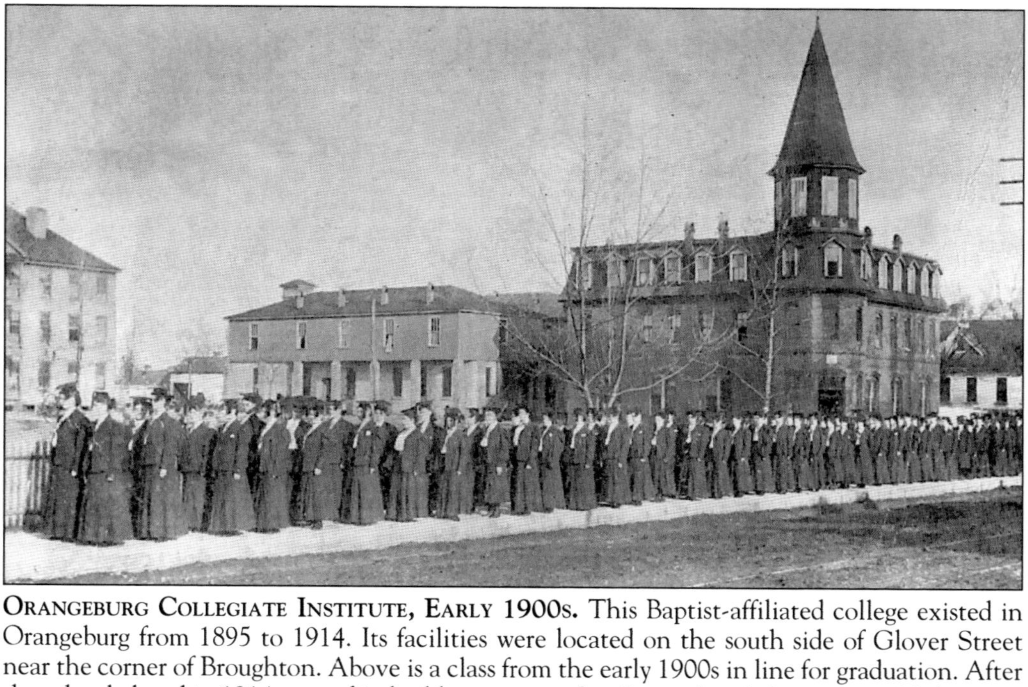

ORANGEBURG COLLEGIATE INSTITUTE, EARLY 1900S. This Baptist-affiliated college existed in Orangeburg from 1895 to 1914. Its facilities were located on the south side of Glover Street near the corner of Broughton. Above is a class from the early 1900s in line for graduation. After the school closed in 1914, one of its buildings was used as Orangeburg's first sustainable hospital in 1919. (Courtesy Orangeburg County Historical Society.)

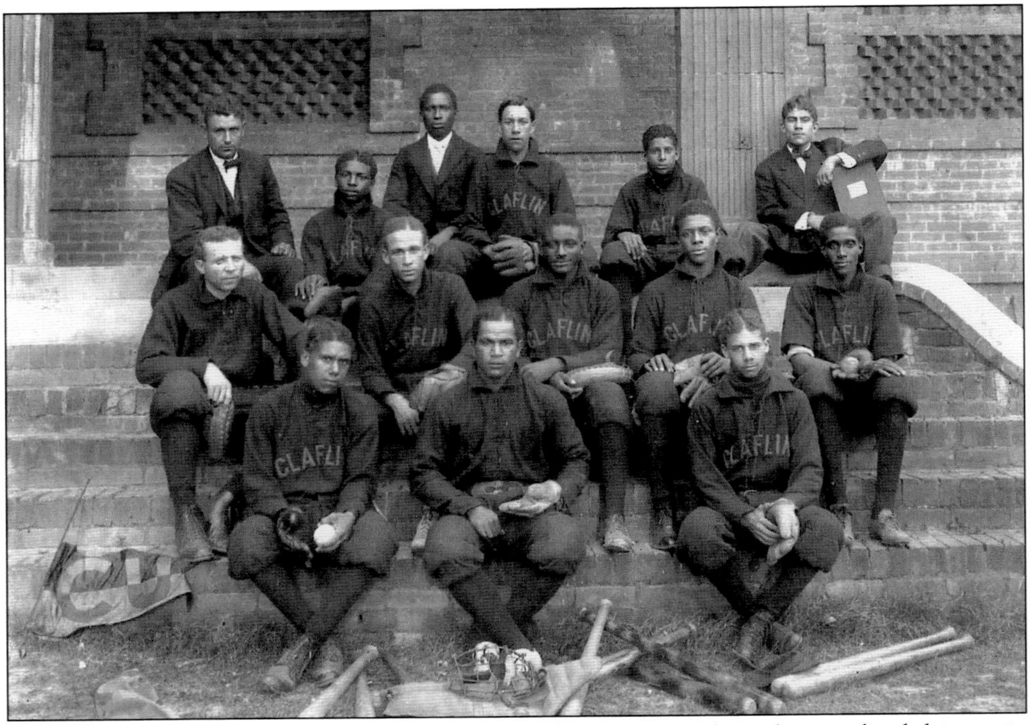

Baseball Team, Claflin University, 1907. Claflin University has a long and rich history in Orangeburg since its founding in 1869. Sports teams have been a part of college life for many years. Here is the 1907 Claflin baseball team. (Claflin University Archives.)

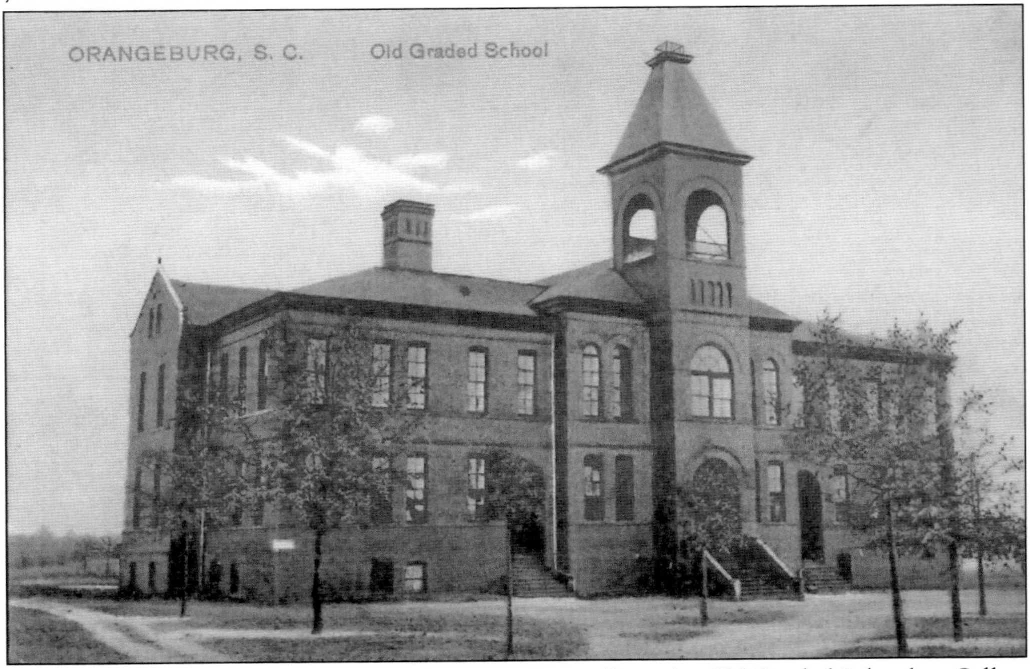

Mellichamp School, 1909. This was known colloquially as the Old Graded School on Sellers Avenue. It was constructed in 1894 and finally had deteriorated enough to be torn down in 1961. (Courtesy Addie Stewart Felkel.)

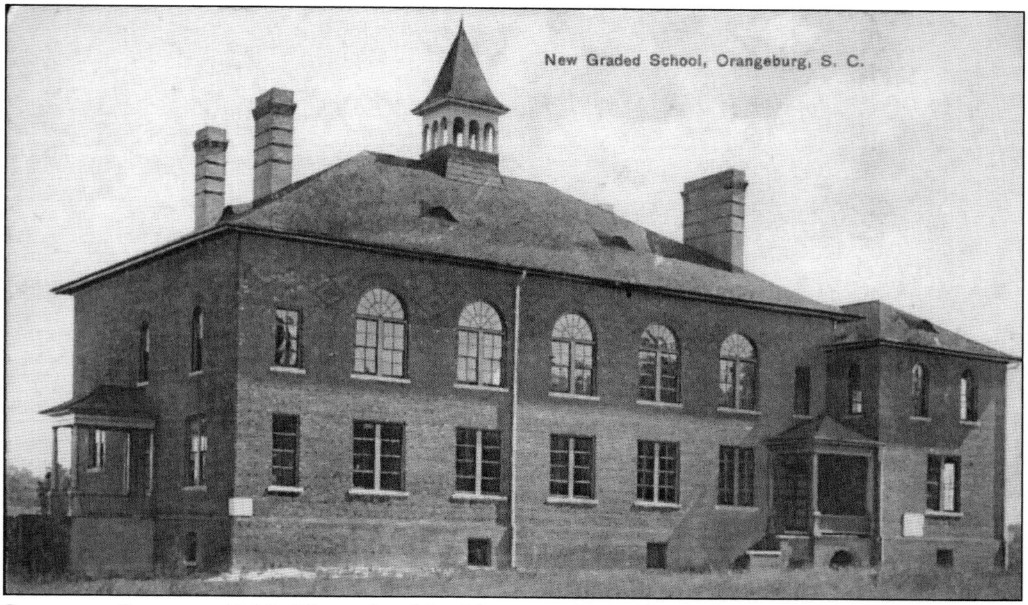

SHERIDAN SCHOOL, 1909. This school building was located on Ellis Avenue at the site where the current Consolidated District Five's administration building is located. Initially after construction in 1905 it was locally called the New Graded School, then later Sheridan School. (Courtesy Anna Lou Wolfe.)

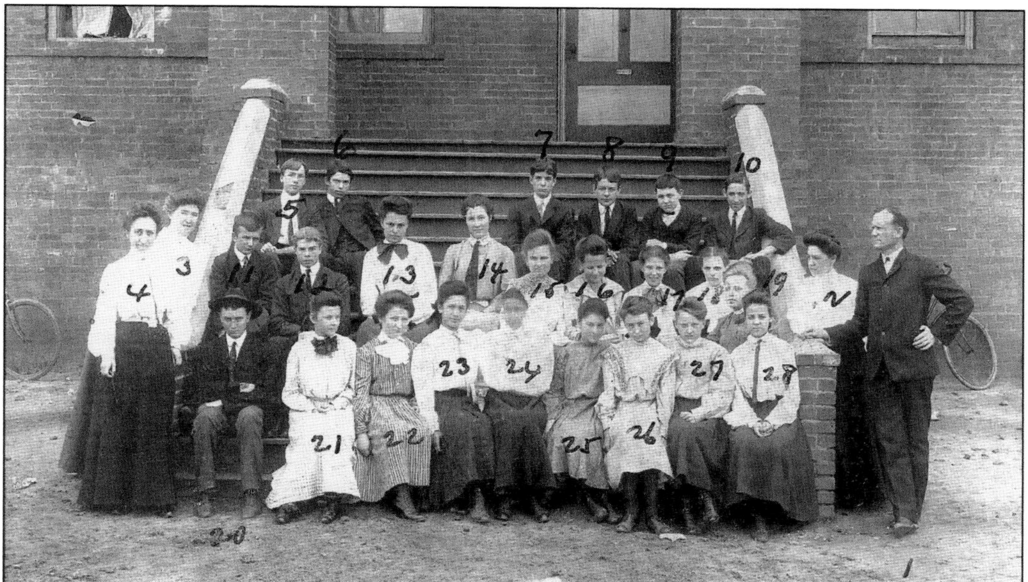

MELLICHAMP SCHOOL, 1905. Pictured above are some of the students with their teachers and superintendent. Identified by number, they are 1) Principal A.J. Thackston, 2) Miss Margaret Daniel, 3) Miss Molly Hope, 4) Miss Fannie Beckman, 5) Kenneth Lowman, 6) Walter O'Cain, 7) Orrin Bowman, 8) Paul Cantwell, 9) Raysor Salley, 10) Willie Dibble, 11) McAlpin Albergotti, 12) LeRoy Izlar, 13) May Lane, 14) Addie Hoover, 15) Alma Davis, 16) Helen Salley, 17) Louise Salley, 18) Laura Copes, 19) Susie Albergotti, 20) Clarence Davis, 21) Rai Zeigler, 22) Reba Albergotti, 23) Rena Wald, 24) Henrietta Kohn, 25) Bessie Ayers, 26) Ella Dukes, 27) Ermine Brunson, and 28) Susie Dibble. (Courtesy Mary Felkel.)

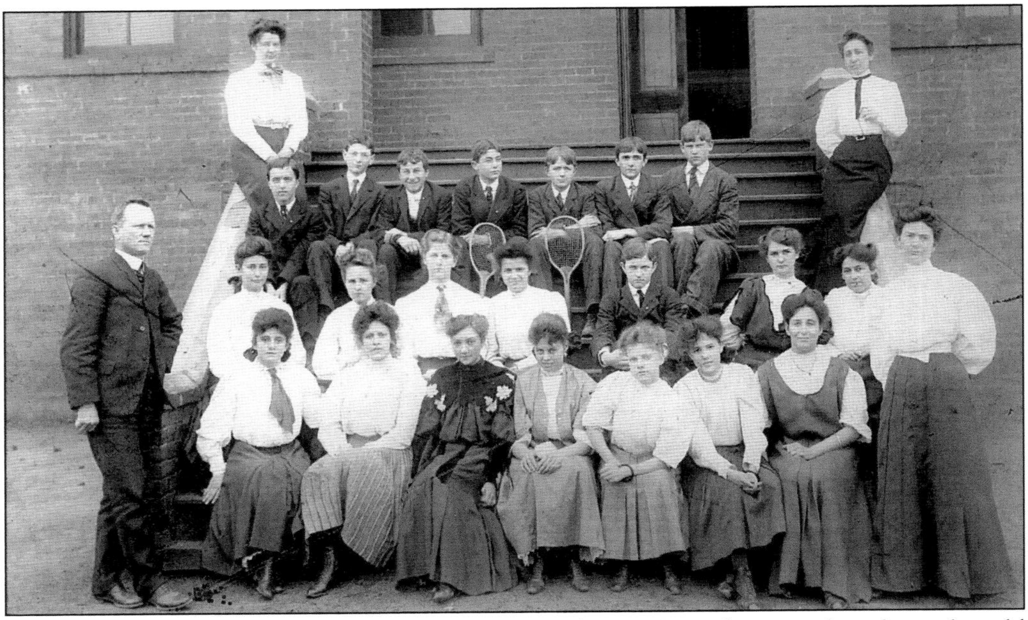

CLASS OF 1907, ORANGEBURG CITY SCHOOLS. The 1907 graduating class from the old Mellichamp School is shown here. Identified are Principal A.J. Thackston on the far left and teachers Miss Molly Hope, top left, Miss Fannie Beckman, top right, and Miss Margaret Daniel, lower right. The only student identified is Russell Wolfe, the only boy in the middle of the second row. (Courtesy Russell Wolfe family.)

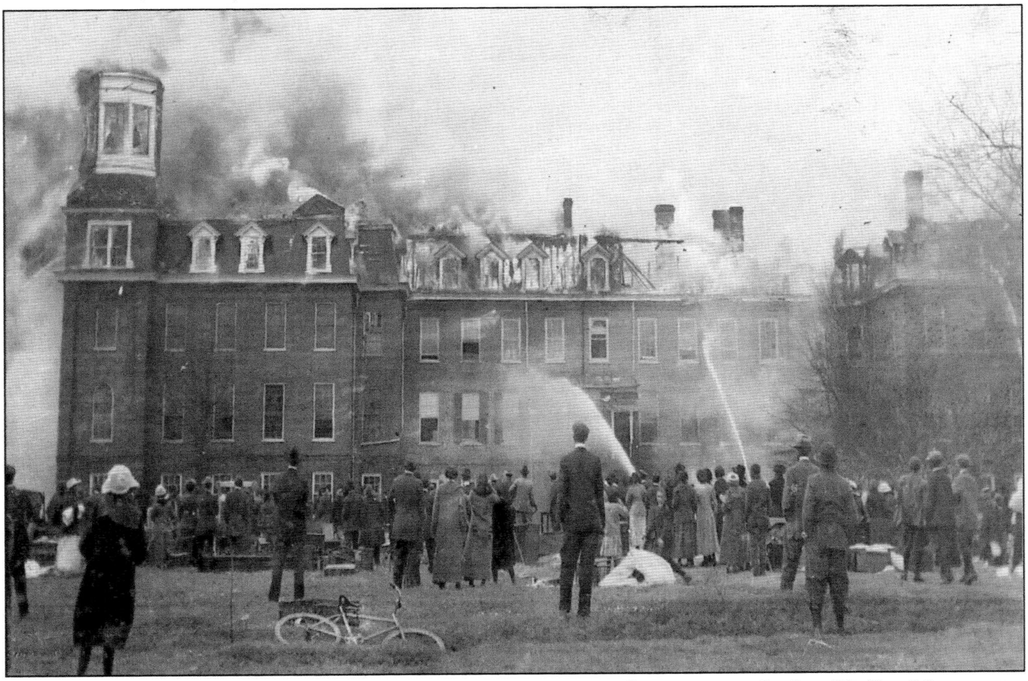

FISK BUILDING FIRE AT CLAFLIN UNIVERSITY, 1913. Misfortune struck the Claflin University Campus in 1913 when the Fisk Building was destroyed by fire. This main campus building contained classrooms, a girls' dormitory, and several offices, including that of Pres. Lewis M. Dunton. (Courtesy Orangeburg County Historical Society.)

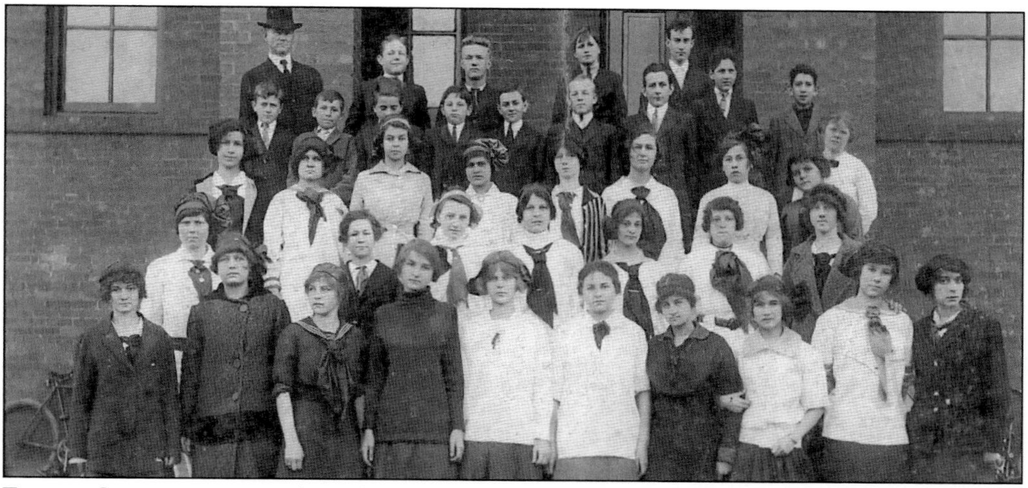

EIGHTH GRADE, 1913. In those days only ten grades of school were required, so this class only had two more to go. Pictured above on Mellichamp's steps, from left to right are (front row) Mae Barsh, Lurline Stroman, Janie Brooks Salley, Emmie Dantzler, Bertha Vaughn, Jessie Copes, Edith Hoffman, Annie Davis, Elizabeth Glaze, and Viola Sawyer; (second row) Willie Mae Kemmerlin, Catherine Sanders, Ralda Sheriff, Amelia Barton, Monteith Smoak, Willie Lou Wannamaker, and Mildred Lide; (third row) Sue Sullins, Lurline Murphy, Jennie McCraw, Elise Kemmerlin, Friezeal Houser, Viola Gardner, Marguerite Liles, Ruby Bryant, and Elizabeth Baskervill; (fourth row) Fletcher Smoak, Wade Freeman, Johnnie Scoville, Joe Gelzer, John McLees, Marion Wannamaker, Lynton Wannamaker, William Stokes, and Herman Wald; (fifth row) Prof. Thackston, Lawrence Thackston, Ingram Lowman, Walter Banks, and Brown Bradley. (Courtesy Orangeburg County Historical Society.)

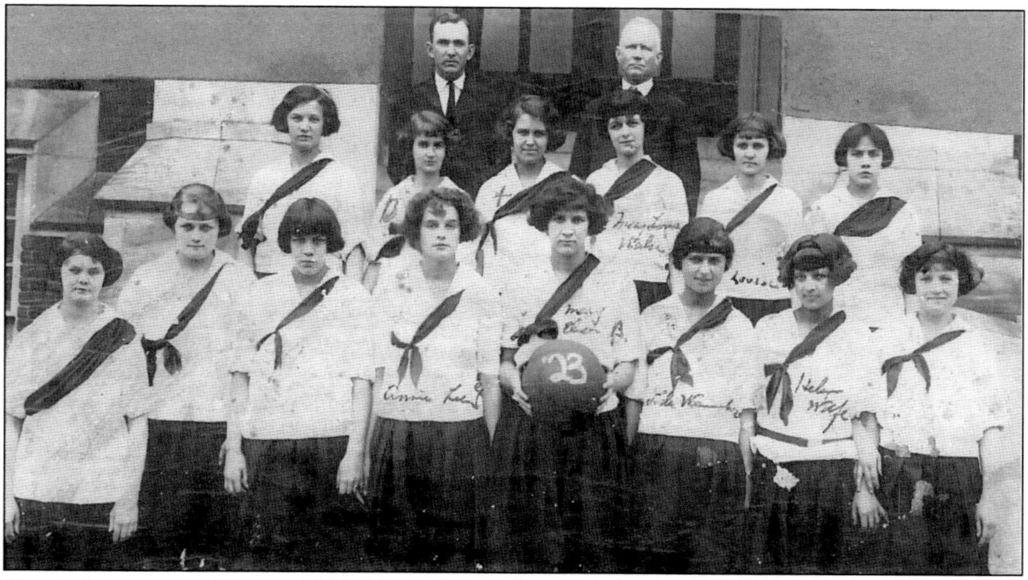

GIRL'S BASKETBALL TEAM, 1923. Note the uniforms of the day in 1923 for the girls' basketball team. Very long bloomers, long middy blouses with flowing ties, and wide ribbon bandeaux for the hair comprised their unique fashion for this relatively new sport. The only people positively identified are Annie Lee Dantzler (later Gramling) just to the left of the girl with the ball, and just to the right of the ball are Lyall Wannamaker and Helen Wolfe. A.J. Thackston, the superintendent, is on the back row, far right. (Courtesy Orangeburg County Historical Society.)

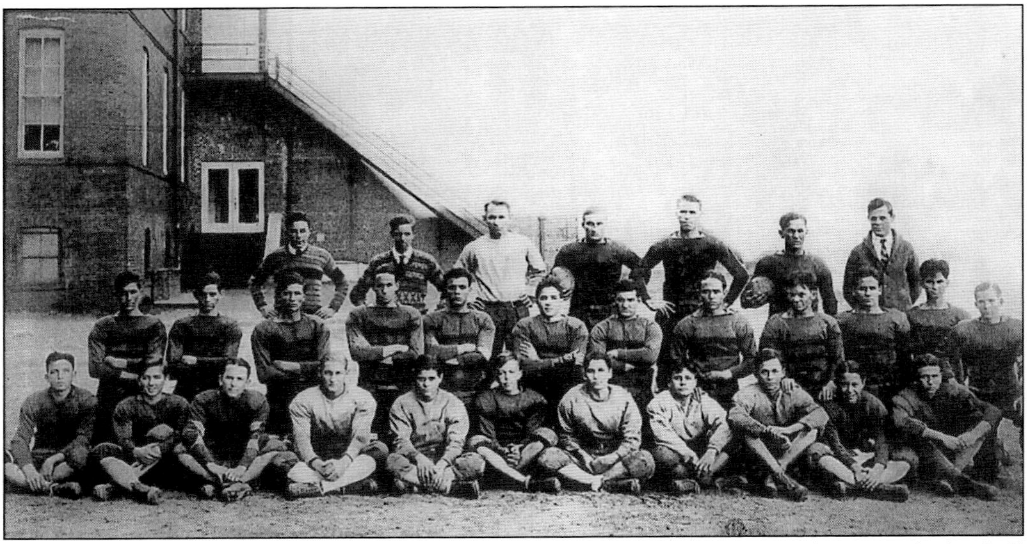

ORANGEBURG HIGH FOOTBALL TEAM, 1926. Here is the 1926 Orangeburg High football team lined up behind the school. They are, from left to right, (front row) Ed Mann, Jimmy Brailsford, Emmett Brown, Roy Hoover, Lewis Stone, J.A. Berry, Tom "Rabbi" Brantley, Marshall Williams, Marvin Cole, Junius Liles, and Paul Way; (middle row) Hollis Ayers, Ralph Owens, Ben Fair, Luther Weeks, Foster Boone, George "Pot" Scoville, Ed Bruner, Kenneth Griffith, Wilbur Pendarvis, Yates Williams, Watson Stewart, and Julian "Dutch" Jeffords; (back row) Ansel Salley (assistant manager), Buck Miller (manager), P.H. Bomar (head coach), Carl Fairey (co-captain), Alvis "Pig" Bomar, Bill Dukes (co-captain), and Teddy Weeks (assistant coach). (Courtesy Bill Dukes.)

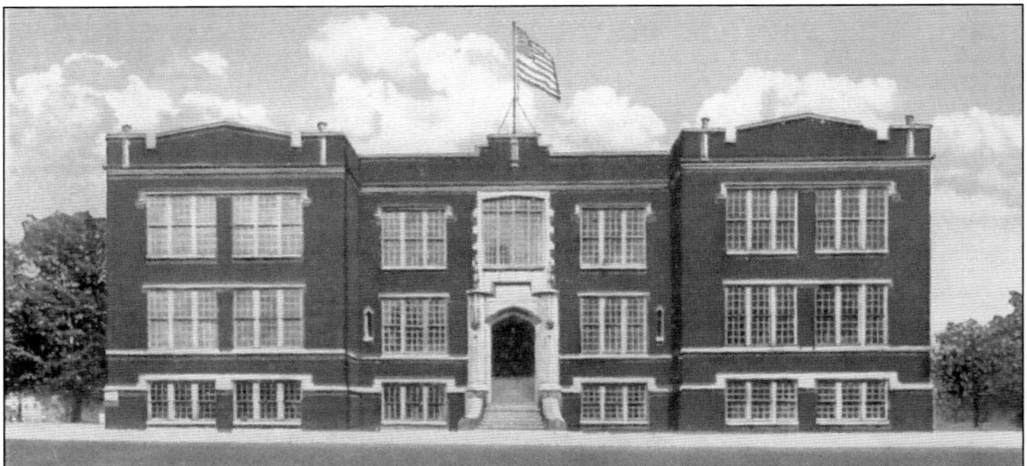

ORANGEBURG HIGH SCHOOL, 1930S. The names Orangeburg High School and Thackston High School were interchangeable back in the era of this 1930s photograph. This separate building for the high school was constructed around 1915 next door to the original Mellichamp School. When Orangeburg High School moved to the new Bennett Avenue campus in 1954, this building was renamed Mellichamp Elementary School. The old Mellichamp building next door was then named Orangeburg Junior High School. In 1961 Mellichamp Elementary moved to a new location on Murray Road and the above building was renamed Thackston Junior High School. The original Mellichamp Building, which had been renamed Orangeburg Junior High, was torn down. (Courtesy Anna Lou Wolfe.)

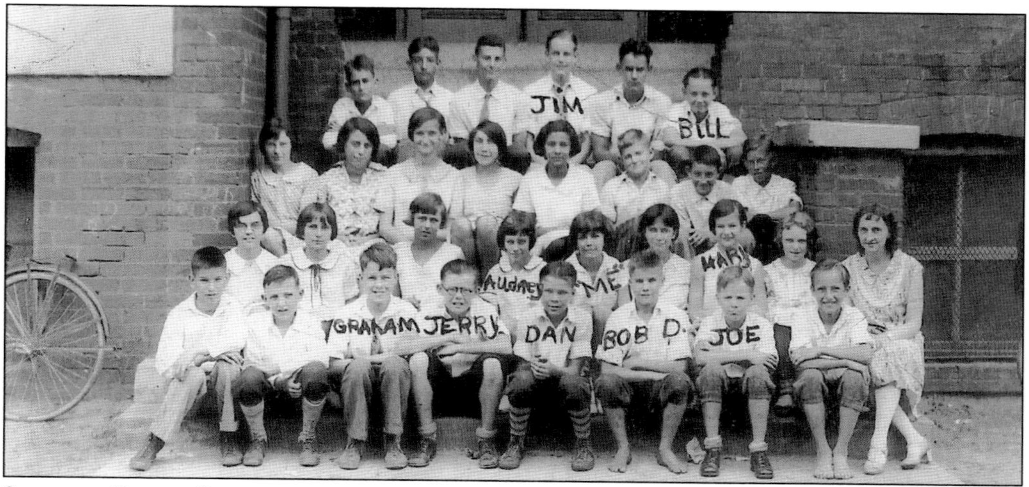

SEVENTH GRADE CLASS, 1930. A seventh-grade class is featured here on the steps of the old Mellichamp building on Sellers Avenue. Identified, from left to right, are (front row) Wardlaw Brodie, Lyle Allen, Graham Culler, Jerry Hughes, Dan Dukes, Bob Dukes, Joe Cannon, and Gordon Dawson; (second row) Rubye Lee Jackson, Ruth Bozard, Cleo Carroll, Audrey Fabian, Georgiana Culler, Chivilette Thomas, Mary Inabinet, Cecelia Gramling, and teacher Ruth Manning; (third row) Inez Collins, Hazel Bozard, Anna Bess Evans, Daisy Brooks, Minnie Lee Bolen, Edward Hoover, Eldred Bair, and Patrick DeMars; (fourth row) Billy Bozard, Christa Edwins, Hoyt Bookhart, James Bryant, Al Ethridge, and Bill Dukes. (Courtesy Gene Atkinson.)

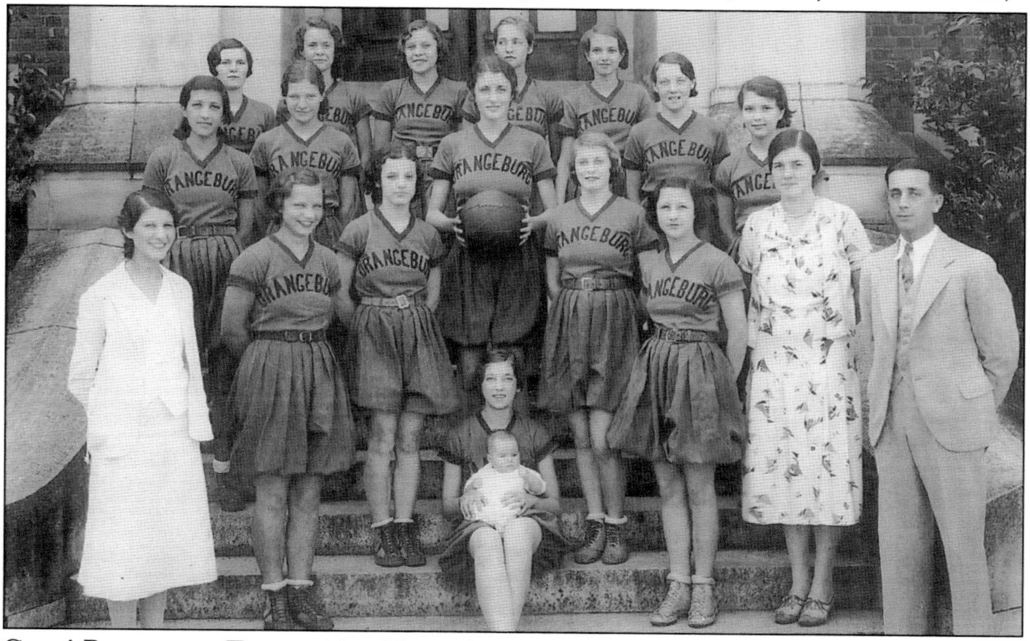

GIRLS' BASKETBALL TEAM, 1931. The 1931 Orangeburg High School girls' basketball team, from left to right, are (seated) Mary Schiffley with Coach Garrison's baby; (first row) Harriet "Sister" Livingston, manager; Ray DeMars; Sunshine Pearce; May Mildred Sandel; Gene Arant; Miss Lucy Love, assistant coach; and Bob Garrison, coach; (second row) Lavern Sharp; Leila Belle Smith; Agnes Watson with ball, Geraldine Lowman, and St. Claire Albergotti; (third row) Dorothy Greene, Annie Louise Renneker, Emilie Crum, June Hodges, and Louise Culler. (Courtesy Mary Schiffley Fairey.)

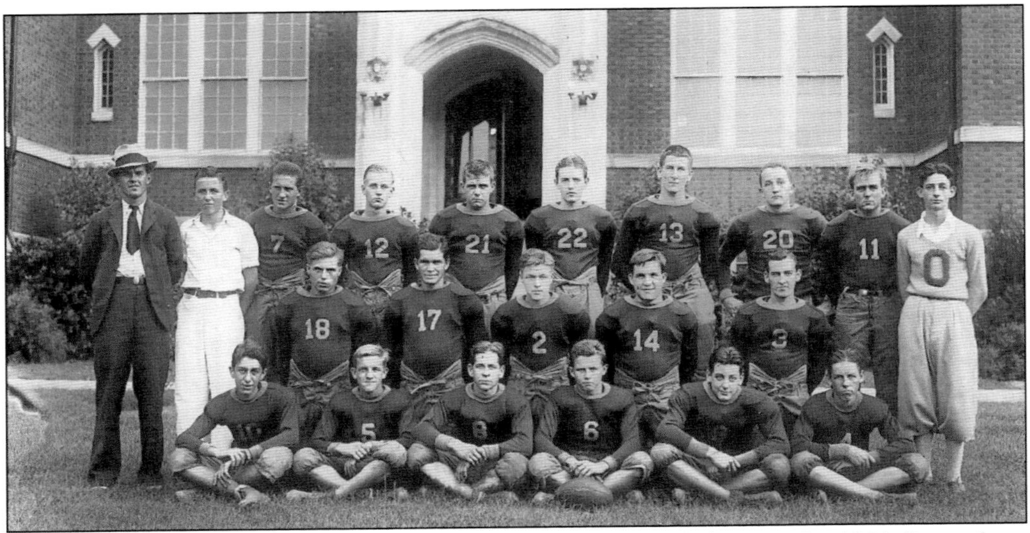

ORANGEBURG HIGH SCHOOL FOOTBALL TEAM, 1931. Featured above is the 1931 Orangeburg High School state championship football team. Members, from left to right, are (first row) Edward Moore, Bubba Dawson, Hydrick Harley, Billy Butler, Robert Furchgott, and Paul Westbury; (middle row) Bonner Hutto, Harold Knotts, Allison Walter, Eugene Richardson, and Colie Hughes; (third row) Bru Boineau (coach), Eddie Langston (assistant manager), Woodrow "Crip" Fair, Jim Bryant, Walter Whisenhunt, John McNamara, Roddy Kissam, C.J. Inabinet, Paul Gwinn, and Sidney Kline (manager). Robert Furchgott achieved further acclaim as the 1998 winner of the Nobel Prize for Medicine. (Courtesy W.C. Ziegler.)

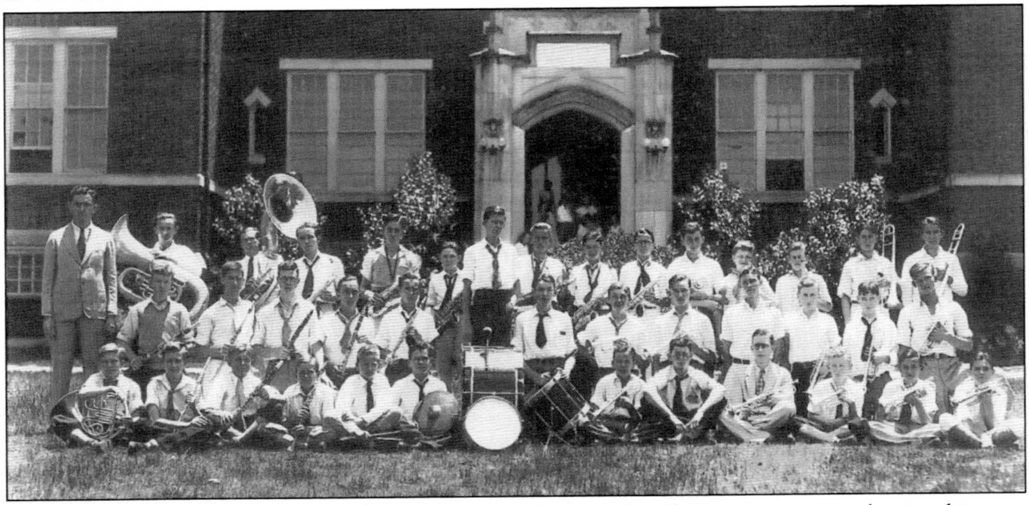

THE 1932 ORANGEBURG HIGH SCHOOL BAND. School bands were very popular in this era. The Orangeburg High School band proudly poses in front of the school. Members, from left to right, are (front row) ? Sharp, Freddie Schiffley, Wilbur Smith, ? Williamson, Billy Boy Salley, Henry Nelms, Dan Dukes, "Spec" Limehouse, Hamp Culler, ? Gramling, John Birney, and Raymond Smith; (middle row) Marchant Smith, Edwin Moseley, Earl Haigler, unidentified, Neil ?, Billy Ziegler, Gillespie Fogle, Edison Fairey, James Slaughter, Herman Spahr, ? Cauthen, and Raymond O'Cain; (back row) band director Victor Jackson, unidentified, Bobby Fogle, Billy Williams, Bill Atkinson, unidentified, Rotie Salley, George Williamson, Neil Price, Norman Avinger, Pete Hunt, unidentified, Russell Wolfe, and two more unidentified students. (Courtesy W.C. Ziegler.)

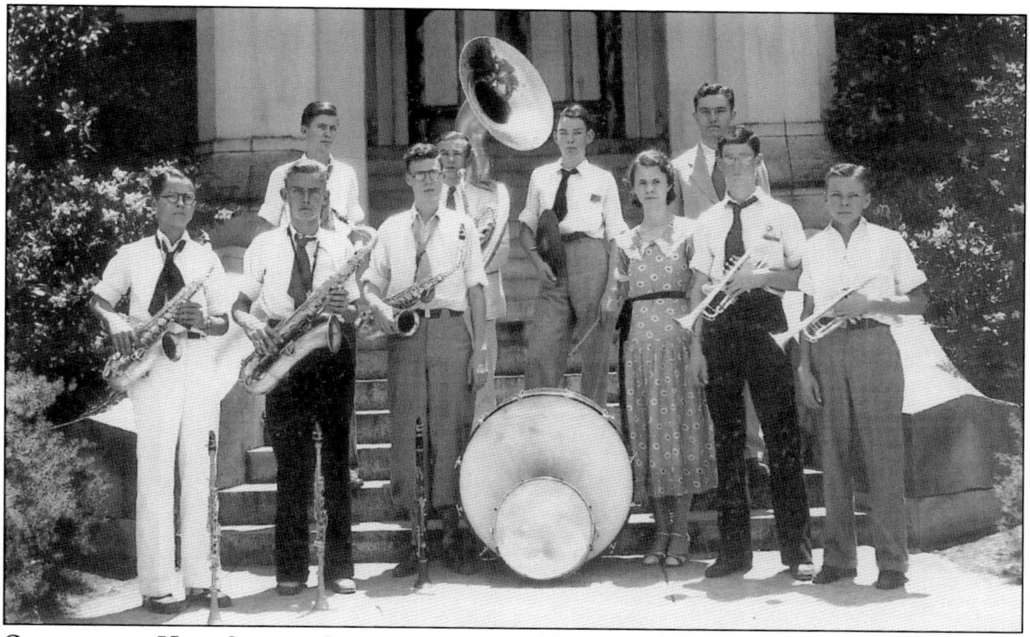

Orangeburg High School Orchestra, 1932. Members of the high school orchestra played at dances and other functions around town during this time period. Members, from left to right, are (front row) Norman Avinger, sax; George Williamson, sax; Earl Haigler, sax; Annie Louise Renneker, piano; Walker Limehouse, trumpet; and Dan Dukes, trumpet; (back row) Rotie Salley, violin; Bobby Fogle, bass; Billy Ziegler, drums; and Victor Jackson, director. (Courtesy W.C. Ziegler.)

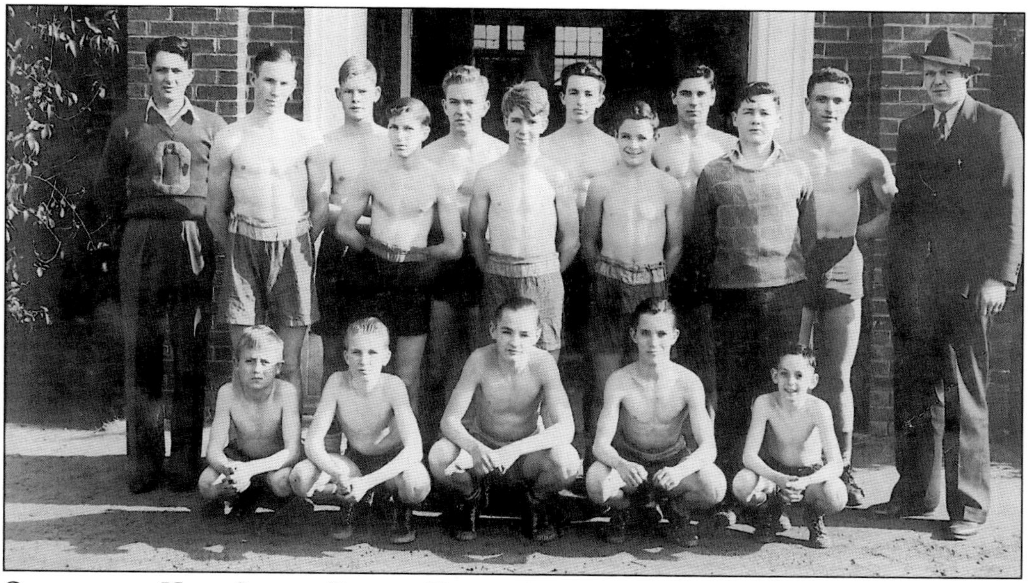

Orangeburg High School Boxing Team, 1937–1938. Boxing was a very popular sport in high school and in amateur leagues during this era. Team members, from left to right, are (front row) Jack Schuyler, Lofton Fanning, Gilbert Hoffman, John Buffkin, and Carroll "Pee Wee" Seawell; (second row) "Boot" Lewis (manager) Johnny O'Cain, Lee Weatherington, J.T. Fanning, Malcolm Carson, Louis Stewart, Henry Edwins, Edgar Seymour, Lloyd Rickenbaker, Briggs Livingston, "Red" Bolen, and Manuel Black (coach). (Courtesy Pat Black.)

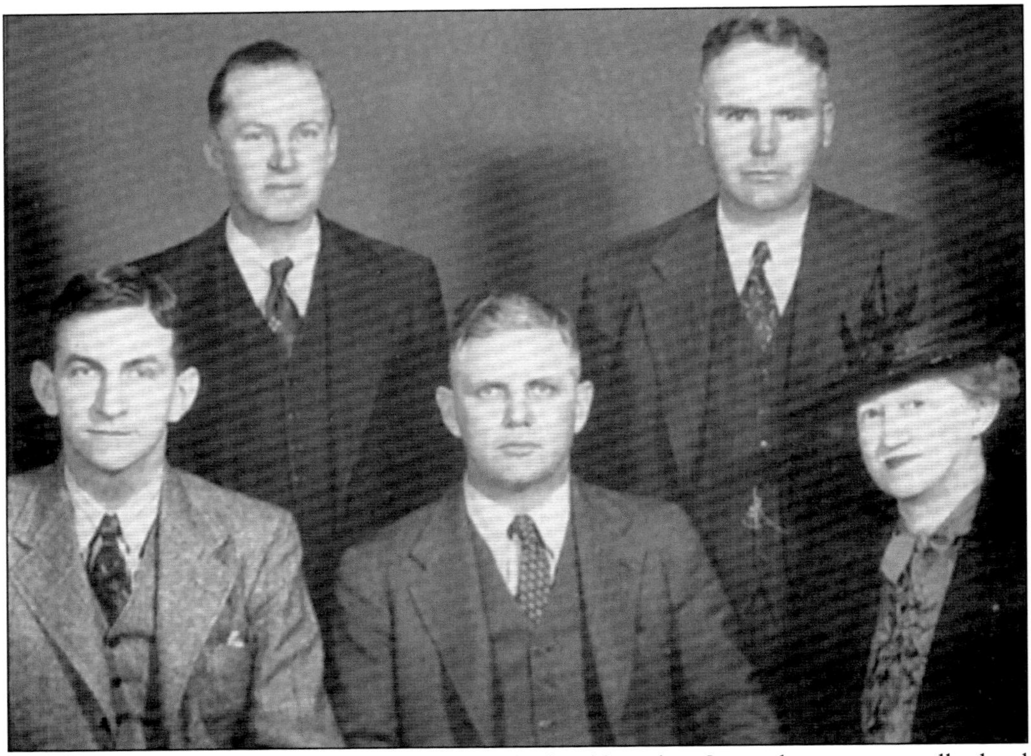

Orangeburg School Board, 1939. The local school board in Orangeburg oversaw all school operations and finances for the district. Pictured here is the 1939 Orangeburg City School Board. The are, from left to right, (front row) James M. Green, Wallace C. Bethea (chairman), and Mrs. Harry Wannamaker Sr.; (back row) Hugo S. Sims and Dr. R.R. Salley. (Courtesy Virginia Till.)

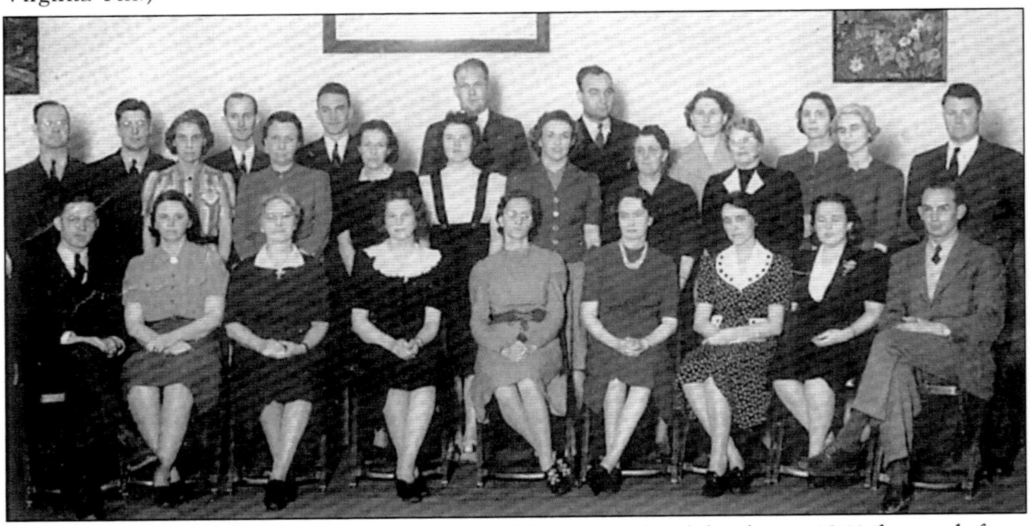

Orangeburg High School Faculty, 1941. The high school faculty in 1941 featured, from left to right, (front row) Burris, Blanton, Walker, Gramling, Bennett, Buchanan, Adden, Richardson, and McGee; (middle row) Cox, Josey, Glaze, Hunter, Hay, Putnam, Metts, Baskervill, Nicholes, and McCallum; (back row) Banister, Ulmer, Williams, Black, McKnight, Salley, and White. (Courtesy Edith H. Kemmerlin.)

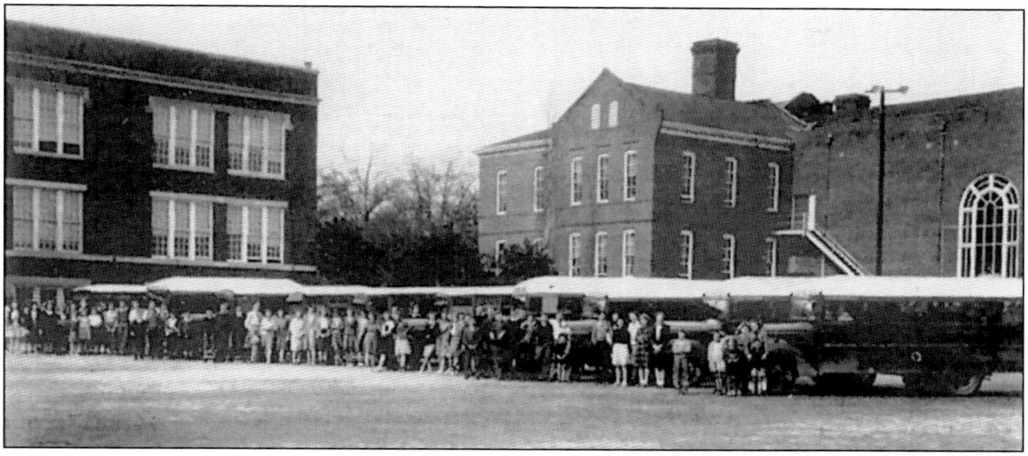

School Bus Transportation, 1941. School buses played an integral role by transporting students in the outlying areas to school, as well as taking athletic teams to their games. Here are some of the school buses and the bus students lined up behind Orangeburg High School in 1941. (Courtesy Edith H. Kemmerlin.)

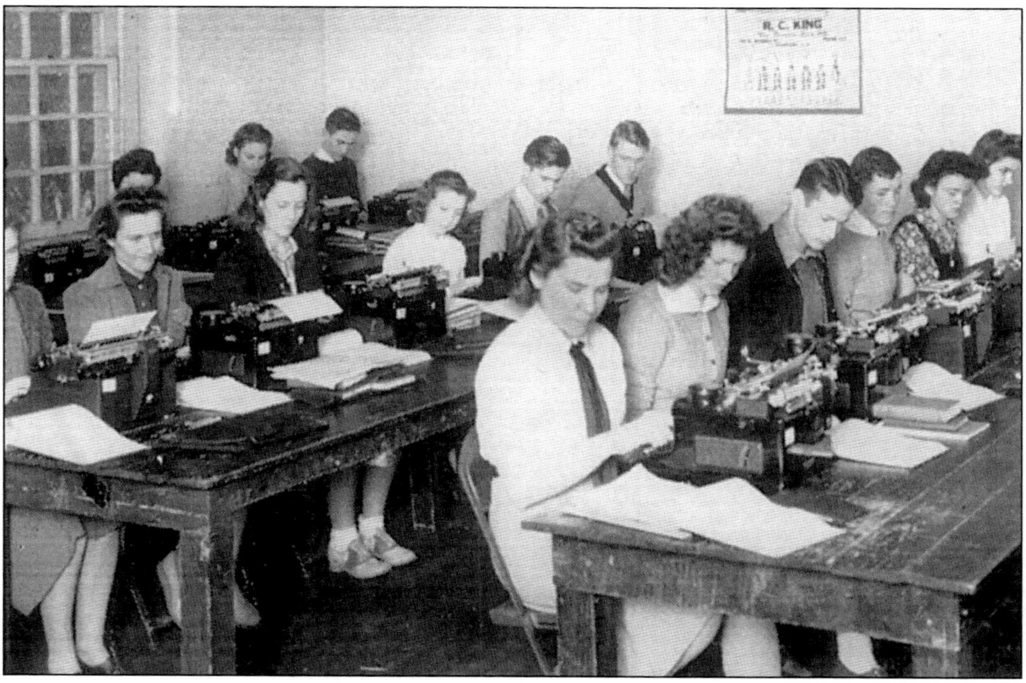

Typing Class, 1941. One of the typing classes at Orangeburg High School is shown here. Manual typewriters were the order of the day then. Note how bare and sparse classroom facilities were back then. (Courtesy Al Fischer.)

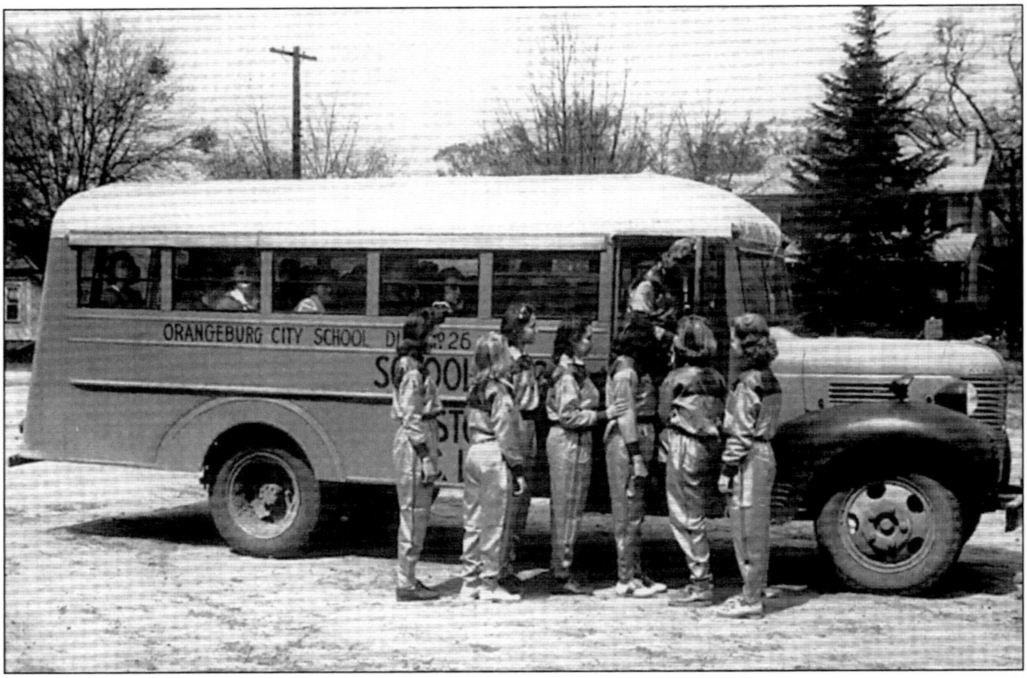

GIRLS' BASKETBALL TEAM, 1941. School buses were needed to transport athletes to out-of-town athletic events. Here the Orangeburg High School girls' basketball team loads up on what was considered a modern bus for that era. (Courtesy Al Fischer.)

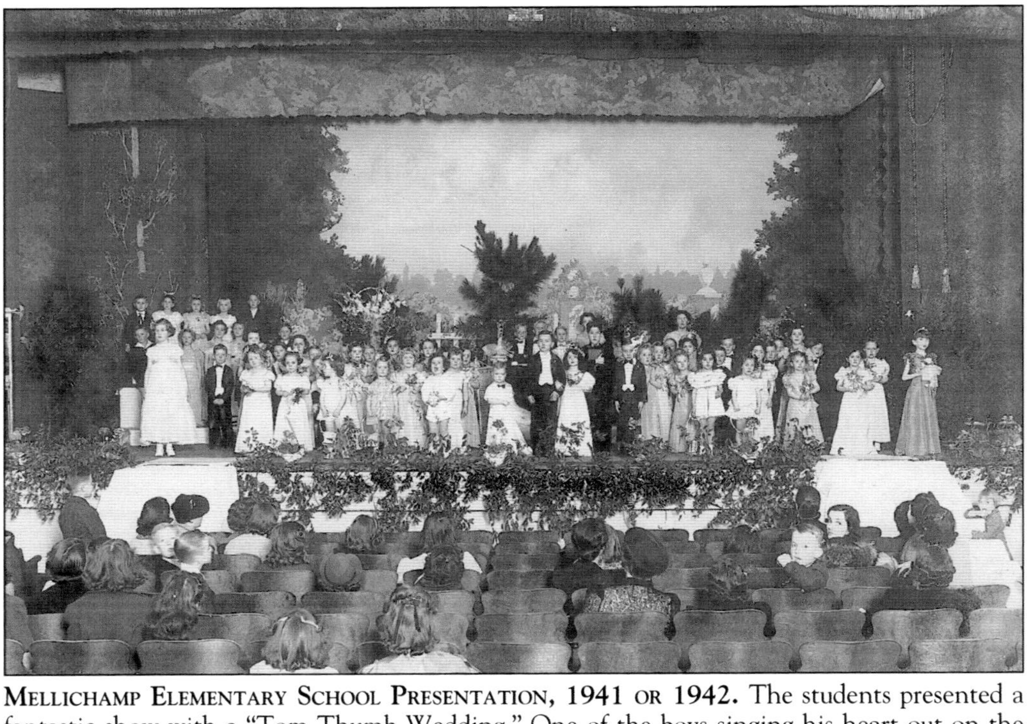

MELLICHAMP ELEMENTARY SCHOOL PRESENTATION, 1941 OR 1942. The students presented a fantastic show with a "Tom Thumb Wedding." One of the boys singing his heart out on the front row was Brown Bradley, who as an adult would sing professionally in presentations and concerts in New York City and throughout the entire United States. (Courtesy Sylvia Boone.)

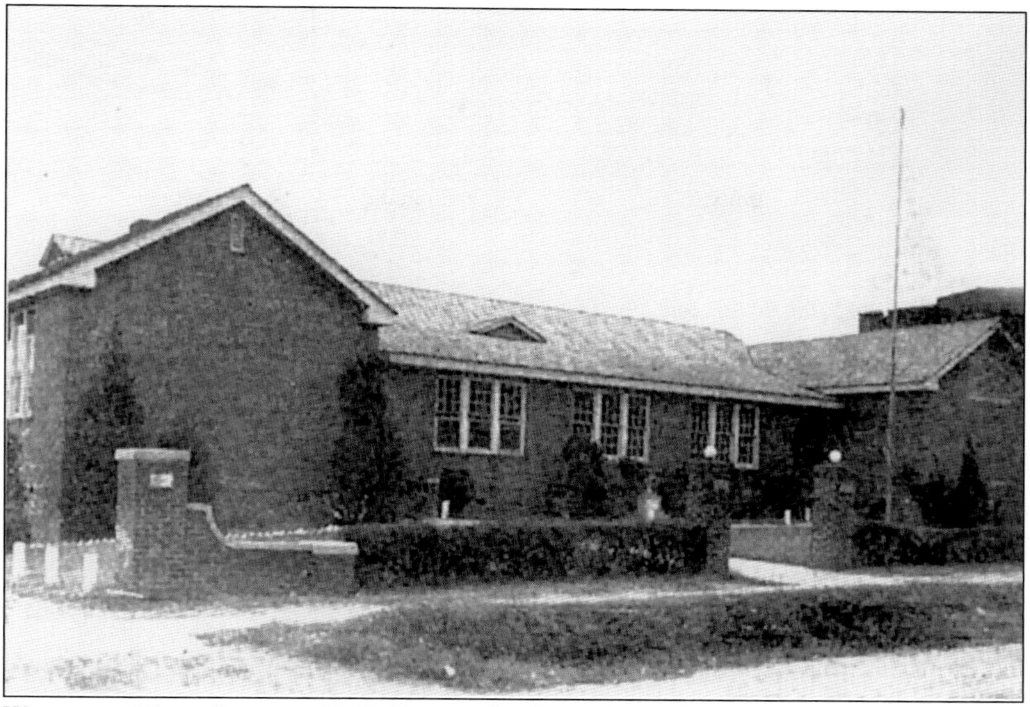

Wilkinson High School, 1946. During the days of racial segregation African-American students attended separate schools. This 1947 photograph shows the academic building at Wilkinson High School on Goff Avenue. Wilkinson High opened at this location in 1937. (Courtesy Cecil Williams.)

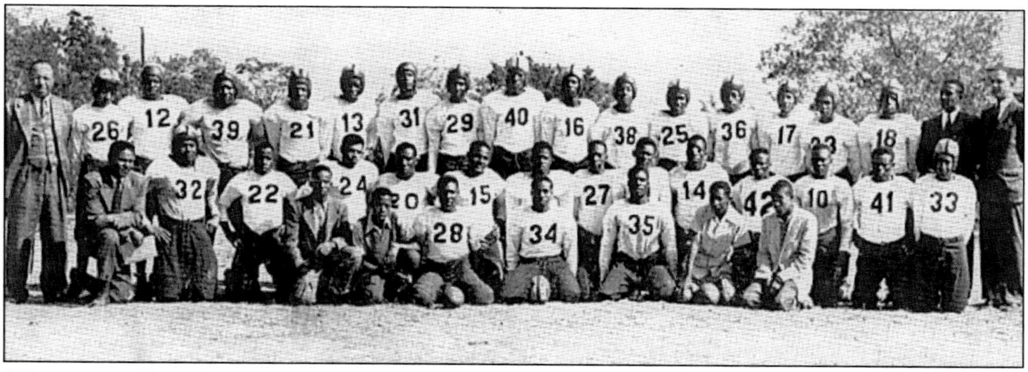

Wilkinson High School Football Team, 1946. Pictured above is the 1946 Wilkinson High School football team. They are, from left to right, (front row) James Brunson, trainer; Lewis Wallace, trainer; Ernest Seawright; Howard Coleman; Samuel Keitt; Willie Green, trainer; and Nathaniel Robinson, trainer; (middle row) Robert Howard, coach; Stoney Toomer; Julius Murphy; Eugene Williams; Austin Gaillard; B.E. Evans; John Haynes; Otto Garner; Albert Williams; James Miller; Earl Jenkins; Thomas Jackson; Harden Zeigler; and Robert Gaffney; (back row) Mr. Harper, assistant coach; Hammie Pinckney; Theodore Johnson; Clyde Moorer; Elijah Jenkins; Milligan Thomas; Willie Aiken; Earl Johnson; Mervin Brown; Lemuel Dantzler; Charles Aiken; Julius Bowman; C.D. Dantzler; Wilbur Green; Thomas Grant; Edward Jamison; J. Pearson, assistant coach; and T.K. Bythewood, assistant coach. (Courtesy Cecil Williams.)

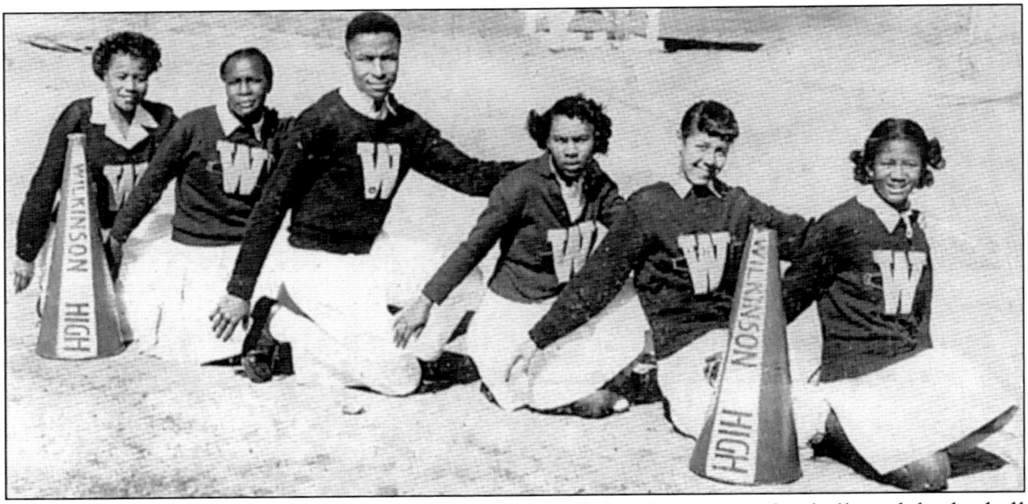

WILKINSON HIGH SCHOOL CHEERLEADERS, 1946. School spirit at football and basketball games was led by these energetic cheerleaders at Wilkinson High School during the school year 1946–1947. They are, from left to right, Minnie Toomer, Mildred Ellis, Cornell Johnson, Rosebud Antley, Sandra Glover, and Geneva Aiken. (Courtesy Cecil Williams.)

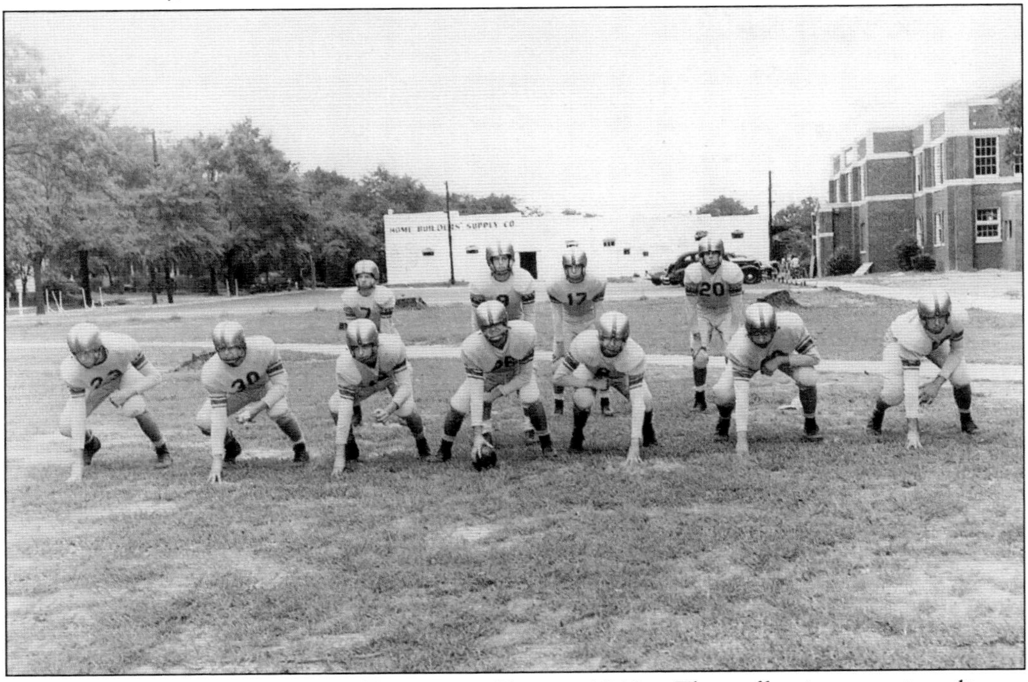

ORANGEBURG HIGH SCHOOL FOOTBALL TEAM, 1948. The offensive starting lineup from the 1948 season is shown here. Quarterback Johnny Gramling went on to star at the University of South Carolina where he set several school records. This was the first year that legendary Coach Bill Clark began coaching in Orangeburg. Altogether seven starters and two reserves from the 1948 team would later be granted full athletic scholarships to various colleges. Pictured from left to right are (linemen) Dreher Gaskin; L.P. Thackston, co-captain; Dean Livingston; Edward "Hank" Mirmow; Tommy Sheriff, co-captain; Bill Spires; and Louis Boone; (backfield) Jimmy Johnson; Johnny Gramling; Bobby Wactor; and Jim Sloan. (Courtesy Louis Boone.)

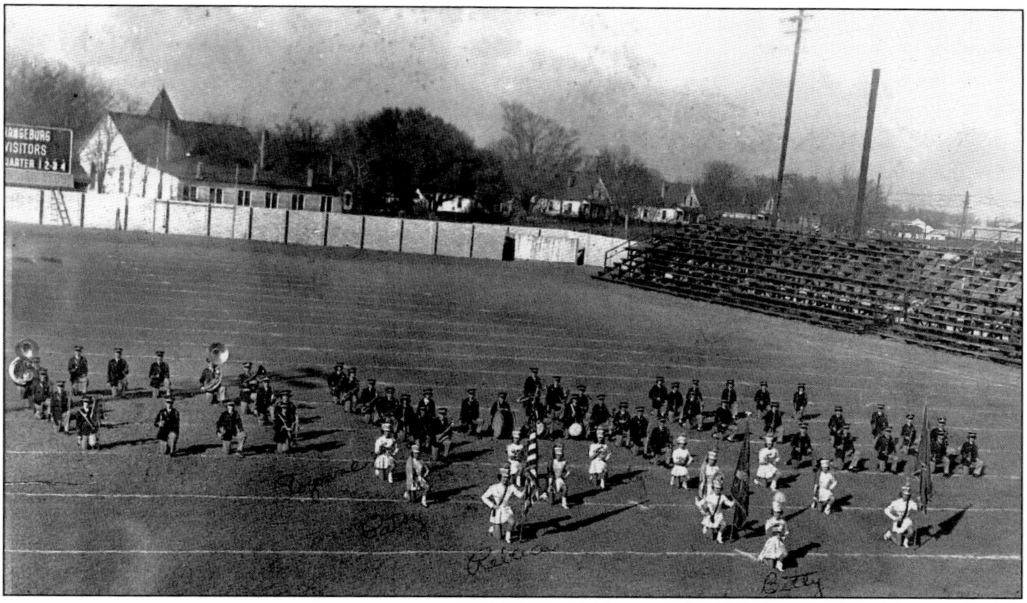

Orangeburg High School Band, c. 1949. The Orangeburg High School Band with their accompanying majorettes are lined up spelling "OHS" at Fairgrounds Stadium, which later became Judge Hughes Stadium, named after longtime fair manager Jerry Hughes. Each year during the fair week, Orangeburg would play a home game and "Big Friday" was set aside for a college game. Some of the participating college football teams through the years were the University of South Carolina, Clemson, Wofford, Citadel, Newberry, and Presbyterian. (Courtesy Sylvia S. Boone.)

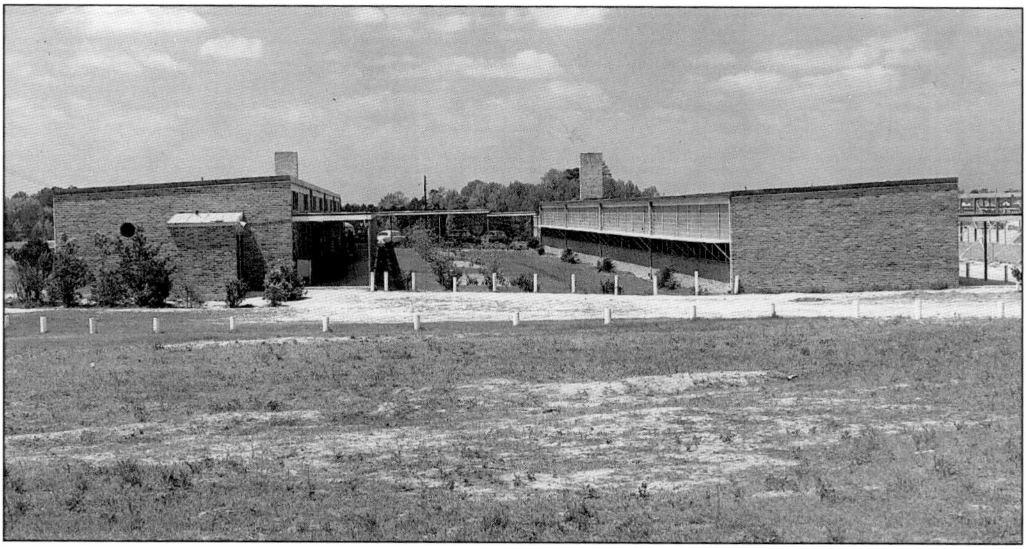

New Orangeburg Junior High School, c. 1953. As the post-war population boom created a shortage of classrooms, a new junior high school was built on Bennett Avenue, which was on the edge of town back then. Only two corridors were built in 1950; however, when it was decided to relocate Orangeburg High School to this campus in 1954, additional corridors had to be built. Notice construction on the right of the picture. The two corridors shown here are the "A" and "B" corridors of the current William J. Clark Middle School. (Courtesy Chamber of Commerce.)

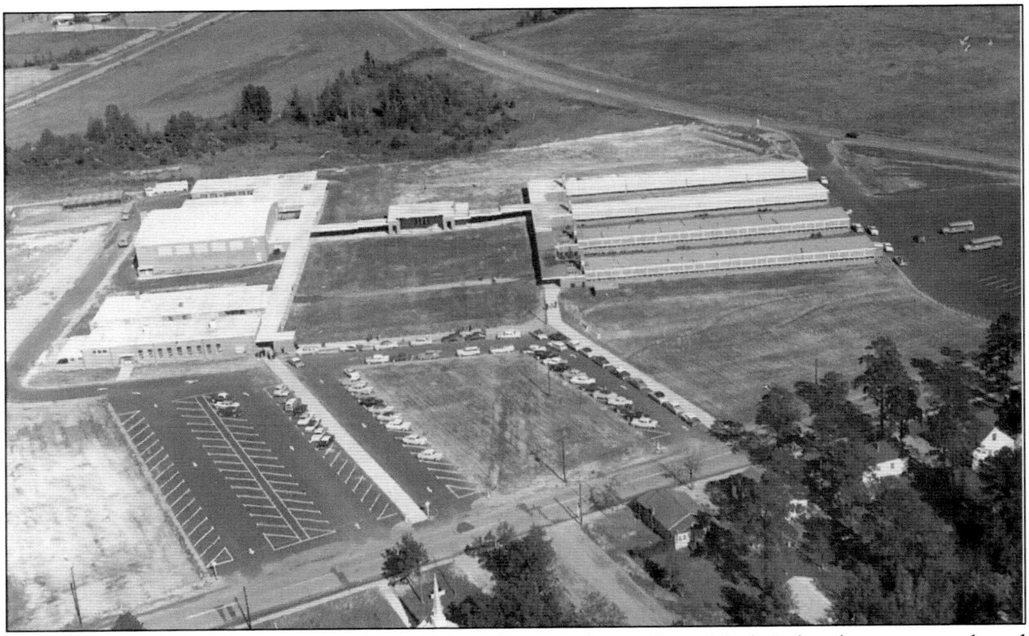

NEW ORANGEBURG HIGH SCHOOL, c. 1954. The new Orangeburg High School campus replaced the Junior High School on Bennett Avenue. Note the vacant field in the upper right that would later become Orangeburg Mall in 1968. Several more buildings and corridors would be added to this school as the years went on. This was also the site of the combined Orangeburg-Wilkinson High School from 1971 to 1984. Beginning in 1984 it became Bennett Middle School and was renamed William J. Clark Middle School in 1991. (Courtesy Chamber of Commerce.)

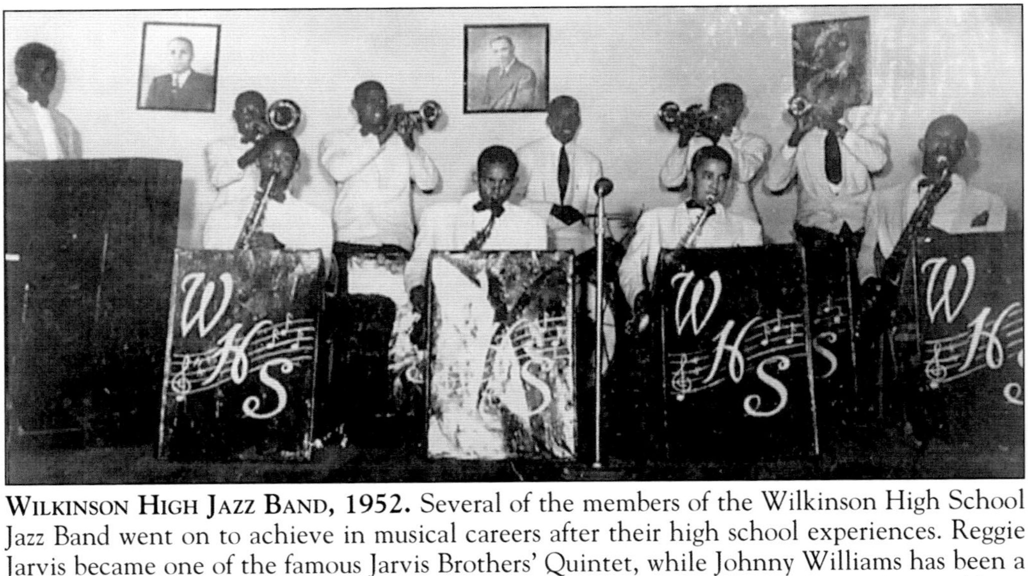

WILKINSON HIGH JAZZ BAND, 1952. Several of the members of the Wilkinson High School Jazz Band went on to achieve in musical careers after their high school experiences. Reggie Jarvis became one of the famous Jarvis Brothers' Quintet, while Johnny Williams has been a member of the Count Basie Band for over 30 years. Shown here, from left to right, are (front row) Bobby Knight, tenor sax; Al Williams, alto sax; Johnny Williams, alto sax; and Nick Brailey, tenor sax; (second row) Reggie Jarvis, vocals; Bobby Sharperson, trombone; Bobby Evans, trumpet; James Funchess, drums; Ben Felder, trumpet; and Nat Howard, trumpet. (Courtesy Johnny Williams.)

Three

CHURCHES

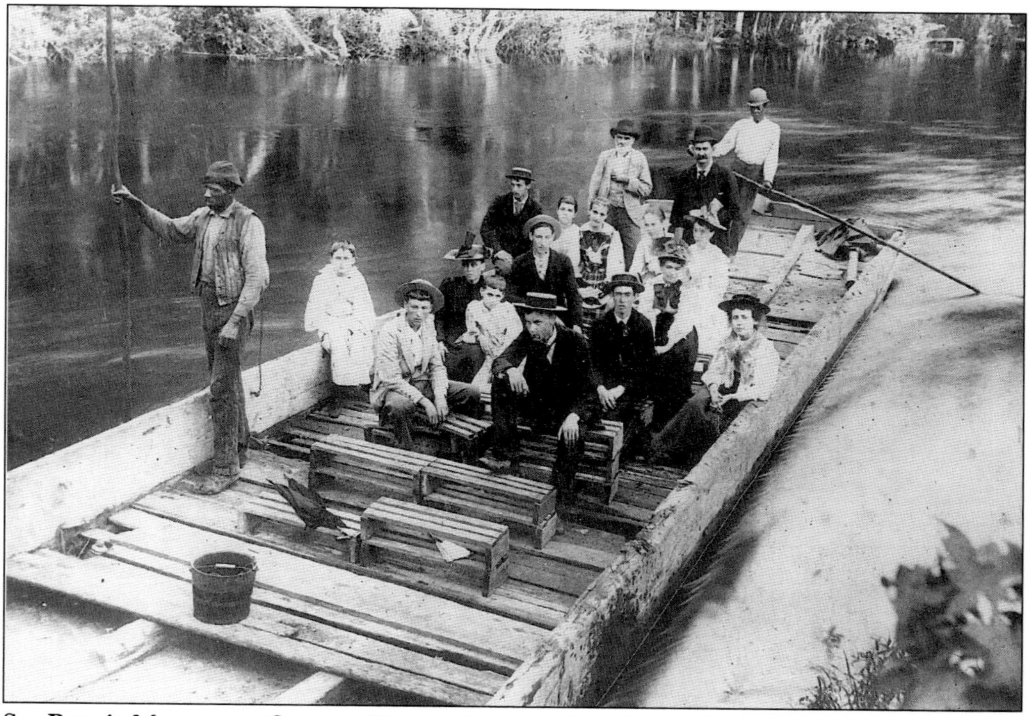

ST. PAUL'S METHODIST CHURCH YOUTH GROUP, 1894. Mr. and Mrs. B.B. Owen taught the youth Sunday School class at the time of this outing on the Edisto River. The class enjoyed an ice cream and cake picnic afterwards at High Hill Landing. They are, from left to right, (first row) Charlie Perreyclear and Emmit Dibble; (second row) Addie Owen, Mrs. B.B. "Betty" Owen, Bessie Owen, Marion "Buck" Inabinet, and Ella Wolfe; (third row) Walter Berry and Belle Wolfe; (fourth row) Allie Webster, Annie Fair Dickson, Agnes Jones, Josie Webster, and Addie Livingston; (fifth row) Joseph P. Harley and B.B. Owen. The boatmen are Charles Frost (father) and Charlie (son, at tiller). (Courtesy Orangeburg County Historical Society.)

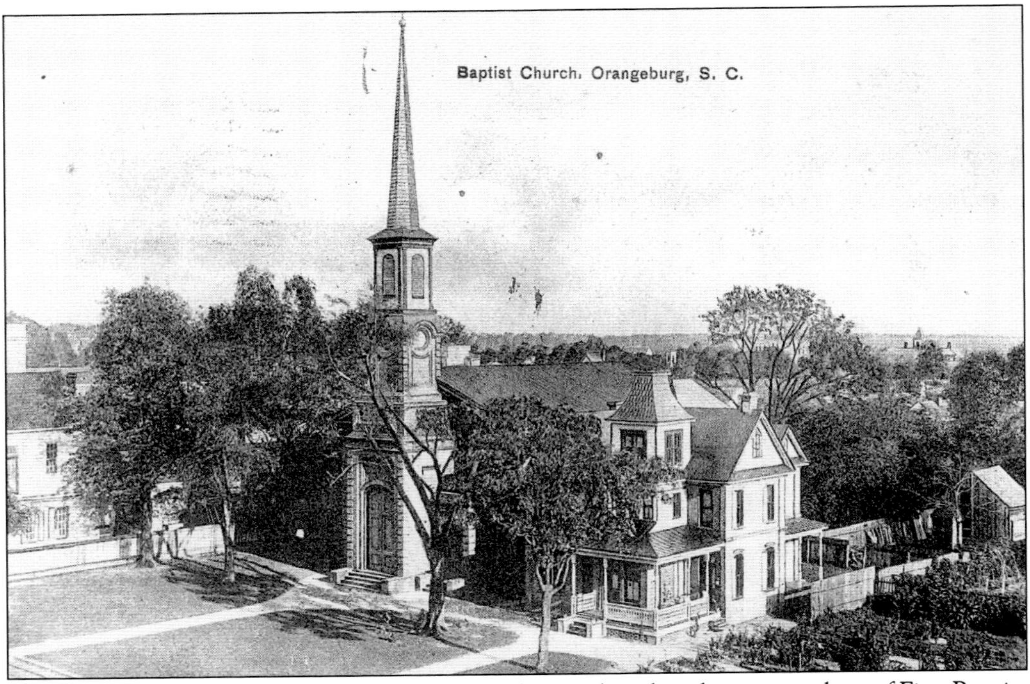

First Baptist Church, c. 1900. Only 15 people were listed as charter members of First Baptist Church in July 1860. The sanctuary here was constructed in 1863 at a cost of $8,000. It was remodeled in 1914, but a major fire in 1939 caused considerable damage. The parsonage was built shortly after 1891. Note the vegetable garden, a common occurrence in those days, at the parsonage. (Courtesy Orangeburg County Historical Society.)

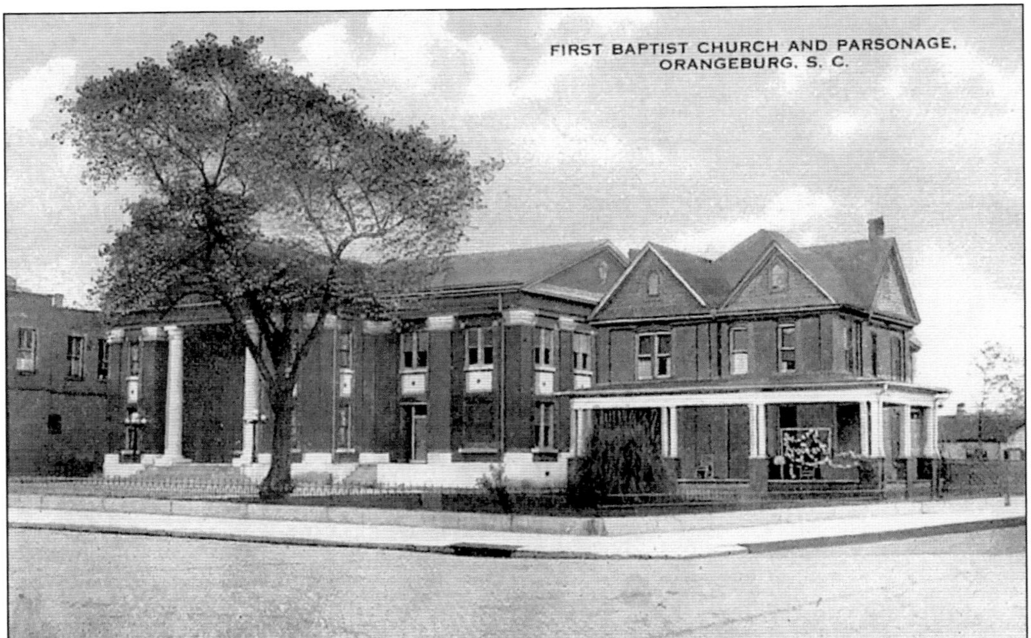

First Baptist Church, 1916. A major renovation of First Baptist Church in 1914 produced this new look for the church. (Courtesy Addie S. Felkel.)

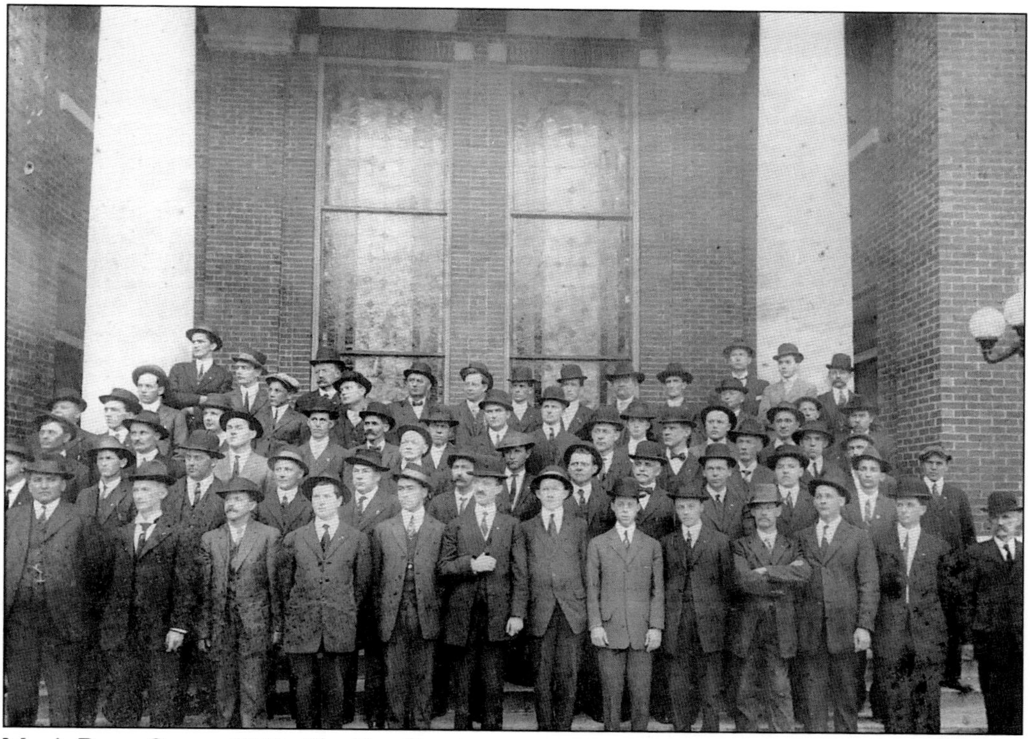

Men's Bible Class, 1925. The First Baptist Men's Bible Class is gathered here on the front steps of the church for this group photograph. (Courtesy Edith Gillam.)

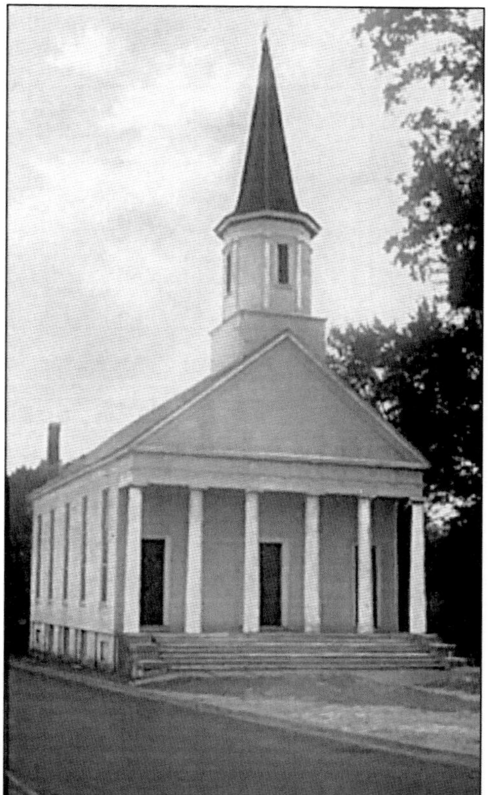

First Presbyterian Church, c. 1920. Founded in 1836 the First Presbyterian Church was located at the corner of Russell and Doyle Streets, just in back of the current location of the Orangeburg Pharmacy building. (Courtesy Orangeburg County Historical Society.)

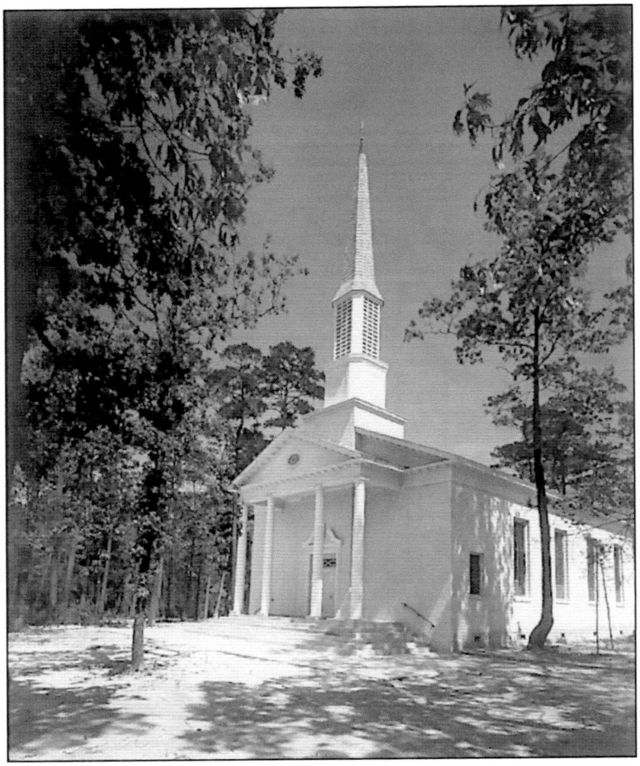

First Presbyterian Church, 1950. The church had outgrown its Russell Street location, and a new sanctuary and education building were constructed on Summers Avenue across from Sunnyside Cemetery in 1950. This view shows the church about the time of its first occupation before any shrubbery and landscaping were done. (Courtesy Chamber of Commerce.)

Episcopal Church of the Redeemer, 1899. Previously located on Railroad Avenue (now Boulevard) near Peasley Street, the sanctuary was moved on rolling logs and pulled by mules to its current location on Russell Street in 1891. (Courtesy St. Paul's United Methodist Church Archives.)

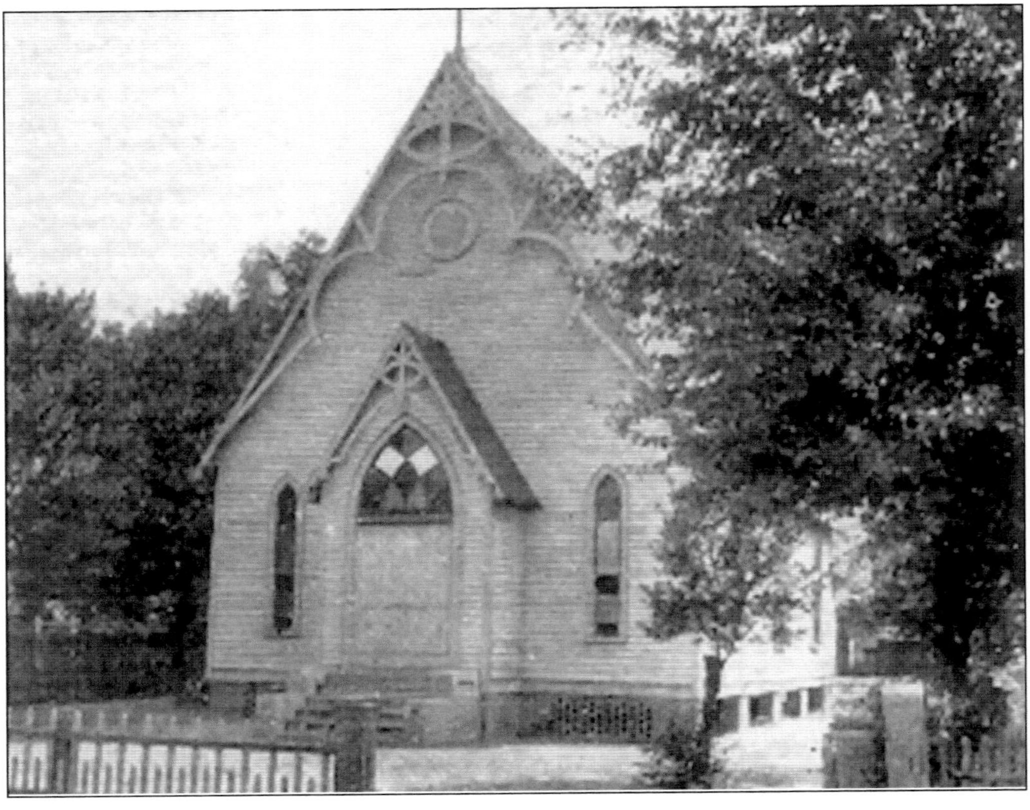

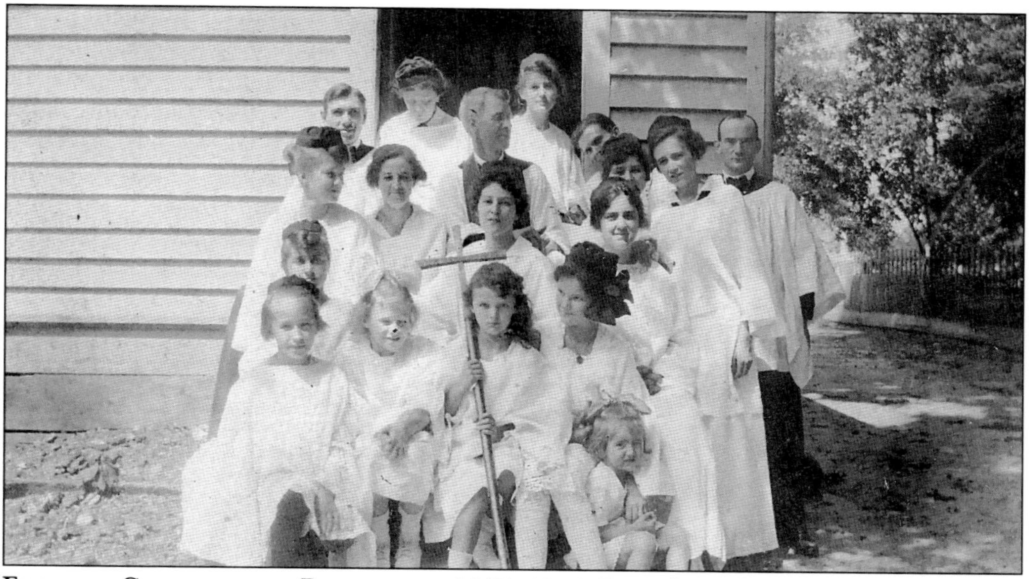

Episcopal Church of the Redeemer, c. 1907–1914. Several members are shown outside the sanctuary with Rev. W.S. Holmes, Rector. The crucifer has been identified as Lydia Glover. The little girl turned sideways in the front is Caroline Schiffley, and her mother, Lula Kate Mewborne Schiffley, is standing to the far right. (Courtesy Episcopal Church of the Redeemer.)

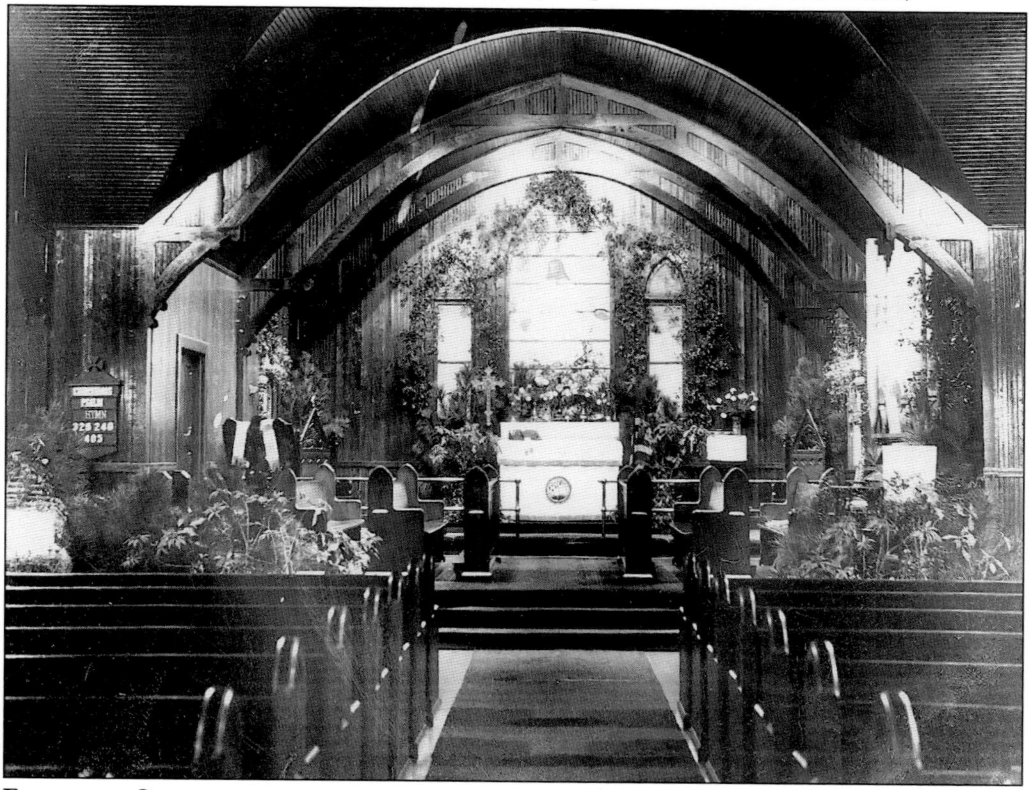

Episcopal Church of the Redeemer, Interior, 1935. The beautiful artisanship in the woodwork of the church interior is shown in this 1935 photograph. (Courtesy Russell Wolfe family.)

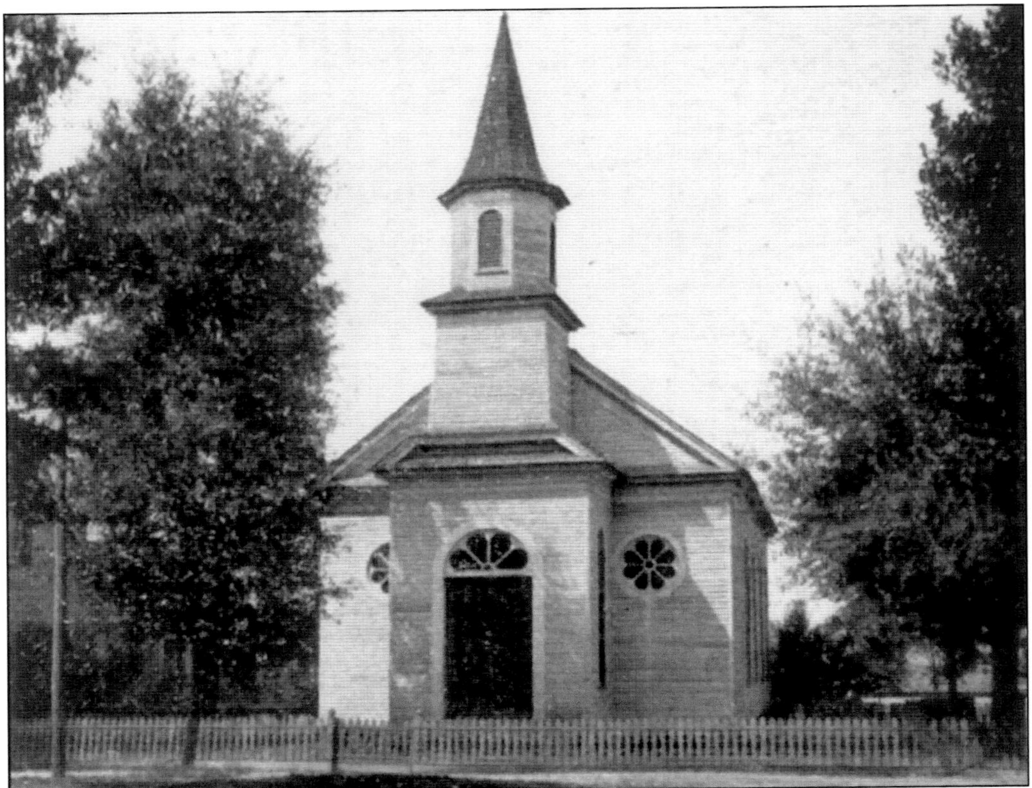

ORANGEBURG LUTHERAN CHURCH, 1899. For many years the Orangeburg Lutheran Church was a fixture at the corner of Amelia and Green Streets. The church sanctuary pictured here was dedicated in 1856, and the congregation was listed as 22 in number at that time. This building faithfully served the needs of its membership until 1950 when the Ellis Avenue sanctuary was built. (Courtesy St. Paul's United Methodist Church Archives.)

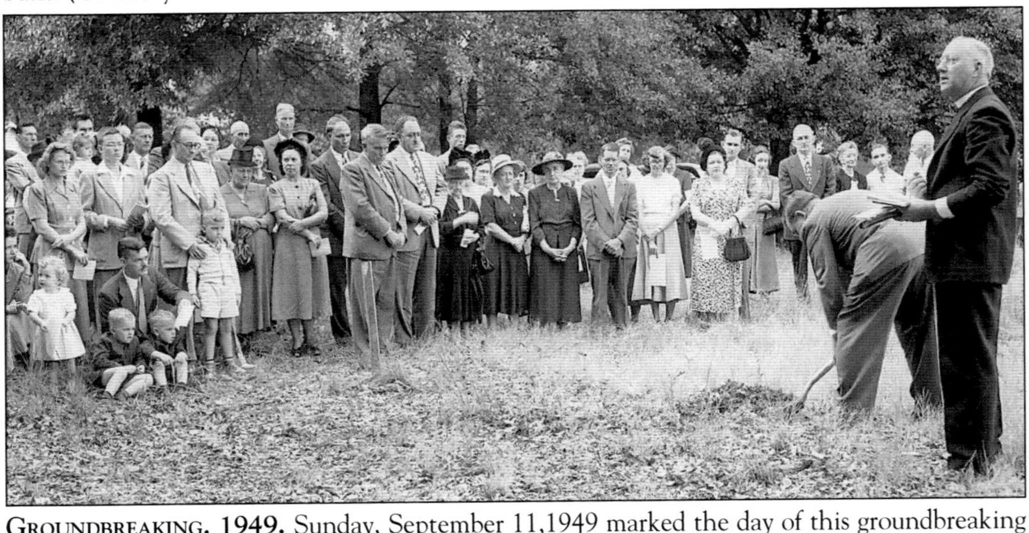

GROUNDBREAKING, 1949. Sunday, September 11,1949 marked the day of this groundbreaking photograph for the beautiful new Orangeburg Lutheran Church on Ellis Avenue. On August 13, 1950 the new church was dedicated and the congregation occupied it for the first time. (Courtesy Orangeburg Lutheran Church.)

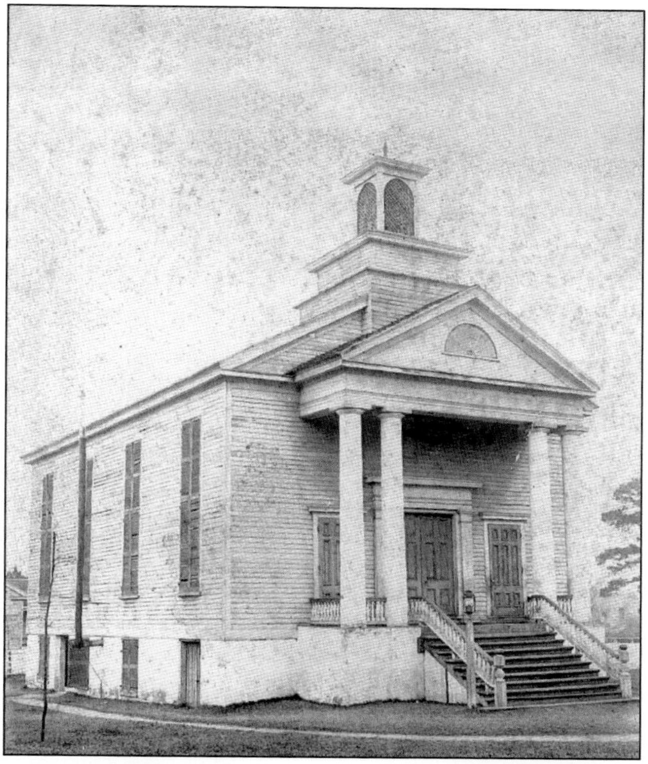

St. Paul's Methodist Church, 1894. This was the second sanctuary for the congregation of St. Paul's and was built in 1859. In 1892 a terrible thunderstorm with extremely high winds blew the steeple off while Sunday School was going on inside. It is said that the congregation then opened their umbrellas and the service continued. A small belfry seen here was built to replace the steeple. At this time a decision was made to build a new and much larger sanctuary building to house the ever-growing congregation. (Courtesy Orangeburg County Historical Society.)

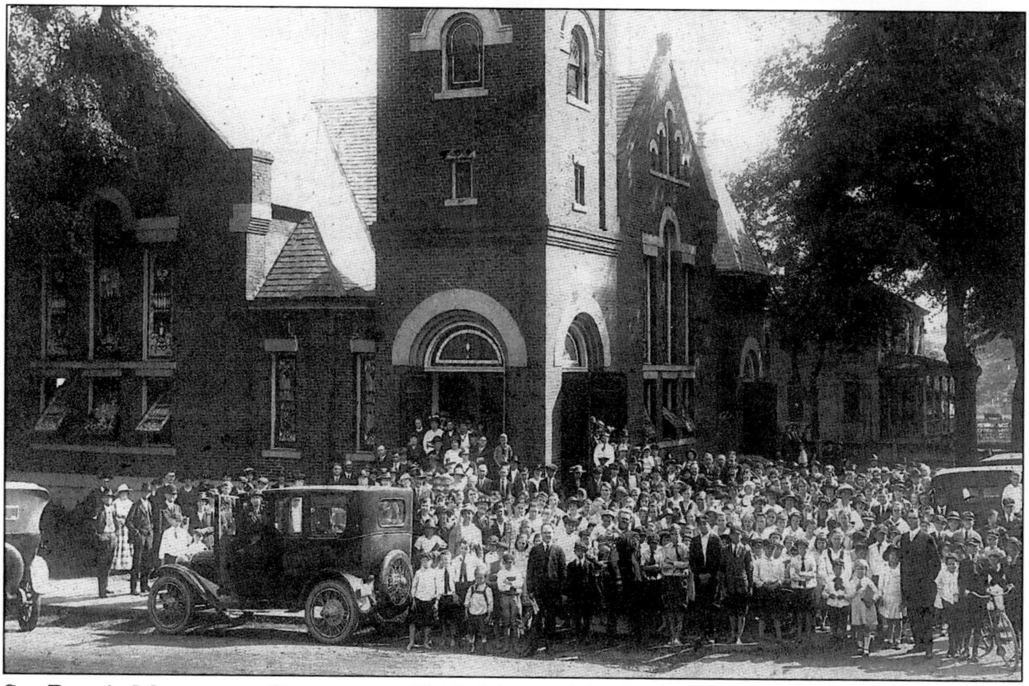

St. Paul's Methodist Church, c. 1920. Many of St. Paul's members are shown posing for this picture right after Sunday church services. Because air conditioning was not existent in that day, note the swiveled stained glass windows that let in fresh air. Hand-held fans were very common in that era during warm weather. (Courtesy St. Paul's United Methodist Church.)

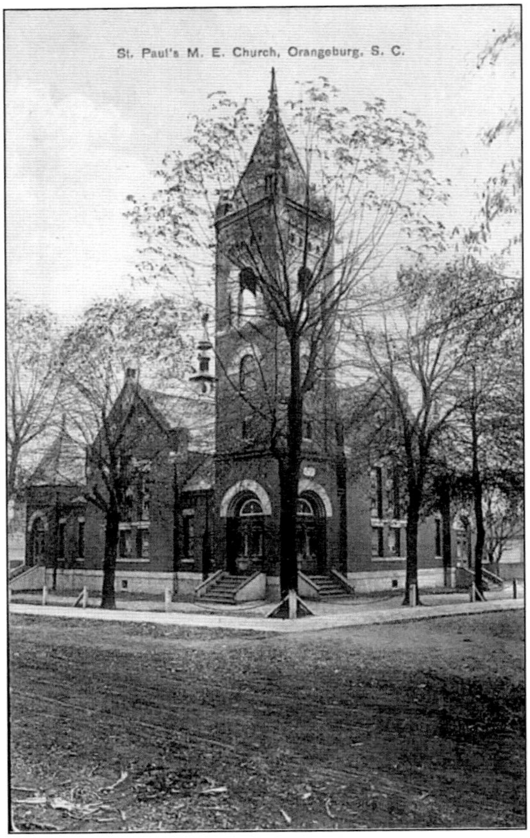

ST. PAUL'S METHODIST CHURCH, 1907. Construction began on this magnificent structure in 1896, and it was dedicated in January of 1898. At the time of construction this was the largest church sanctuary in Orangeburg, and St. Paul's had the largest church membership in town too. (Courtesy Anna Lou Wolfe.)

ST. LUKE'S PRESBYTERIAN CHURCH, 1940s. African-American Presbyterians established St. Luke's Presbyterian Church in the 1860s. The sanctuary building pictured here on Lowman Street faithfully served the congregation for 69 years before a new church was built on Mingo Street. (Courtesy St. Luke's Presbyterian Church.)

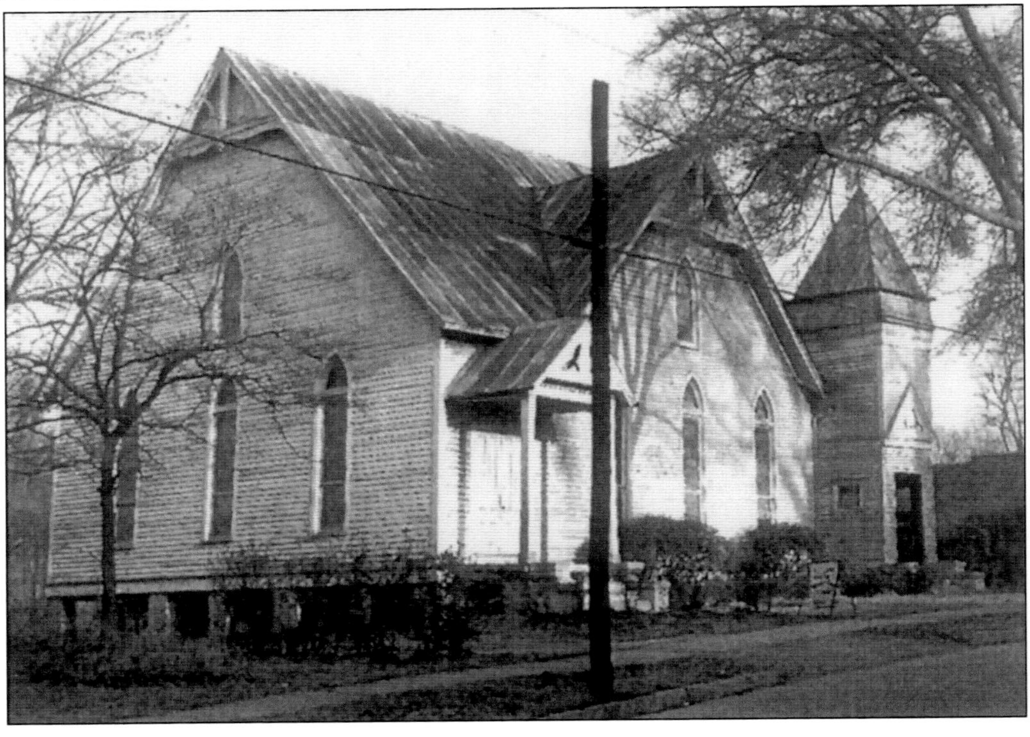

HOLY TRINITY CATHOLIC CHURCH, 1899. This beautiful edifice was constructed in 1893 on Amelia Street. Three of the four corners here were then occupied by churches; the others were St. Paul's Methodist Church and Orangeburg Lutheran Church. Also, Trinity Methodist Church was located across the street on the next block. This area could truly be called "Amen Corner." (Courtesy St. Paul's United Methodist Church Archives.)

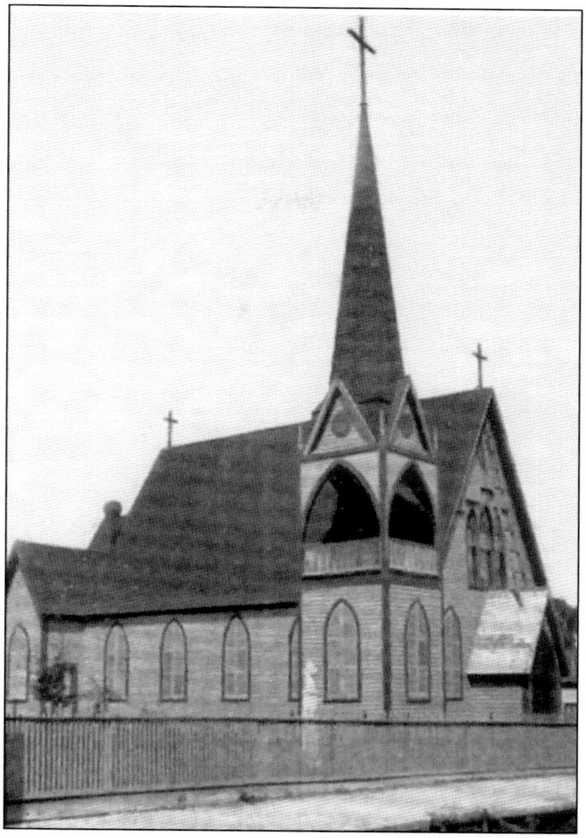

HOLY TRINITY CATHOLIC CHURCH, 1934. The rectory to house the priests was built next door a year or so before this 1934 photograph was taken. Also major renovations were needed on the church itself, and the exterior was bricked up to match the adjacent new rectory. Church members are featured here out front after the 1934 re-dedication ceremony. (Courtesy Holy Trinity Catholic Church.)

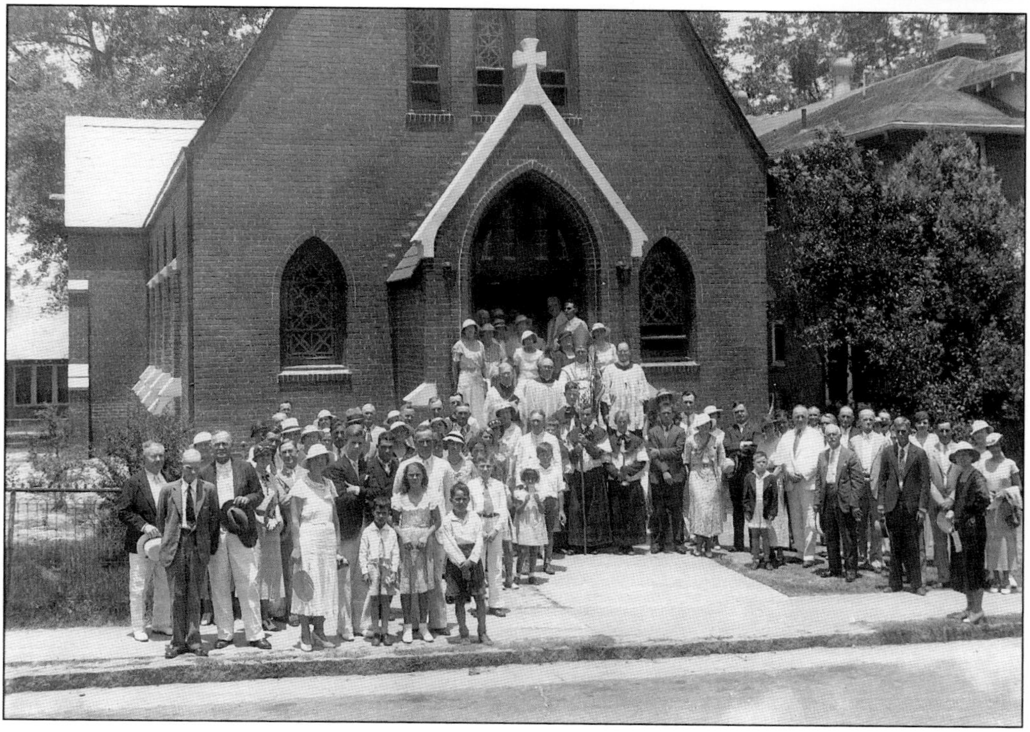

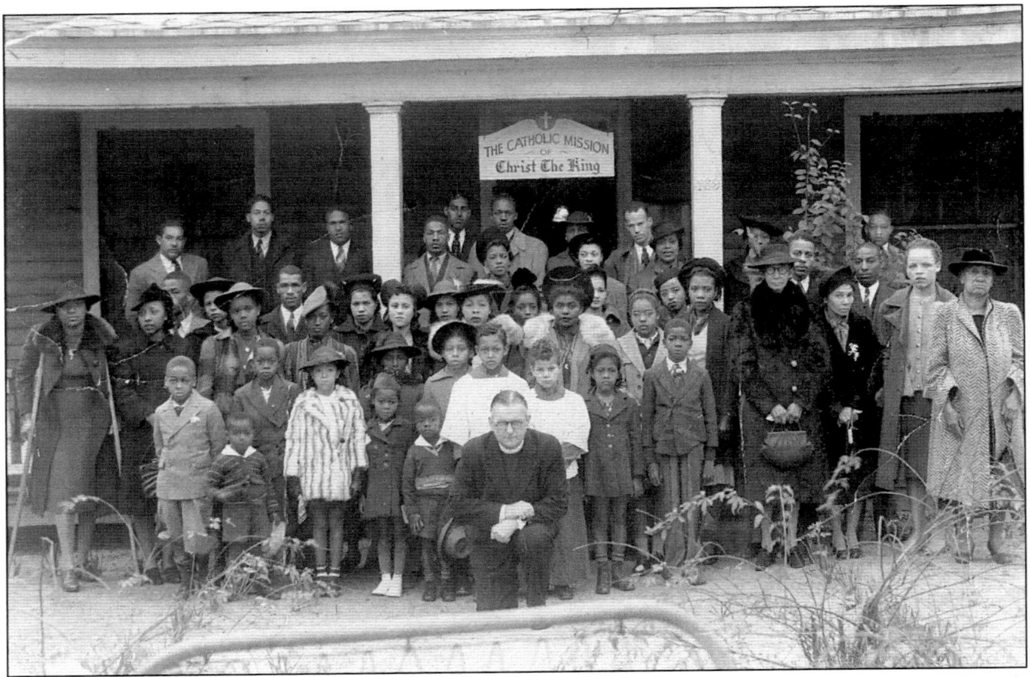

Christ the King Church, 1939. Holy Trinity Catholic Church established a Catholic church for African Americans in Orangeburg in 1939. It was located at first in a rented house at the corner of Boulevard and Oaks Street. Father Martin Gilhooly, pictured in the foreground, was the local priest who helped lead these efforts. (Courtesy Holy Trinity Catholic Church.)

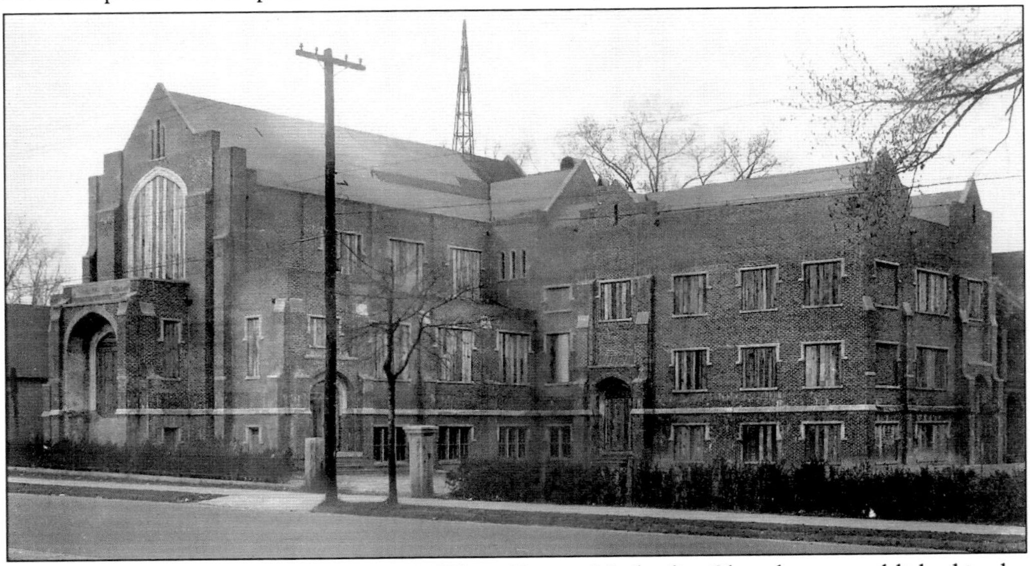

Trinity Methodist Church, c. 1935. When Trinity Methodist Church was established in the 1860s, it was located on the block next to St. Paul's Methodist Church. In 1927 it moved to a new location on Boulevard across the street and railroad tracks from what is now South Carolina State University. The old location was used for the new Orangeburg County Courthouse. This picture shows the windows boarded up as fund-raising took many years for construction of this new church and education building, so the entire structure was not completed until 1942. (Courtesy Russell Wolfe family.)

Four

Orangeburg County Fair

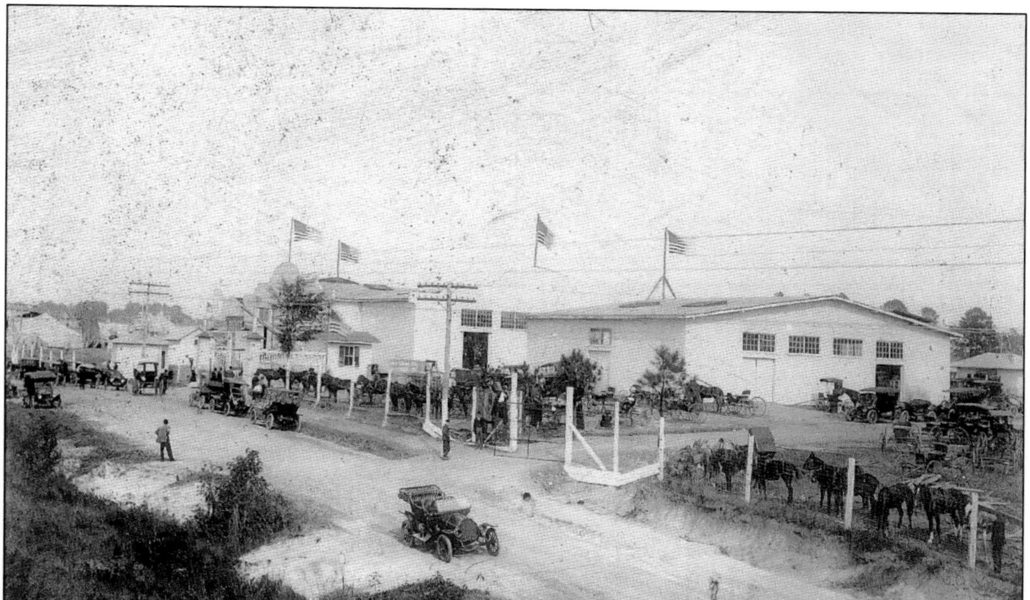

Orangeburg County Fair, c. 1916. The Orangeburg County Fair was established in 1911 to provide a forum in the fall for everyone to come together not only for fun, but to display and compete with their best canned goods, quilting, flower displays, and other goods, as well as with their livestock. Forerunners to the county fair were the Orangeburg Agricultural and Mechanical Association Fair established in 1873 and later the annual Fall Festival. The Orangeburg County Fair today has the distinction of being the oldest continually run fair in all of South Carolina. (Courtesy Orangeburg County Fair Association.)

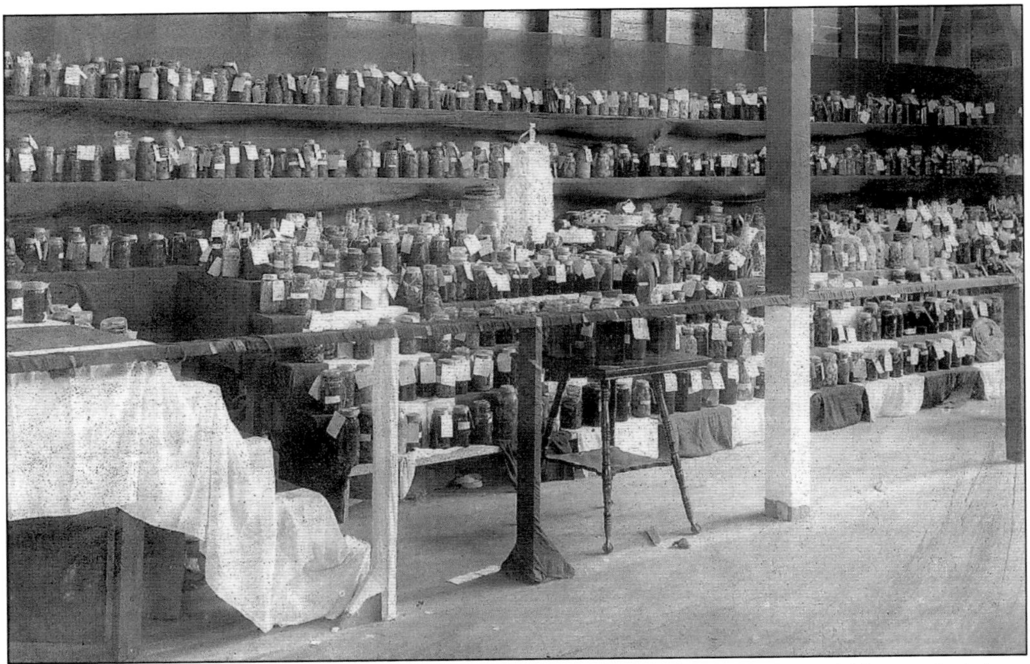

Canned Goods Competition, c. 1915. Ladies from all over the county would bring their best canned goods for display and competition each year at the fair. (Courtesy Orangeburg County Fair Association.)

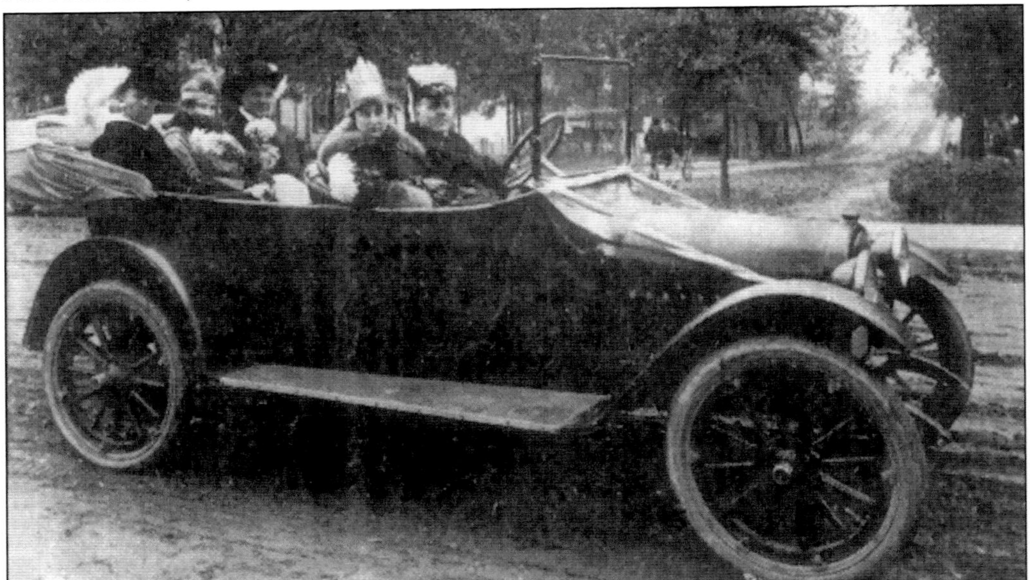

Fair Parade, 1916. A parade was held in conjunction with the fair in the early years of its existence. This car features several members of the queen's court all decked out in plumes and streamers for the big occasion. Pictured from left to right are Henry Sims (who later became a state senator and president of Winthrop College), Miss Mana Claffey, Willie Bates, Miss Mamie Zeigler, and A. Hydrick Hildebrand. The location of this photo was the corner of Broughton and Lindale Streets. The Oakland car was a gift to Miss Zeigler from her grandfather prior to her marriage to Mr. Hildebrand. (Courtesy Virginia Hildebrand Jeffcoat.)

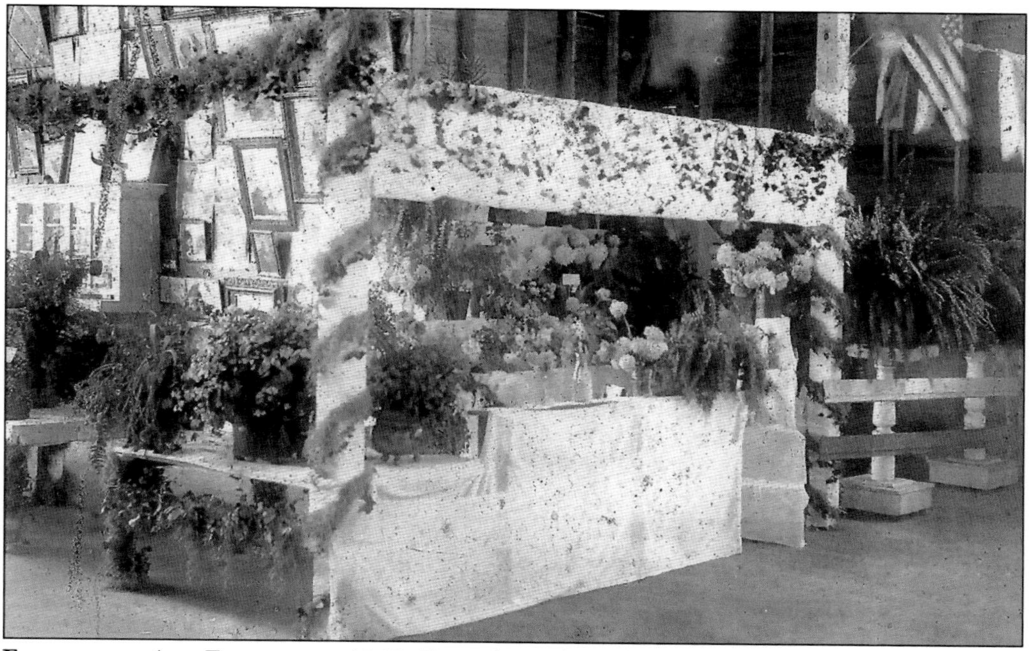

FLOWER AND ART EXHIBITS, c. 1917. From the earliest days of the fair, county citizens would bring their best flower displays and artwork to be displayed as well as be judged competitively. This tradition continues today. (Courtesy Orangeburg County Fair Association.)

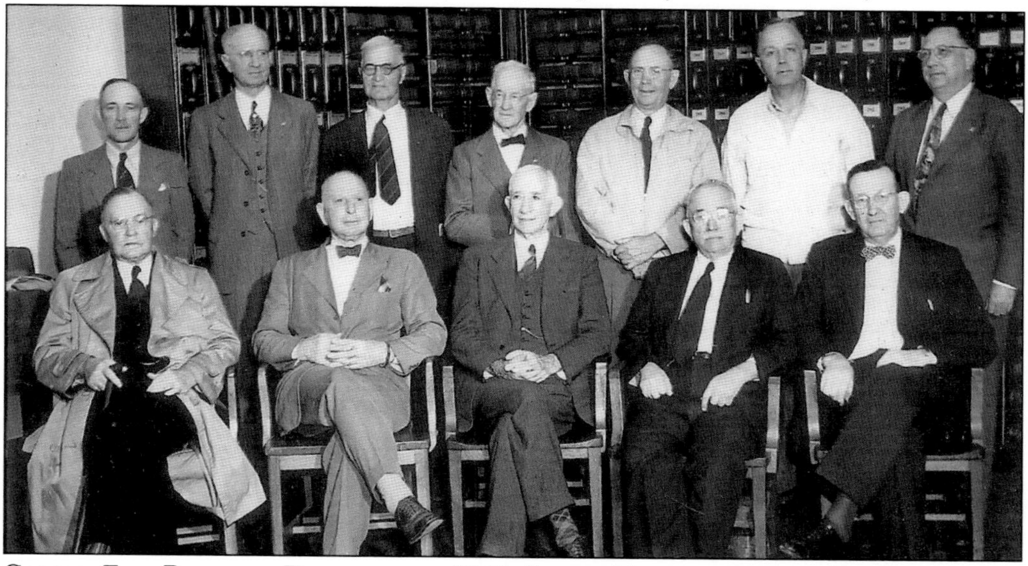

COUNTY FAIR BOARD OF DIRECTORS, c. 1940. Featured here are the fair's board of directors around 1940. They were responsible for coordinating all the events including the livestock shows, floral competitions, handiwork contests, and canned goods and artwork displays. They were also in charge of building and maintaining the excitement of the carnival. Pictured from left to right are (front row) George R. Bowman; J.E. Gramling; J.W. Smoak, President; Reverend G.W. Dukes; Jerry M. Hughes, Secretary and Manager; (back row) C.Y. McCants; I.W. Bull; N.N. Hayden; J.F. Cleckley; H.R. Fairey; Woody Culler; and W.A. Schiffley. The legendary Judge Hughes managed the fair from the beginning in 1911 up to the early 1970s. (Courtesy Orangeburg County Fair Association.)

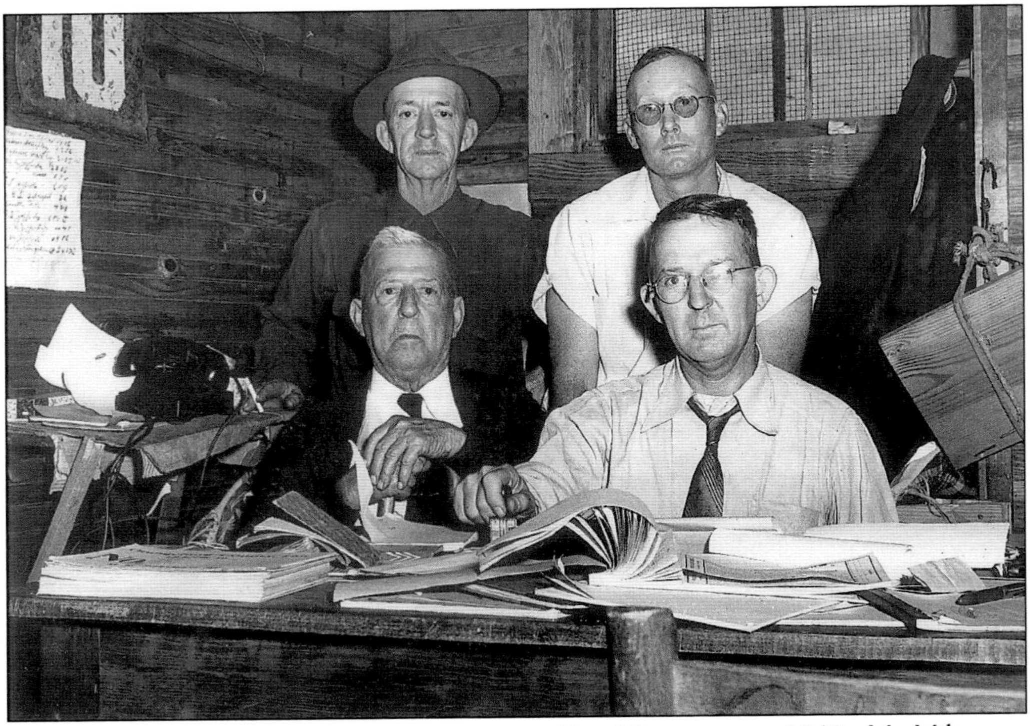

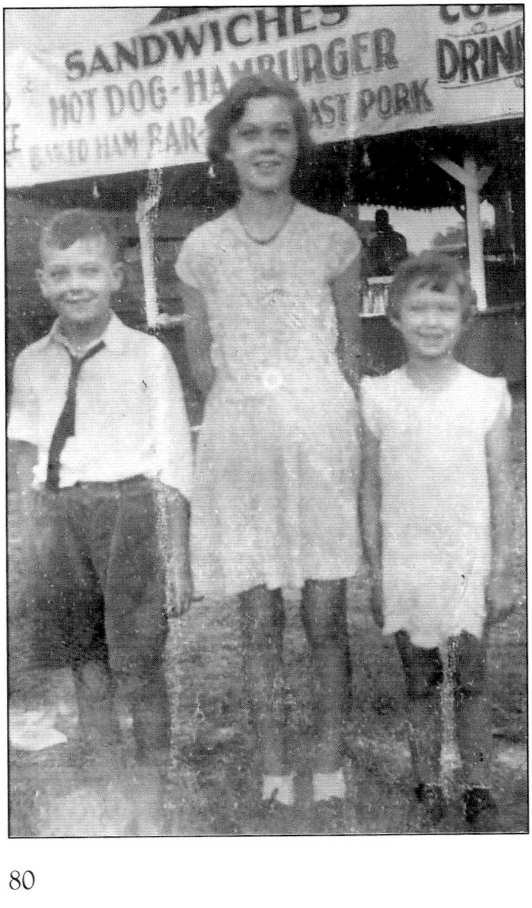

Fair Management, 1940s. Mr. Milton K. Jeffords Sr. was the Midway Secretary for many years at the Orangeburg County Fair. He was assisted by his son T.T. "Son" Jeffords, who later succeeded his father and went on to become the overall manager in the 1970s. Pictured here, from left to right, are (front row) Milton K. Jeffords Sr. and T.T. "Son" Jeffords; (back row) Eddie Langston and Harold Zeigler. (Courtesy Orangeburg County Fair Association.)

Fun at the Fair, Mid-1930s. From the smiles on the faces of these children, it appears a fun time was had by all at the fair. Featured are Smith Fogle, Anne Beckwith Fogle, and Newell Fogle in front of one of the food booths in the mid 1930s. Their parents were very involved with the fair association: John R. Fogle ran the poultry department from the beginning in 1911 until his death after the 1946 fair and Mrs. Annie Fogle was in charge of the canned goods department from 1913 until about 1975. Another one of their sons, Sam Fogle, was the manager of the entire fair for over 15 years from the 1970s into the 1990s. (Courtesy Sam T. Fogle.)

Five

POLICE AND FIRE DEPARTMENTS

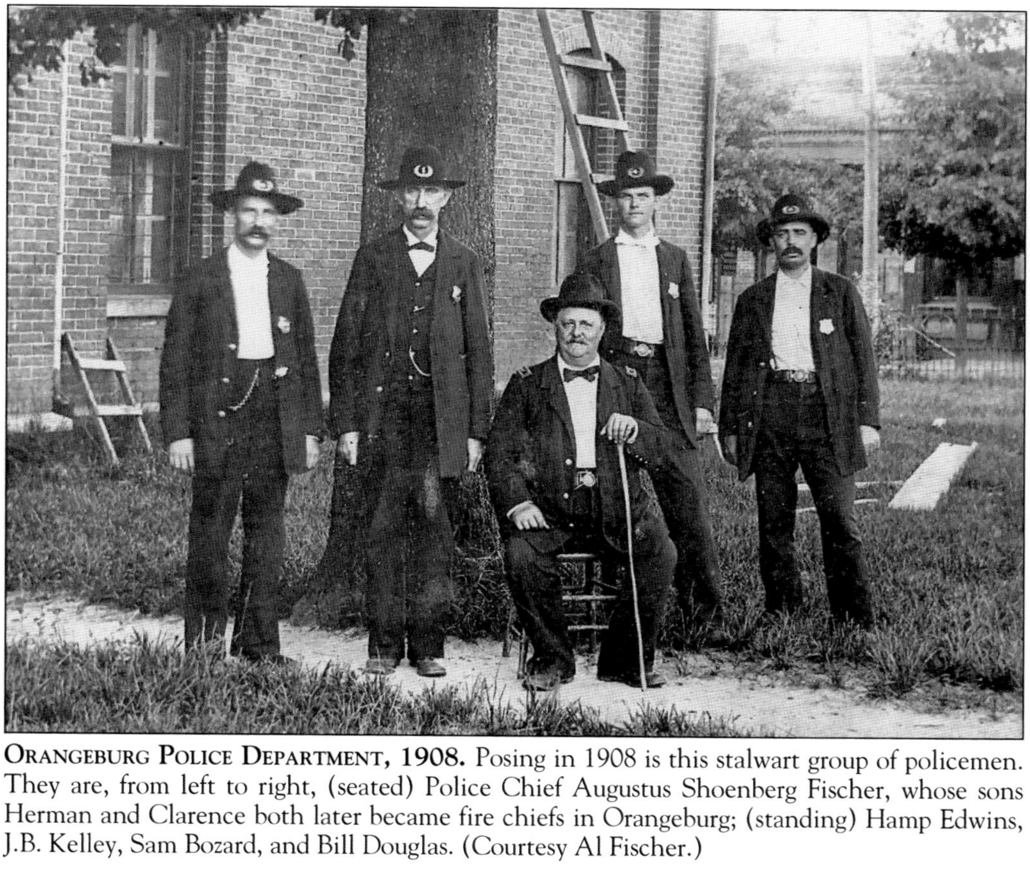

ORANGEBURG POLICE DEPARTMENT, 1908. Posing in 1908 is this stalwart group of policemen. They are, from left to right, (seated) Police Chief Augustus Shoenberg Fischer, whose sons Herman and Clarence both later became fire chiefs in Orangeburg; (standing) Hamp Edwins, J.B. Kelley, Sam Bozard, and Bill Douglas. (Courtesy Al Fischer.)

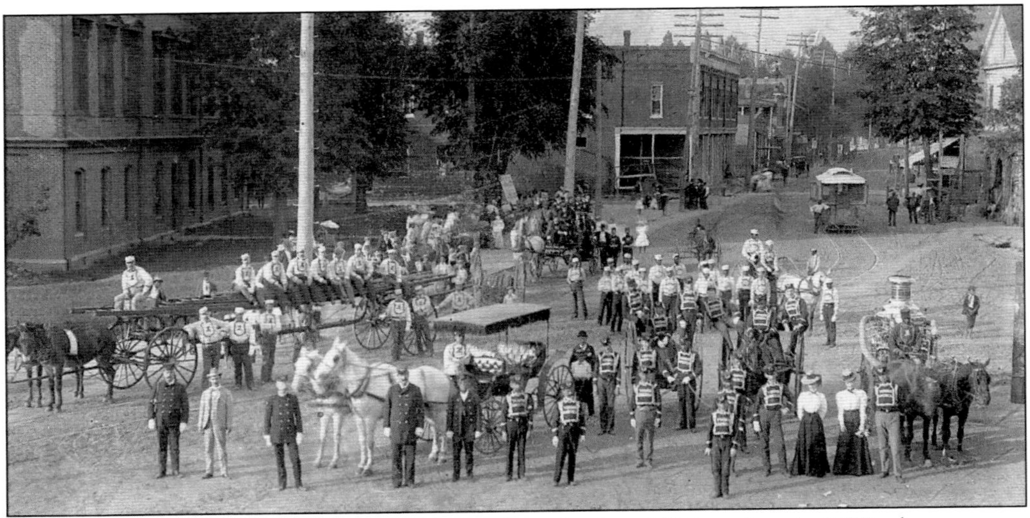

VOLUNTEER FIRE DEPARTMENTS, c. 1900. Back in the late 1800s and early 1900s there was no official city fire department. Instead, fire protection was provided by the following volunteer fire departments: East End Reel Co., Young America Steam Fire Engine Co., Elliott Independent Hook and Ladder Co., and the Phoenix Hose Co., which was an African-American company. This photograph shows all of the groups posing between the courthouse on the square and First Baptist Church. (Courtesy Chamber of Commerce.)

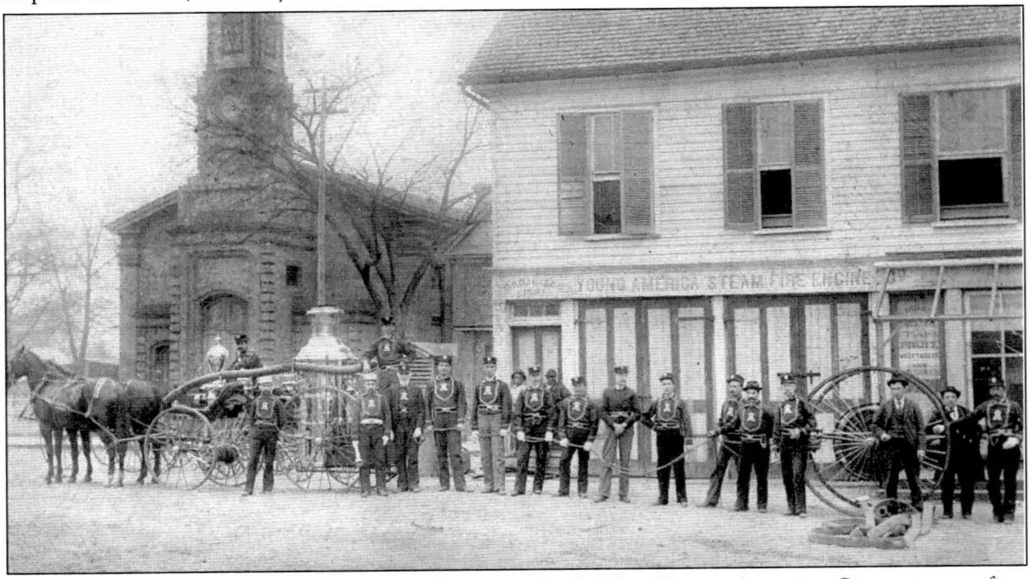

YOUNG AMERICA STEAM FIRE ENGINE CO., c. 1896. The Young America Co. as it was first known, was established in 1854. Their fire station pictured here was erected in front of the parsonage of First Baptist Church at the corner of Russell and Middleton Streets. In 1879 this progressive volunteer group purchased Orangeburg's first steam fire engine pumper at a cost of $6,000. Their station building was torn down around the turn of the century, and later the historic fireman's monument was located at that same spot for many years. The only firemen identified are T.O.S. Dibble, who stands on the engine just to the right and who was the head of this organization for many years; and in front of him, George Dexter and "Uncle Jo" Harley (with the white beard); Gus Hallongren, fifth from the right; Frederick S. Dibble, next to the far right; and W.L. Harley, far right. (Courtesy Orangeburg County Historical Society.)

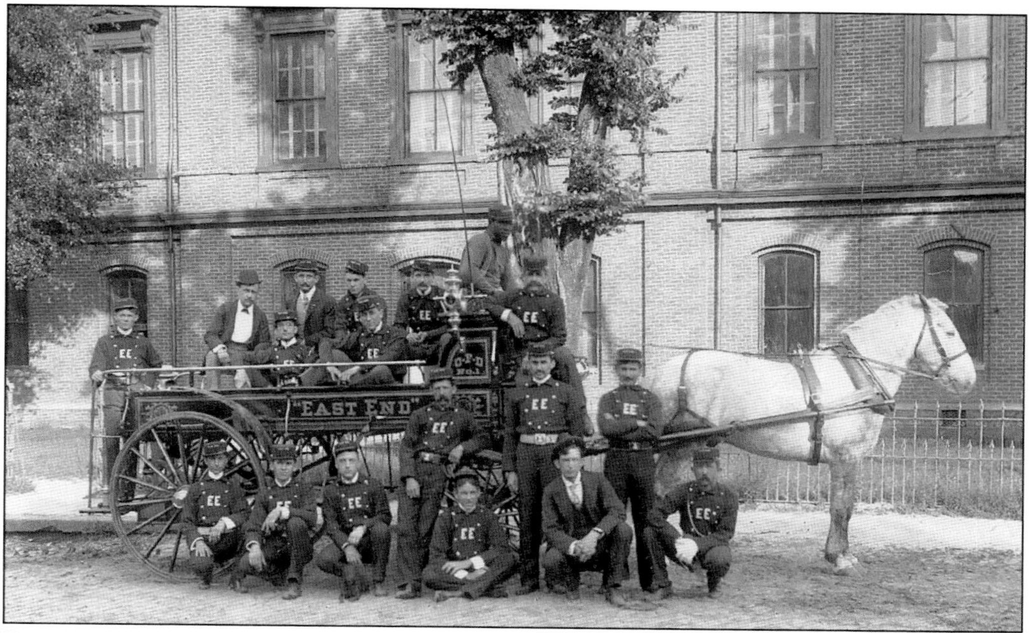

East End Reel Co. This volunteer fire company was organized in 1889. Its headquarters was located on Railroad Avenue, now Boulevard, near the South Carolina Railway tracks, later Southern Railroad. The East End Reel Co. acquired a modern "automobile hose wagon" in 1912. The date of this picture is unknown, but believed to be around the turn of the 20th century. (Courtesy Orangeburg County Historical Society.)

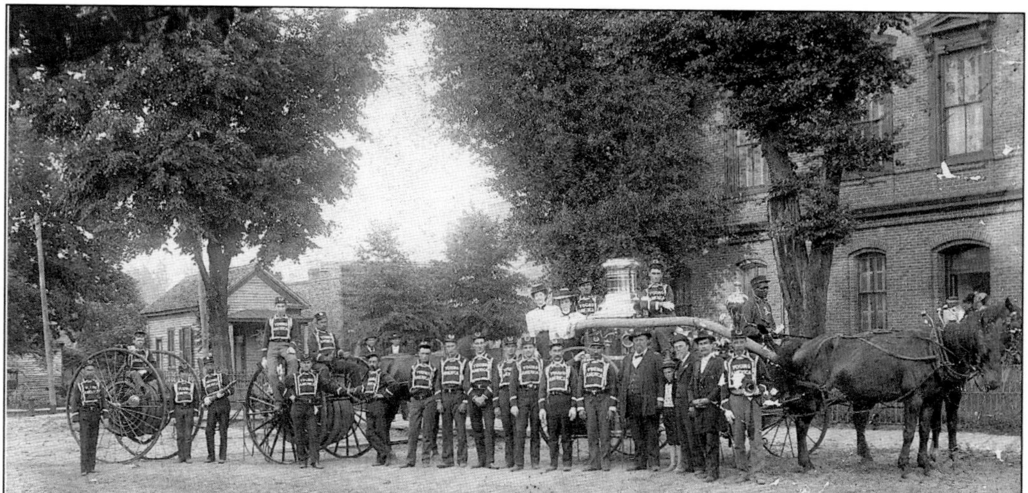

Young America Steam Fire Engine Co. This 1902 photograph shows the "Young Americas" as they were called on the north side of the courthouse. They are, from left to right, George J. Dexter; unidentified; David K. Robinson; W.L. Harley; three unidentified people; Dr. Sheldon Scoville; two unidentified people; Walter Berry; two unidentified people; Jack Sorentrue; Gus Hallongren; Augustus Fischer, chief of police; Fred W. Dibble, boy; Frederick S. Dibble, Rev. W.A. Rogers, preacher of St. Paul's Methodist; and T.O.S. Dibble, fire chief. Several in the rear on the engine and driver are unidentified. The streets around the courthouse were dirt in this picture. Later they were paved with wooden bricks. (Courtesy Orangeburg County Historical Society.)

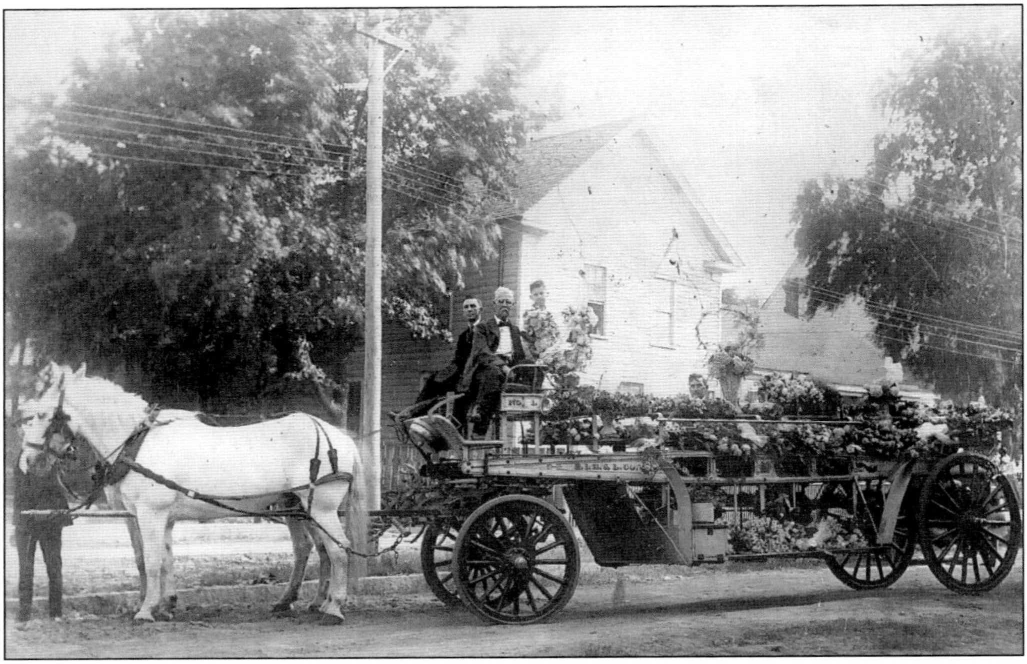

ELLIOTT INDEPENDENT HOOK AND LADDER CO. This ladder wagon all adorned with flowers is believed to be part of the funeral procession for one of Elliott Independent's members. The date appears to be from the 1910s. (Courtesy Orangeburg County Historical Society.)

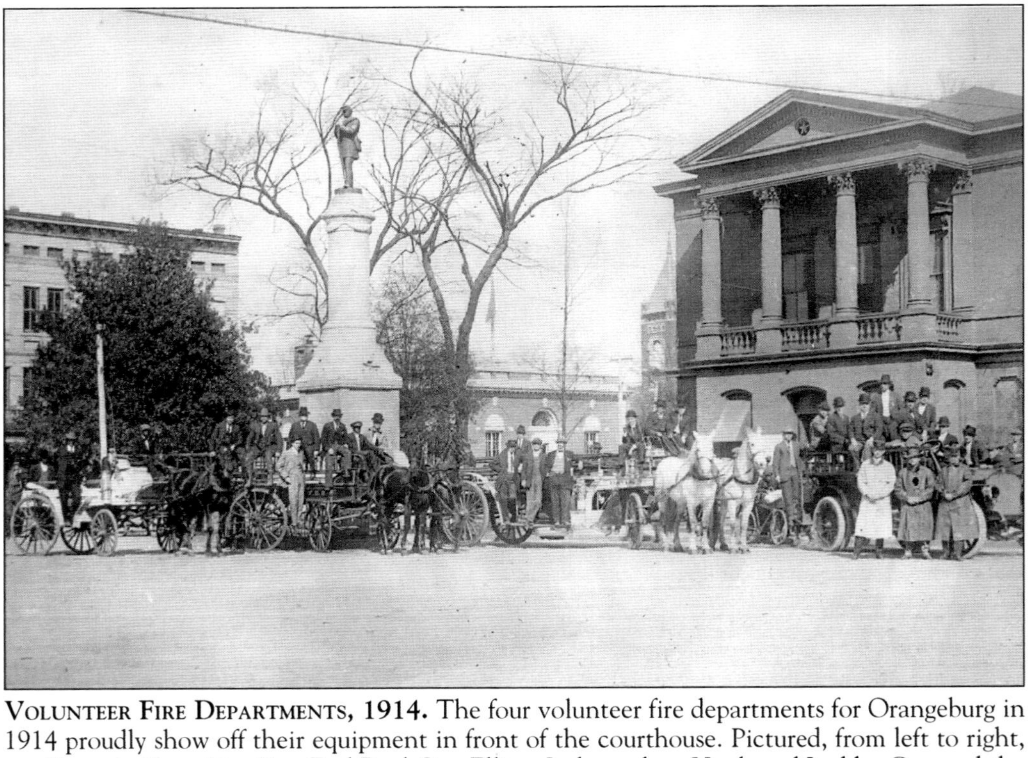

VOLUNTEER FIRE DEPARTMENTS, 1914. The four volunteer fire departments for Orangeburg in 1914 proudly show off their equipment in front of the courthouse. Pictured, from left to right, are Phoenix Hose Co., East End Reel Co., Elliott Independent Hook and Ladder Co., and the Young America Steam Fire Engine Co. (Courtesy Chamber of Commerce.)

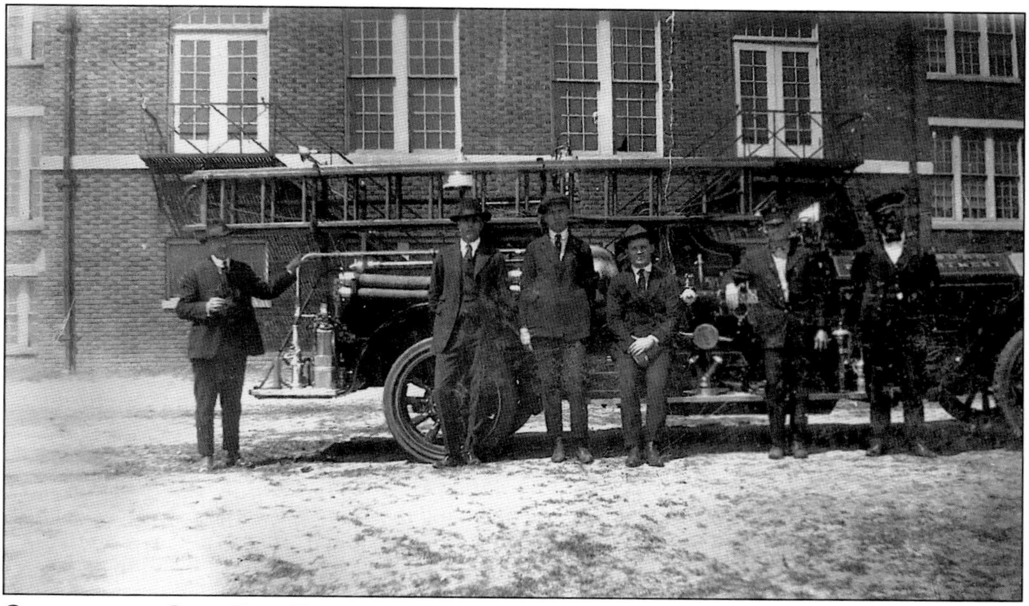

ORANGEBURG CITY FIRE DEPARTMENT'S FIRST TRUCK. In 1920 all of the volunteer fire departments were consolidated into a new city run fire department. The first new truck acquired by the department was this 1921 American LaFrance fire engine. This truck is still in the possession of the city today because of its historical significance. (Courtesy Al Fischer.)

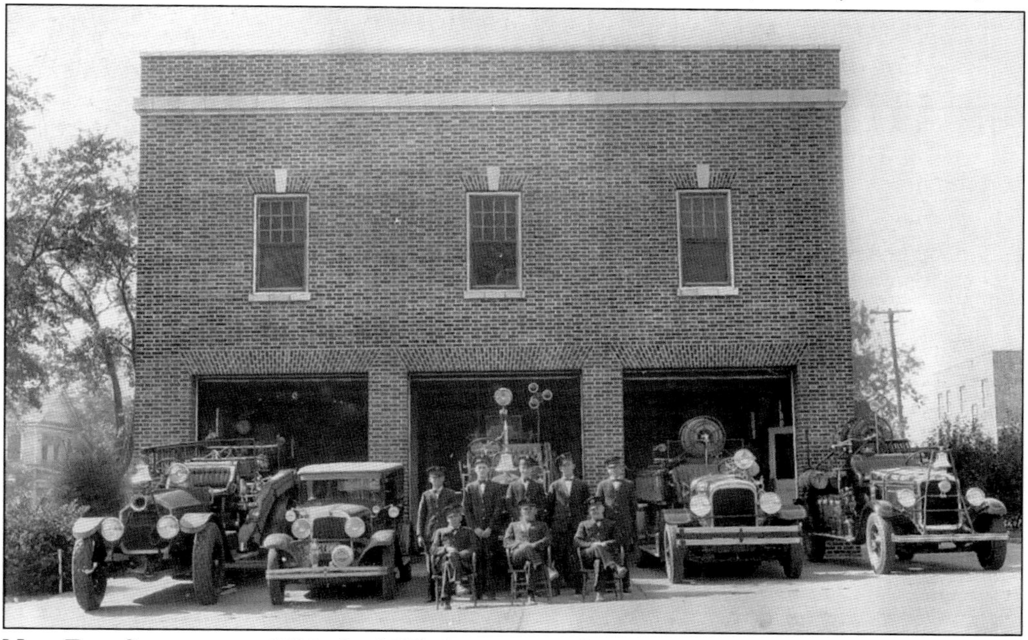

NEW FIRE STATION, c. 1930. In 1927 the municipal group of buildings was built for a total of $175,000. Included in this project were a new fire station, Orangeburg City Hall and The Carolinian auditorium and theatre, and a city jail and police headquarters. Members of the fire department pose proudly with their fire trucks in front of their new station around 1930. Fire Chief Herman Fischer, who served as chief from 1920 to 1945 is seated in the center and his brother Clarence A. Fischer, who served from as chief from 1945 to 1965 is seated to the right. (Courtesy Al Fischer.)

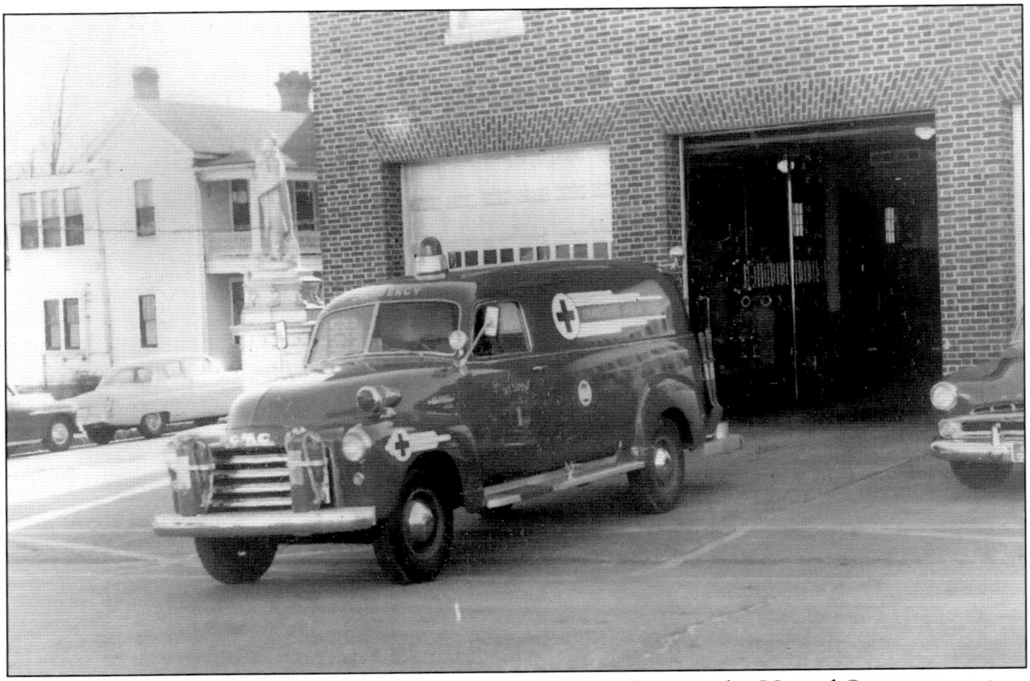

Fire Rescue Truck. In the early 1950s there was a trend across the United States to equip a rescue truck to be used in various emergencies. Orangeburg acquired its rescue truck in the early 1950s, too, and custom installed all the necessary modifications and equipment. Many citizens can also recall seeing this rescue truck at area football games to assist in case of an injury. (Courtesy Al Fischer.)

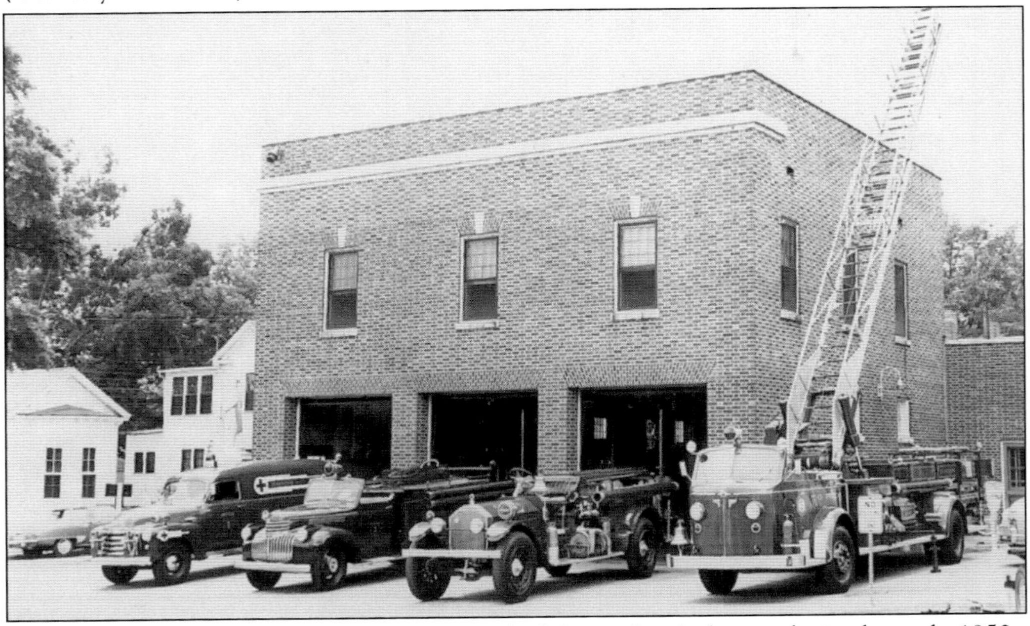

Fire Trucks, 1951. Pictured here are several of Orangeburg's fire trucks in the early 1950s. Featured are the rescue truck, a 1947 or 1948 Chevrolet pumper, the 1921 American LaFrance pumper, and an early 1950s American LaFrance hook and ladder truck with its ladders extended. (Courtesy Edith Gillam.)

Six

Businesses

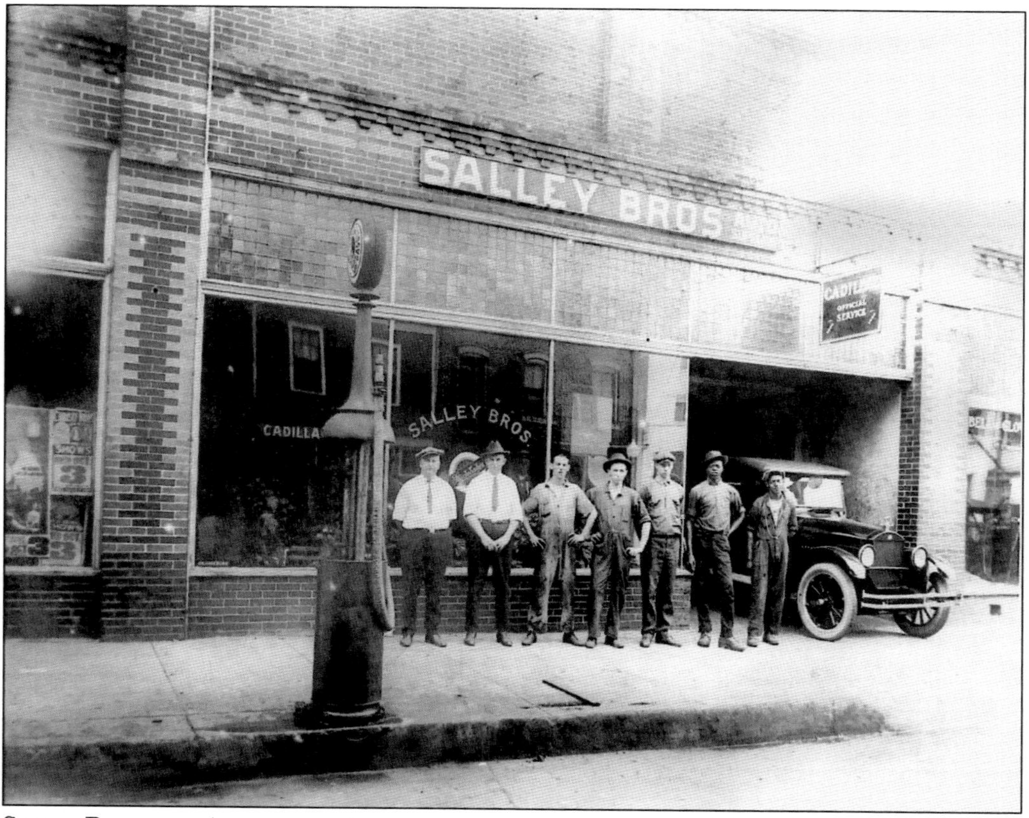

Salley Brothers Automobile Dealership. Norman and Julian Salley, the two men at the far left, operated a car dealership in the 1920s and early 1930s that was located on Russell Street near the intersection with Doyle Street. Currently Palmetto Office Supply occupies this site. The Salleys sold Cadillacs, Willys Overlands, and Whippets at their dealership. Note the old-type gasoline pump on the sidewalk. (Courtesy Orangeburg Historical Society.)

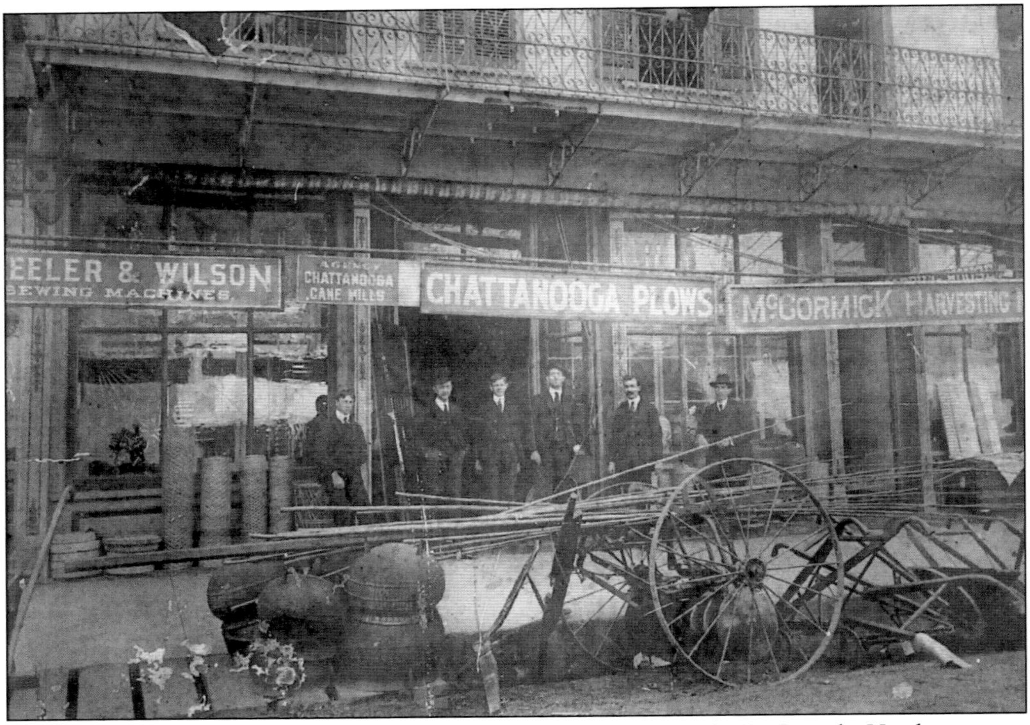

J.W. Smoak Hardware Co., 1905. Established in 1895, J.W. Smoak Hardware was an Orangeburg institution until it closed in the 1980s. Everything from farm machinery to heating systems to hardware was sold here. Pictured, from left to right, are ? Heesemann, John McNamara, John Varn, Ross Ayers, John Jones, and J.W. Smoak. (Courtesy Lillian Bethea Rembert.)

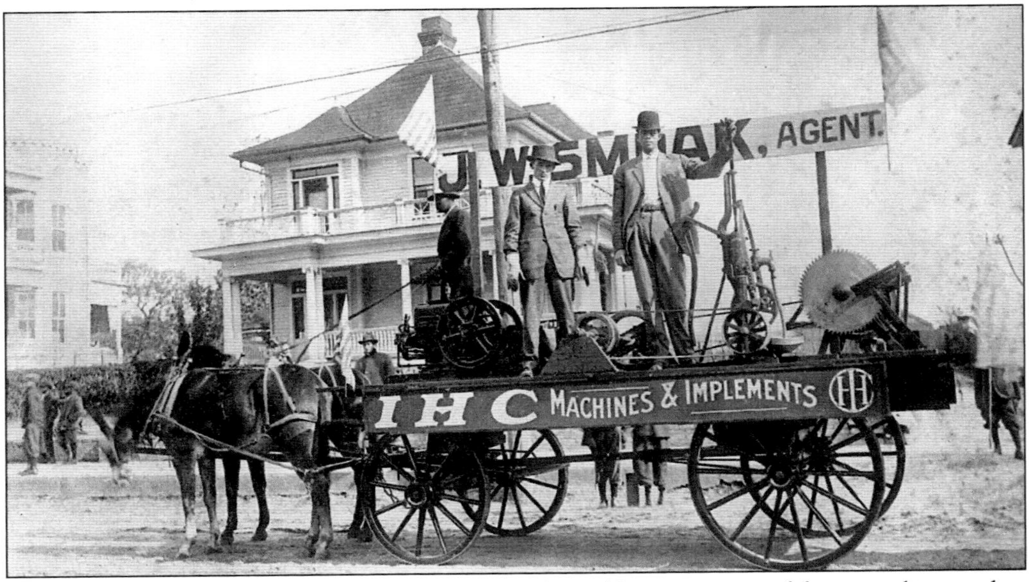

J.W. Smoak Parade Float, 1910s. J.W. Smoak's sold many items of farm machinery that mechanization brought about. Pictured here is a float demonstrating some of the machines available. It is unknown whether this is from a parade during fair week or some other circumstance. (Courtesy Lillian Bethea Rembert.)

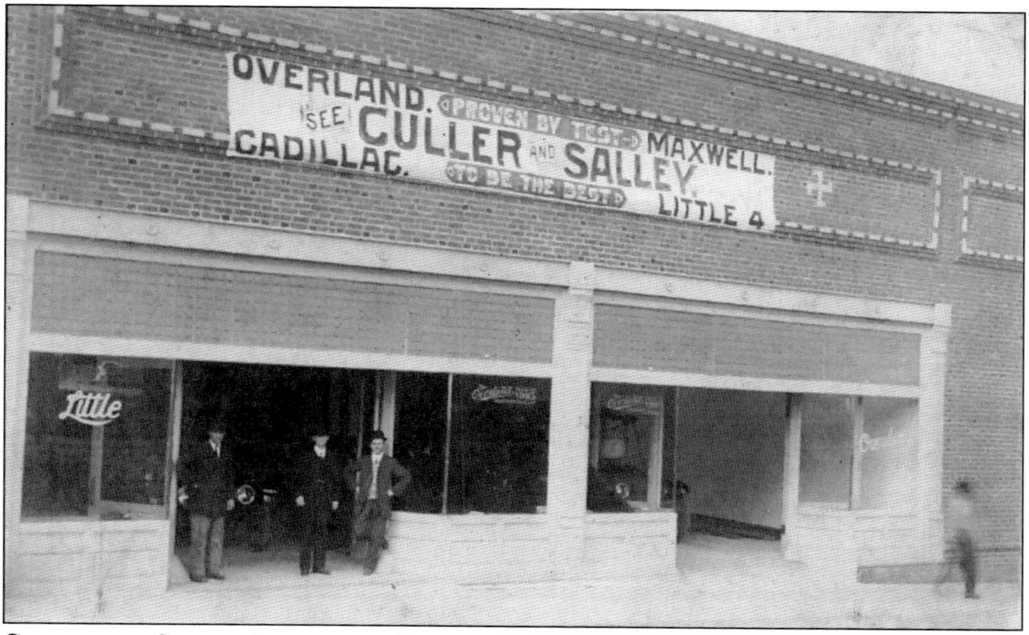

CULLER AND SALLEY AUTOMOBILE DEALERSHIP, c. 1918. Cecil Culler and Norman Salley established their car dealership in the 1910s on Russell Street at the location of Palmetto Office Supply today. They sold Overlands, Maxwells, Cadillacs, and Little 4s. One notable sale of a Cadillac was made to the legendary baseball player Ty Cobb. (Courtesy Mae Louise C. Viola.)

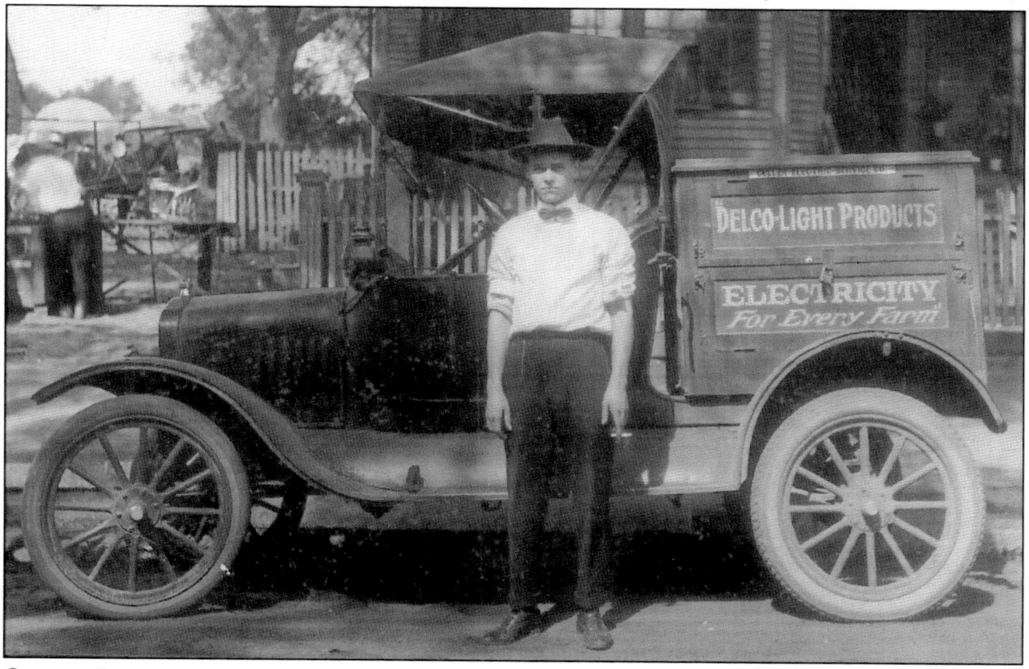

CULLER ELECTRIC SERVICE CO., c. 1920. Cecil and Rudolph Culler, pictured here, operated the Culler Electric Service Co. that installed Delco Light Plants for farms and rural homes. This allowed rural areas to enjoy some of the same comforts and amenities with electricity that city residents enjoyed. Years later rural electricity lines gradually replaced the need for these small generators. (Courtesy Taylor Garick.)

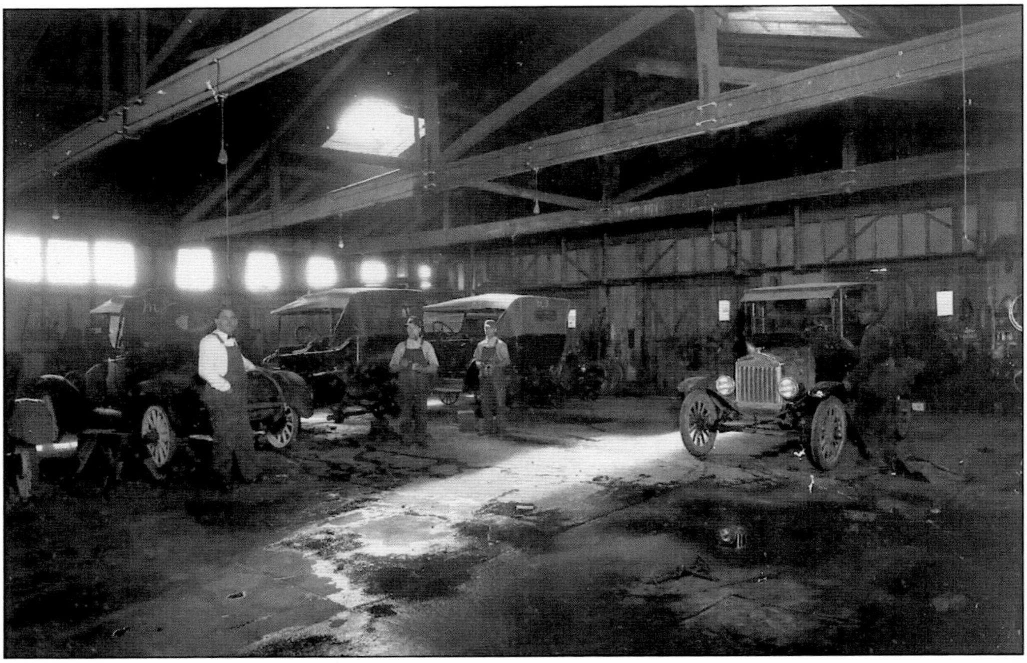

GILLAM'S AUTO TRIMMING. In the 1920s the Gillam brothers, David, King Joseph, and Fitzhugh established a business that made cloth tops for automobiles, as well as painted and lacquered metal parts for car bodies. One of their advertisements read "High Grade Auto Painting and Trimming." Their shop was located on Windsor Street near the current Department of Public Utilities complex. (Courtesy Cleveland Dempsey.)

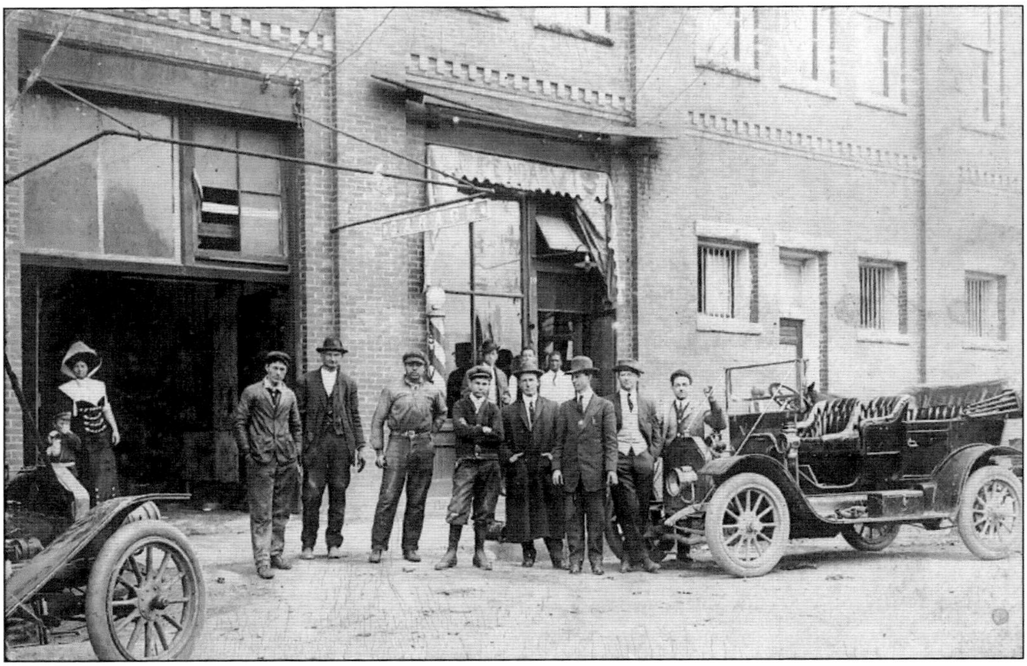

L. BENNETT AUTOMOBILES AND AUTO PARTS, 1920s. L. Bennett was a name long associated with an automobile parts supply business in Orangeburg until the 1970s. It also sold cars back in its early days of business. (Courtesy Catherine Senn.)

EDISTO NATIONAL BANK, 1920s. Orangeburg was served by several banking institutions until the Great Depression. Unfortunately none of the city banks survived this terrible economic time. Judge B.H. Moss was Edisto National's president and W.L. Glover was vice president and cashier. This bank was located in the same building that Ferse's variety store is located in today. (Courtesy Russell Wolfe family.)

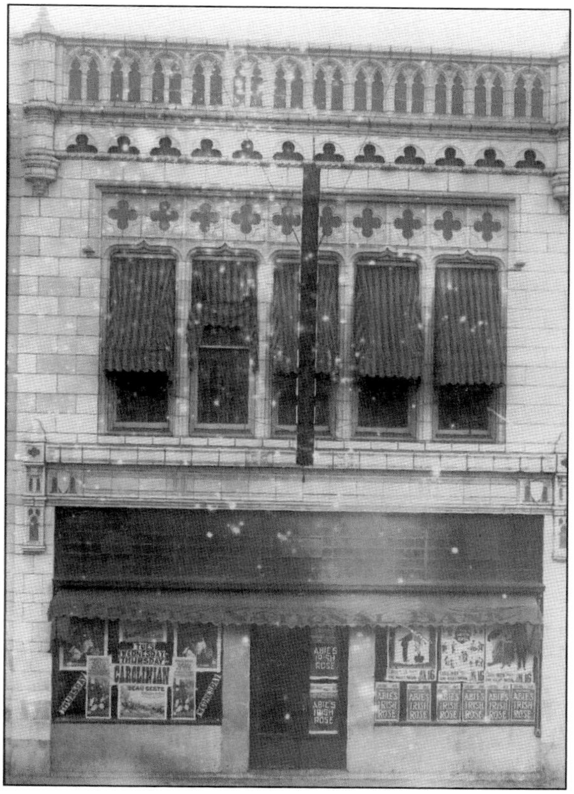

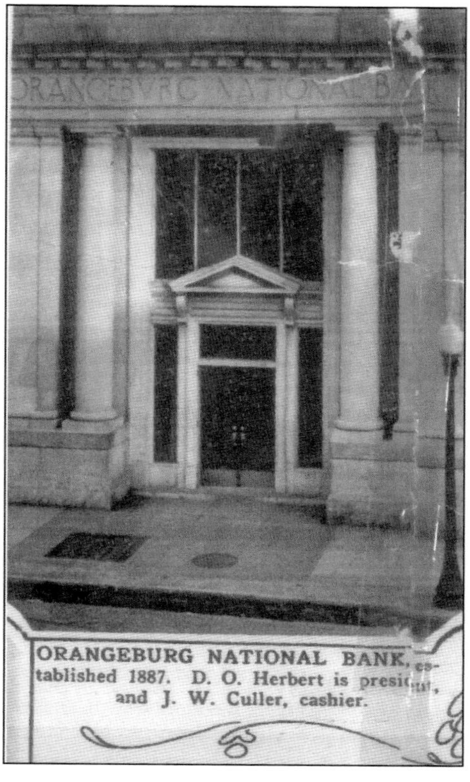

ORANGEBURG NATIONAL BANK, 1920s. This bank was a mainstay in the community until the hard times of the depression. Its location was later taken over by the newly formed First National Bank around 1933. D.O. Herbert was Orangeburg National's president and J.W. Culler was cashier. (Courtesy Downtown Orangeburg Revitalization Association.)

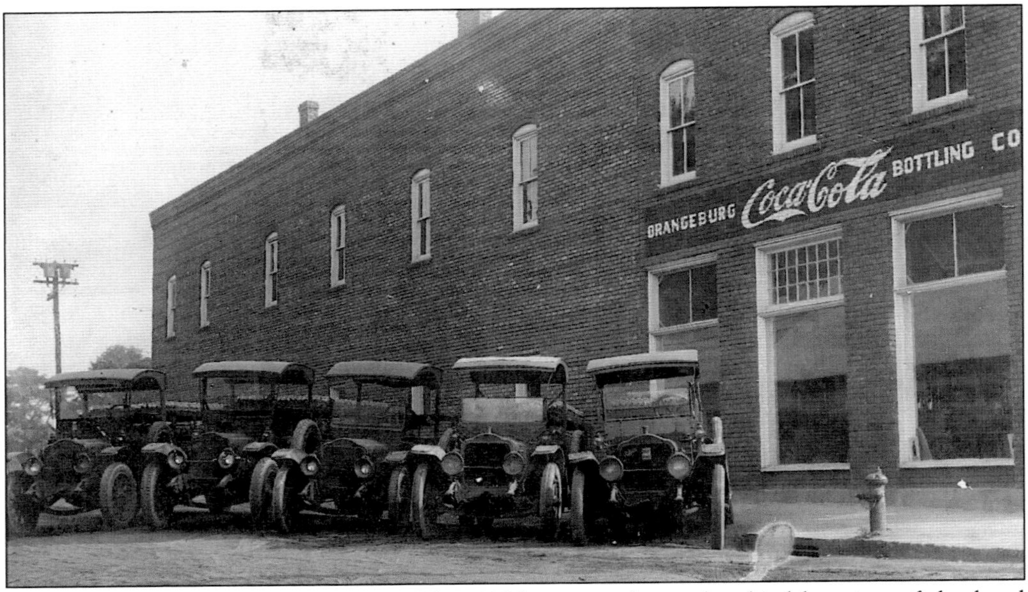

ORANGEBURG COCA-COLA, c. 1920. This 1920 picture shows the third location of the local Coca-Cola plant on Russell Street at the corner with Seaboard Street. Four enterprising men, Robert H. Jennings Sr., P.M. Smoak, Fletcher Fairey Sr., and W.S. Barton established the first Coca-Cola franchise in Orangeburg in 1904. That plant was located on Middleton Street just off the square and behind the old WTND Building, which is currently E-Mart. (Courtesy Orangeburg Coca-Cola Bottling Co.)

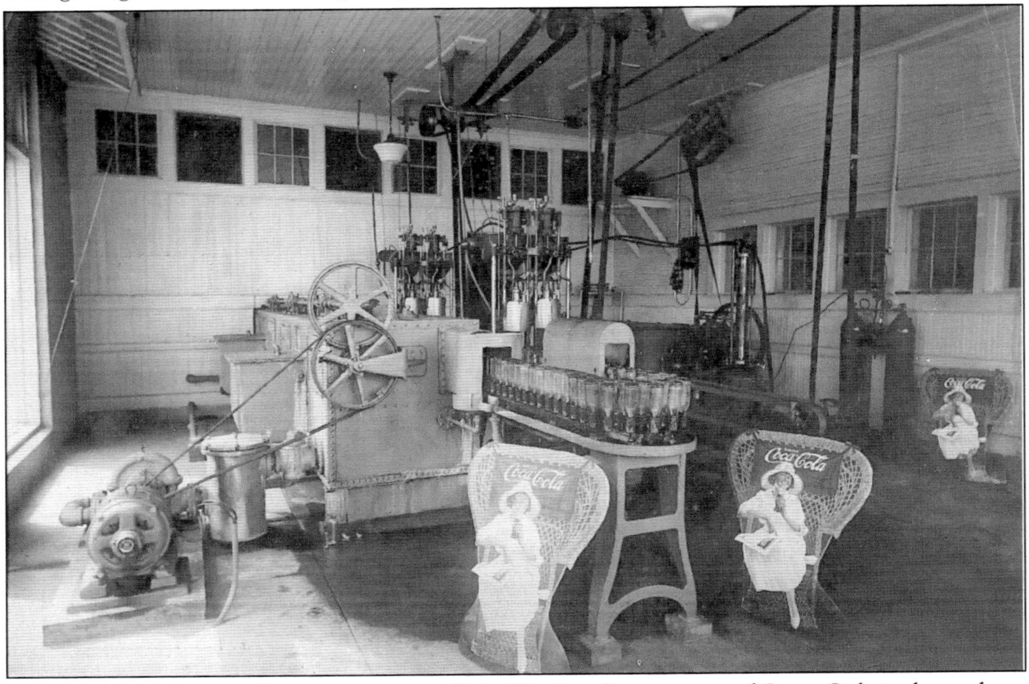

COCA-COLA BOTTLING PRODUCTION, c. 1920. The bottling process of Coca-Cola is shown here in this c. 1920 scene. This location of the local Coca-Cola bottling plant served our community from 1918 until 1981 when all operations were moved to a new location on the St. Matthews Road. (Courtesy Orangeburg Coca-Cola Bottling Co.)

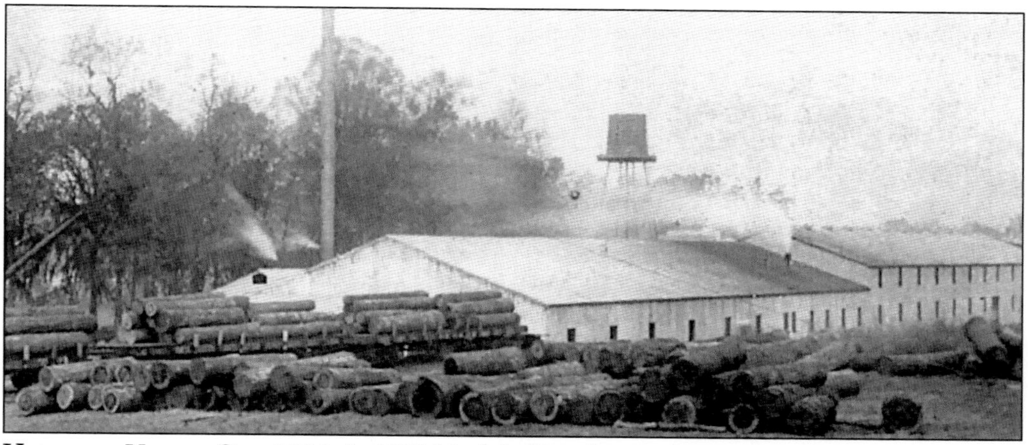

HAMILTON VENEER CO., 1926. In 1923 Mr. L.L. Hamilton and several associates built a veneer plant that was located approximately where today's Quality Inn and the Edisto Village Shopping Center are located off John C. Calhoun Drive. The plant closed down for several years during the depression, reopened, and was sold in 1936. It ultimately became U.S. Plywood. (Courtesy Harry Wannamaker III.)

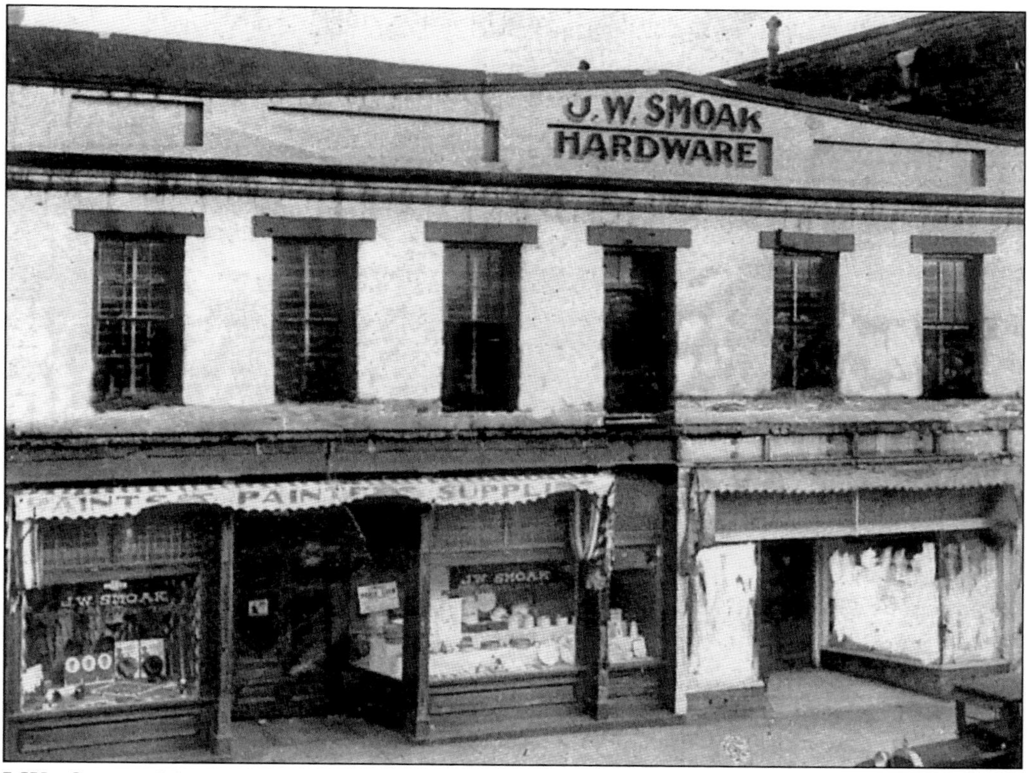

J.W. SMOAK HARDWARE, 1926. In addition to being a leader in the hardware business, Mr. J.W. Smoak was also quite a civic leader in the community. His son-in-law, Wallace Bethea, who followed him in the hardware business also shared this civic spirit. (Courtesy Harry Wannamaker III.)

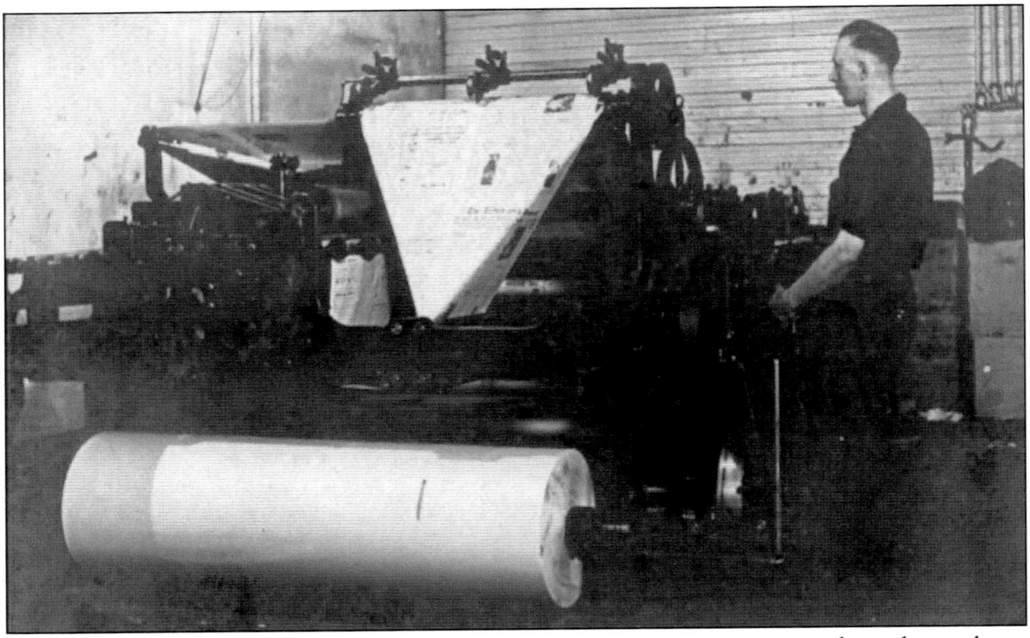

The Times and Democrat Press, c. 1933. A new type press was used in the early to mid-1930s at *The Times and Democrat* newspaper facility. Beginning in the early 1930s local pictures were able to be printed in our newspaper here. Prior to that the technology allowed only national wire photos to be produced. (Courtesy Cleveland Dempsey.)

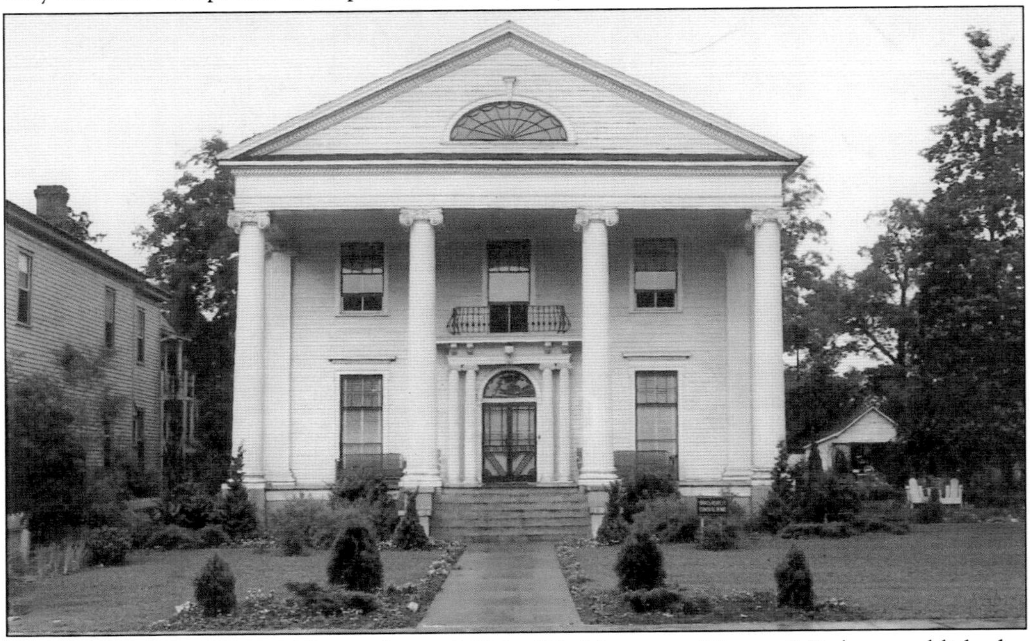

Dukes Harley Funeral Home, Late 1930s. W. Hampton "Hampy" Dukes established a funeral home business on St. John Street in 1896. In 1927 and 1930 he was joined in the business first by Clifton and then I.S. Harley. They moved to this Russell Street location shown here in 1936. This building was originally built as a private residence by Mr. and Mrs. W.S. Lining around 1904. Mr. Lining was a prominent cotton broker in Orangeburg. (Courtesy Cleveland Dempsey.)

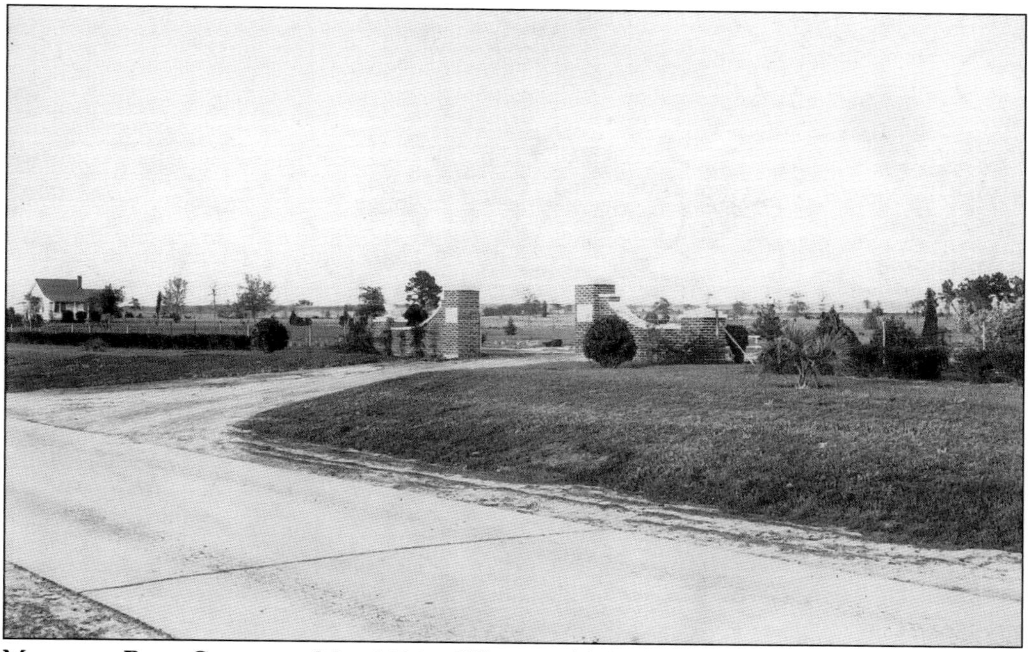

MEMORIAL PARK CEMETERY, MID 1930s. When established by Clifton and I.S. Harley around 1934, Memorial Park Cemetery was a largely undeveloped area just outside of town on Broughton Street. There were very few trees and a fairly narrow concrete road was in front. (Courtesy Cleveland Dempsey.)

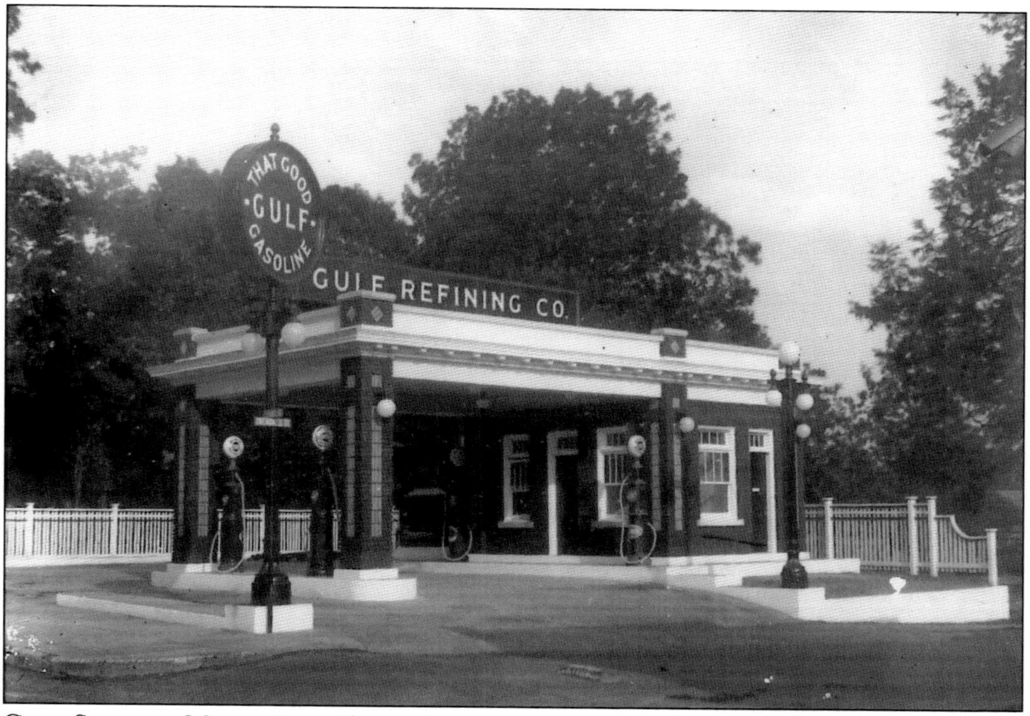

GULF STATION, MID 1930s. This Gulf service station was located at the corner of Russell and Treadwell Streets. For many years it was run by Charlie Way, who also had several other business enterprises here in Orangeburg. (Courtesy Dr. Clemmie Webber.)

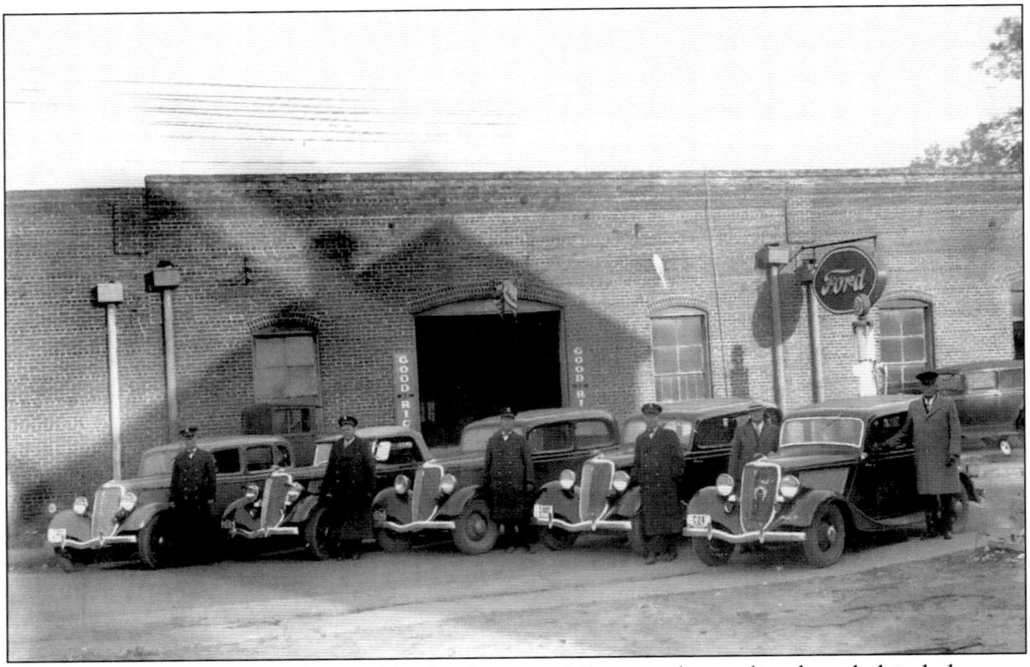

HORNE MOTORS, 1934. These 1934 Ford automobiles are shown lined up behind the rear entrance to Horne Motors on St. John Street. Mr. J.E. "Dick" Horne, the owner, is the man next to the far right with the light colored hat in this picture. Horne Motors was located for many years in this same building that is now occupied by Palmetto Office Supply. Prior to Mr. Horne acquiring the Ford dealership it was known as J.M. Sifly Ford. Mr. Sifly, a city councilman, was credited with the creation of Edisto Memorial Gardens in 1926. (Courtesy Russell Wolfe family.)

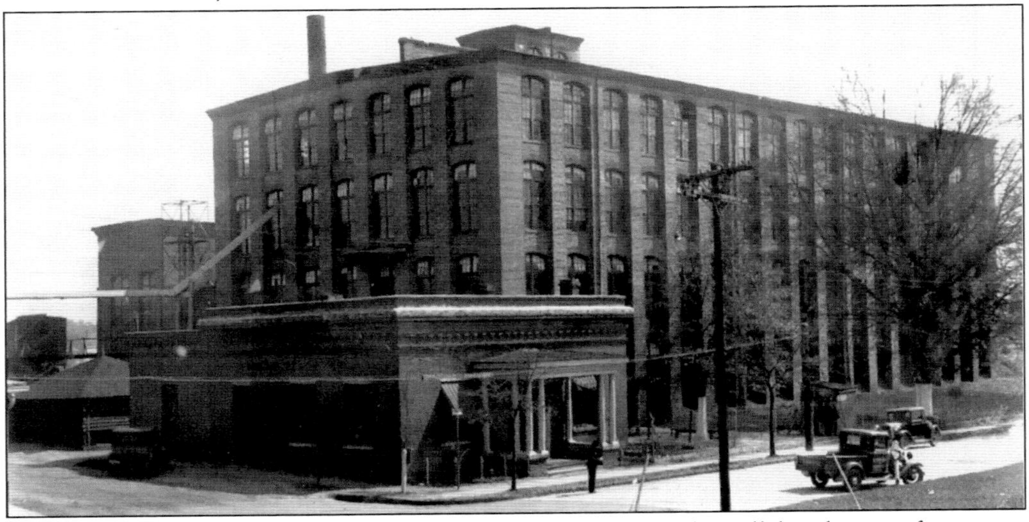

SOUTH CAROLINA COTTON MILL, c. 1935. This large textile mill has been a fixture on Boulevard, now Magnolia Street, for the last century. Back in the early 1900s it was known as Orangeburg Manufacturing Co. Later on it came to be known as Santee Cotton Mills, and it finally became South Carolina Cotton Mill. After it closed in the 1970s, Zeus Industrial Products acquired this facility and now manufactures precision Teflon tubing products there. (Courtesy Russell Wolfe family.)

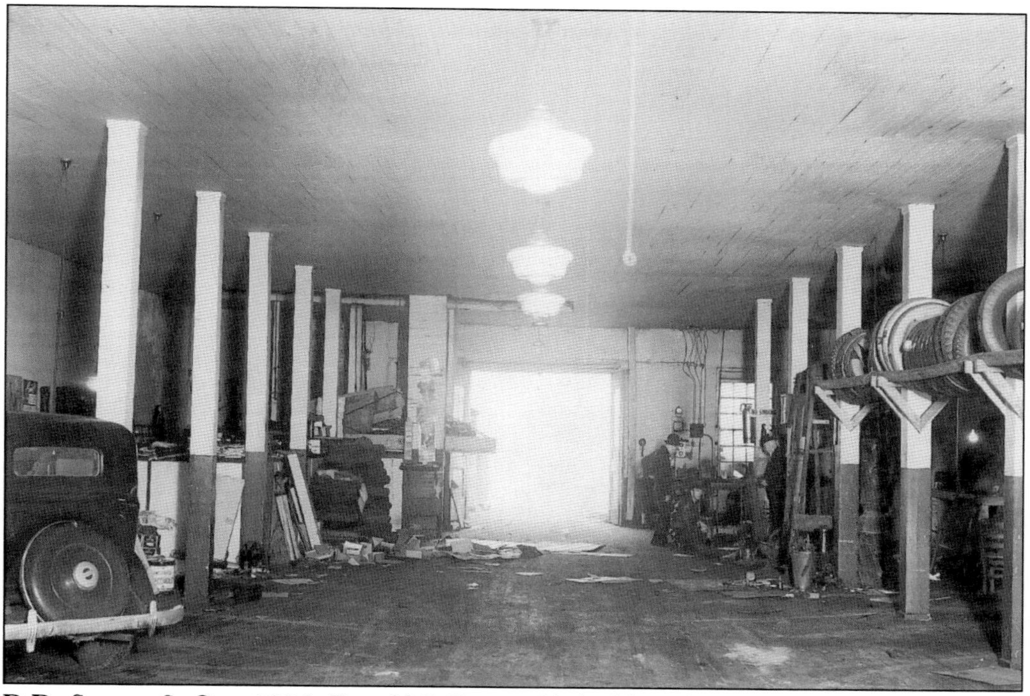

D.D. Salley & Co., 1936. Donald Salley established his Plymouth, Dodge, and Chrysler dealership in the early 1930s. This photo shows the service bay area in 1936. The building was located at the corner of Russell Street and Pitthan Alley, now Wall Street. (Courtesy D.D. Salley III.)

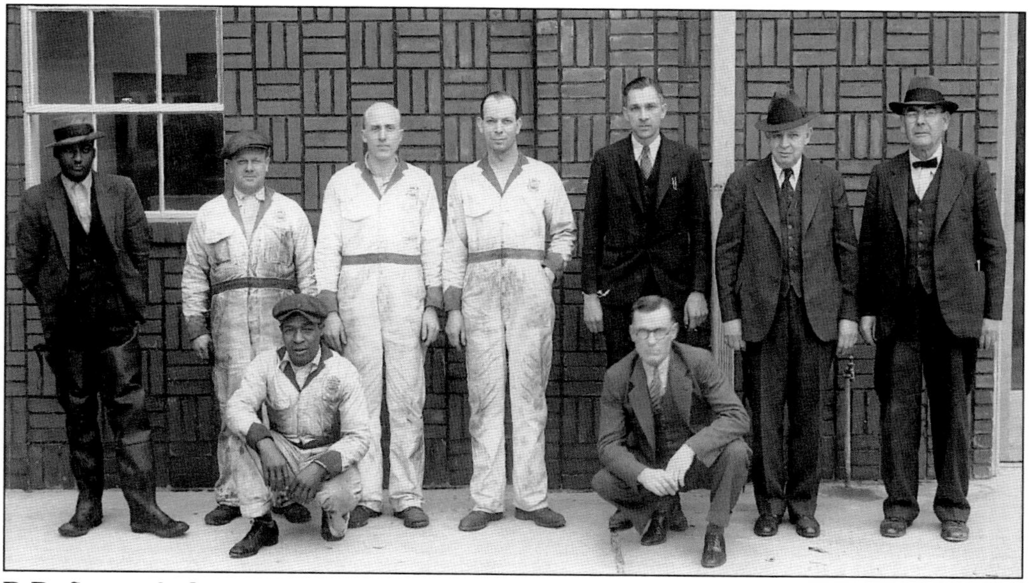

D.D. Salley & Co. Employees, 1937. Donald Salley is shown here with his employees at his new location on Russell Street. He was told when moving there that this location was too far from the center of town to be successful. His skeptics were proven to be quite wrong. Pictured above, from left to right, are (kneeling) George "Whipsaw" Thompson and ? Hyatt; (standing) unidentified, Lloyd Jamison, Ben Brickle (who later established Orangeburg Auto Co.), Kate Williams, Donald Salley, Julian Salley, and Cap Gardner. (Courtesy D.D. Salley III.)

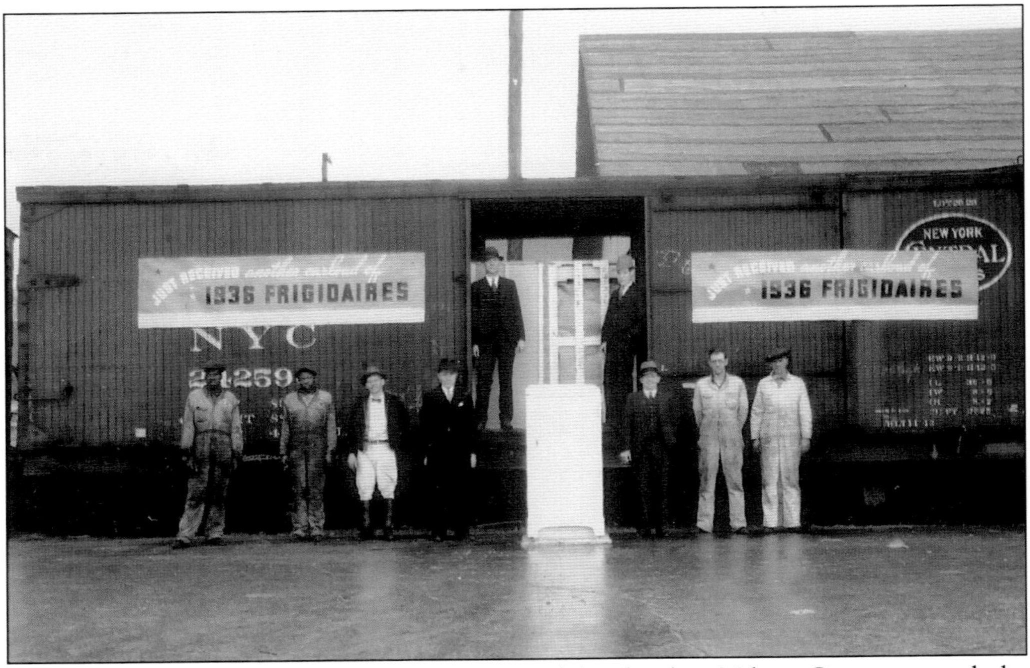

CRUM BROTHERS, 1936. W.C. "Bill" Crum and his brother Milton Crum operated the Frigidaire appliance dealership in Orangeburg, as well as an automobile dealership. These 1936 refrigerators were being unloaded at a local railroad freight yard. Pictured, from left to right, are (front row) Will Stroman, unidentified, Rudolph Culler, Bill Davis, Charlie Scoville, Buck Wactor, and Nolan Livingston; (back row) W.C. Crum and unidentified. (Courtesy the Hub Covington family.)

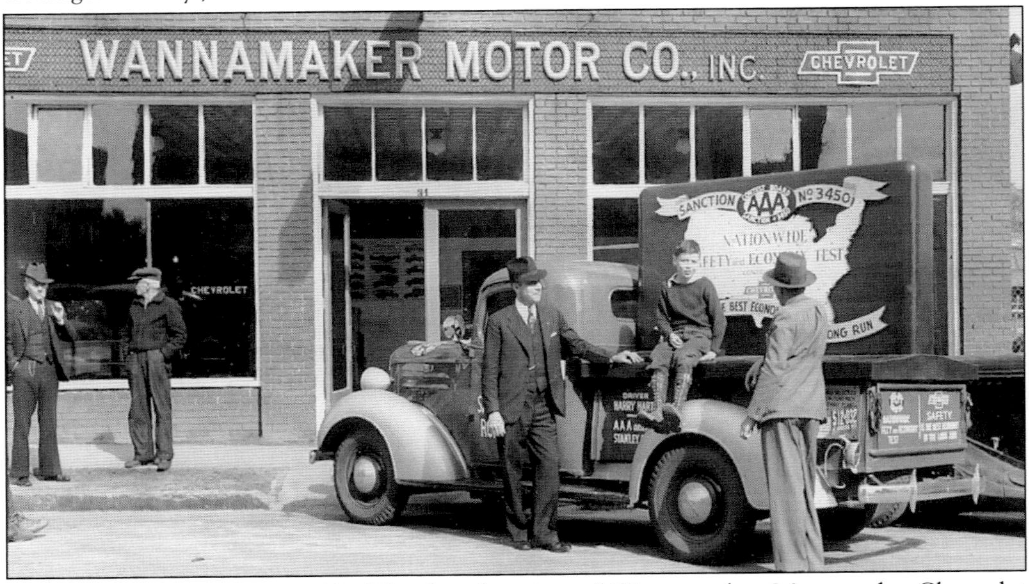

WANNAMAKER MOTORS, 1937. The first location of Wannamaker Motors, the Chevrolet dealership, shown here was on Middleton Street right across from city hall. Pictured above, from left to right, are Welborn Berry, unidentified, W.C. Wannamaker, W.C. "Bill" Wannamaker Jr., and Harry Hart, an Indianapolis race car driver who was on a nationwide tour with this 1937 Chevy truck promoting Chevrolet products. (Courtesy Bill Wannamaker.)

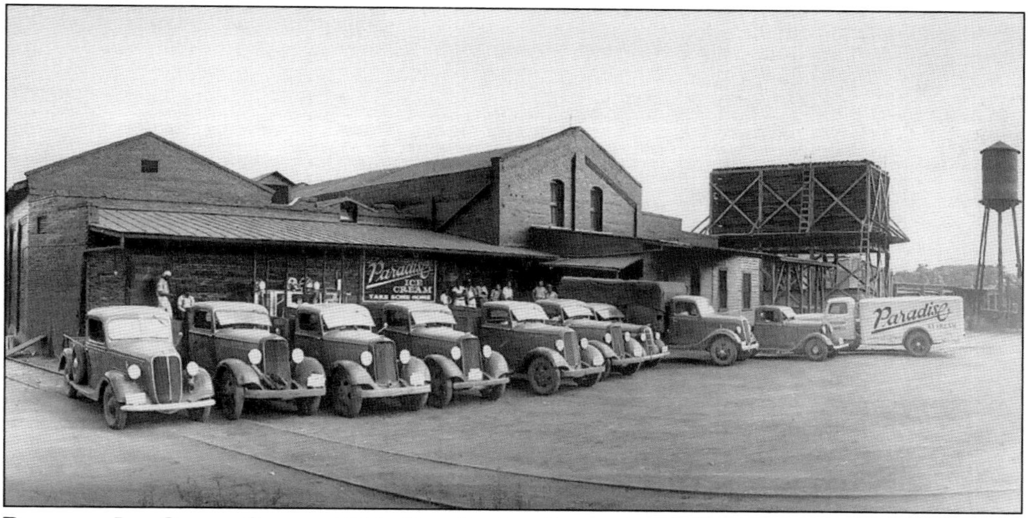

Paradise Ice Cream Co., c. 1940. Paradise Ice Cream Co. did a thriving business during its heyday before the advent of air conditioning. Located off Dukes Street near the Atlantic Coast Line Railroad, it added milk products to its line in the 1950s. This was the era when home delivery of milk was a normal occurrence. (Courtesy Cleveland Dempsey.)

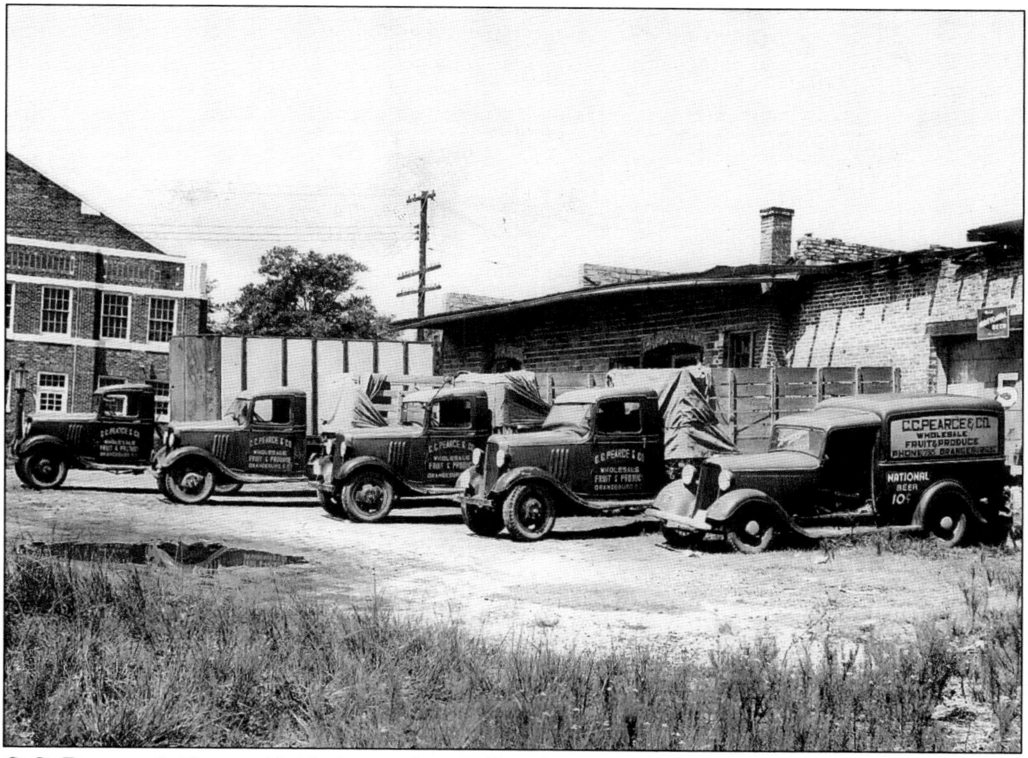

C.C. Pearce & Co., c. 1940. Located on Sellers Avenue in the facilities where Home Builders Supply is located today, the C.C. Pearce & Co. was a wholesale distributor of fruits and produce, plus National Beer. Note the old Orangeburg High School gymnasium in the background. (Courtesy Cleveland Dempsey.)

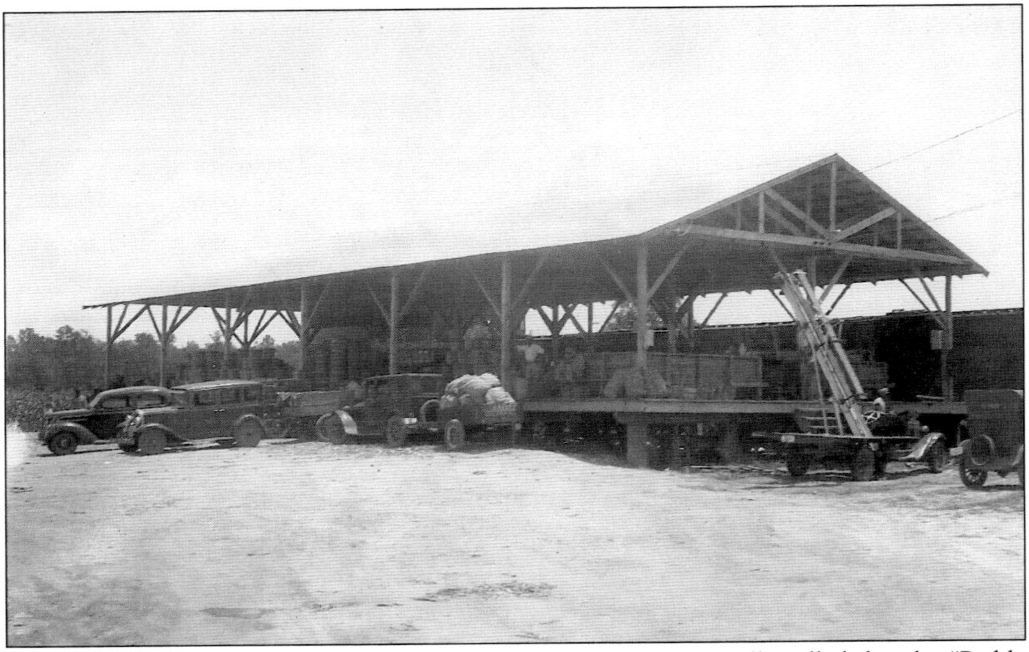

Green Vegetable Market, c. 1940. Some local citizens colloquially called this the "Pickle Factory." Located off Whaley Street beyond the fairgrounds, it was a shipping stand where farmers would bring their vegetables to market. A railroad siding serviced this facility to ship some of the products brought here. (Courtesy Cleveland Dempsey.)

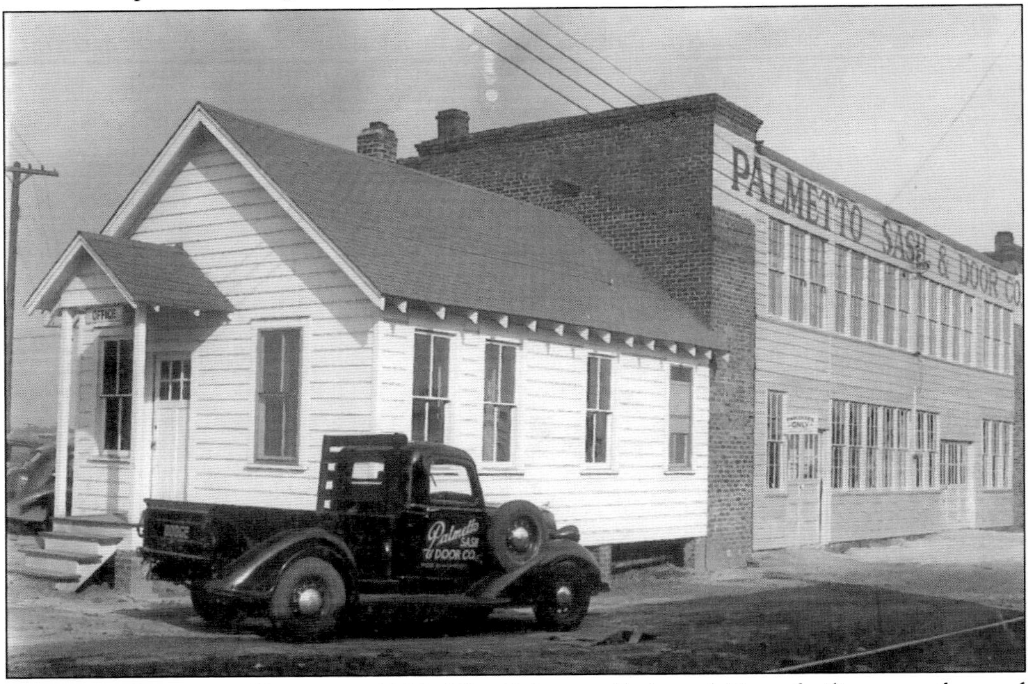

Palmetto Sash and Door, c. 1940. The Palmetto Sash and Door facility manufactured windows, doors, and wood trim for the building industry. Operated by the James Green family, its first location is seen here on Mill Street near the old South Carolina Cotton Mill. (Courtesy Cleveland Dempsey.)

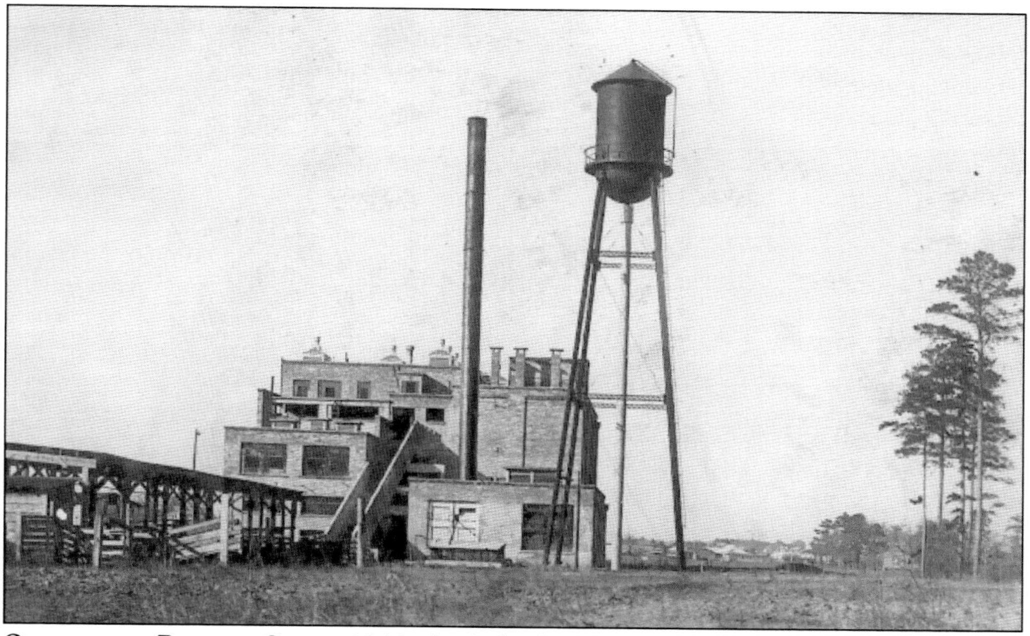

ORANGEBURG PACKING CO., c. 1940. A wholesale meat distributorship and slaughter house , Orangeburg Packing Co. was located off Whaley Street about a mile behind the fairgrounds. Through several ownership changes, the name became Kingan and later Hygrade. (Courtesy Catherine Senn.)

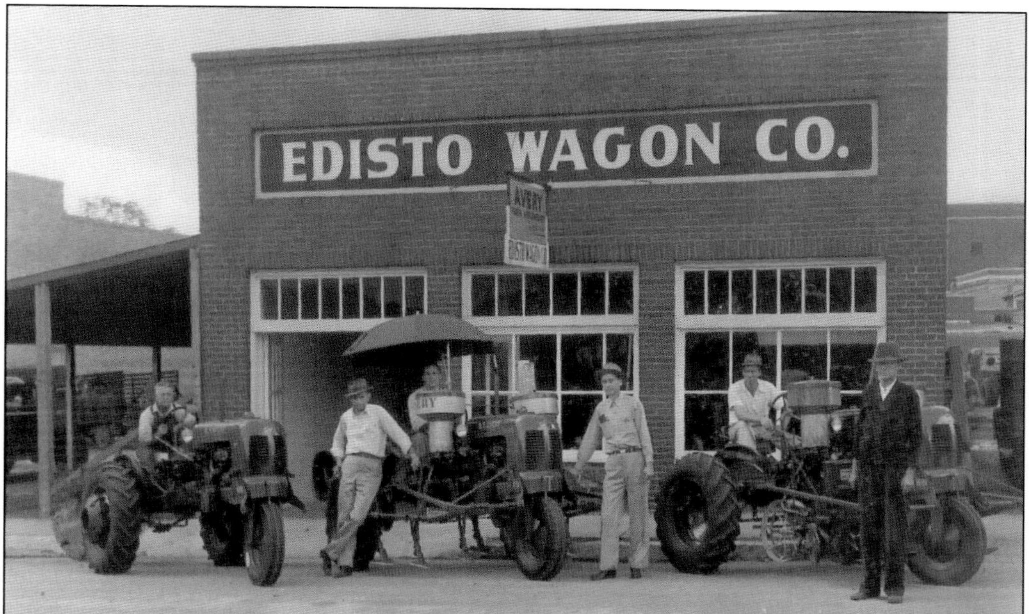

EDISTO WAGON CO., 1940S. The Edisto Wagon Co. began as a business making custom-made wagons, as well as selling the Hackney brand of wagons in the days when horses and mules were common. Owned by Thomas B. Smoak, it later began to sell Avery tractors and other farm machinery. The Edisto Wagon Co. was located on Meeting Street across from the county jail. Those identified are Tillman Smoak, second from left; Gene Smoak, fourth from left; and Thomas B. Smoak, far right. (Courtesy Taylor Garick.)

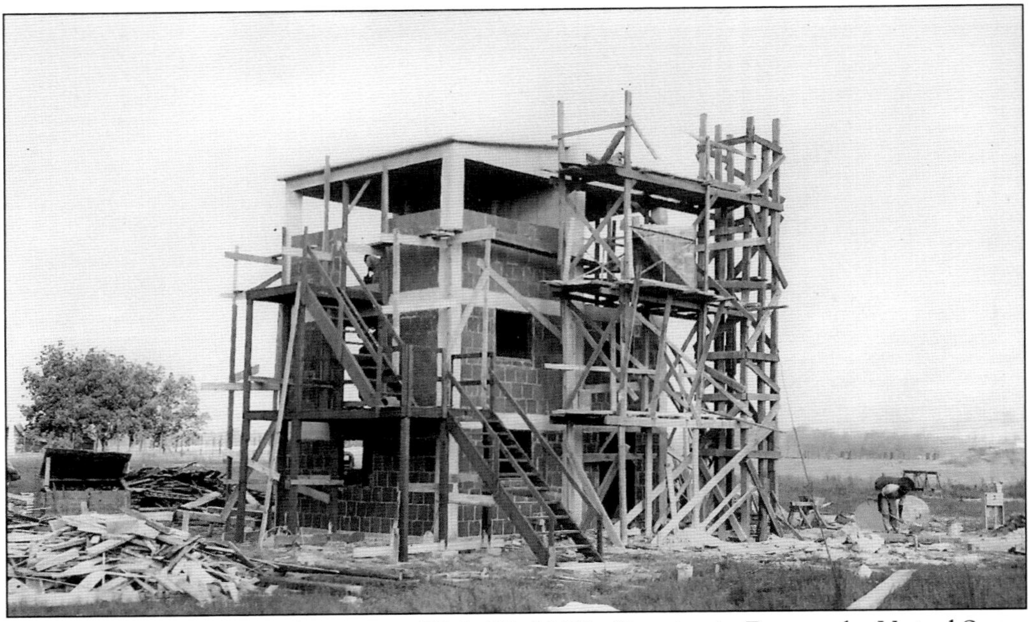

Wannamaker Chemical Co., 1941. With World War II raging in Europe, the United States began to prepare for the inevitable. T.E. Wannamaker established his chemical plant on the Cannon Bridge Road to manufacture military munitions. Here is the first building being constructed on the premises in 1941. In 1954 Ethyl Corporation purchased this thriving plant, but kept Dr. Wannamaker under contract to operate it. Today this same facility continues to operate as the Albemarle Corporation after it was spun off from the Ethyl Corporation. (Courtesy Albemarle Corporation.)

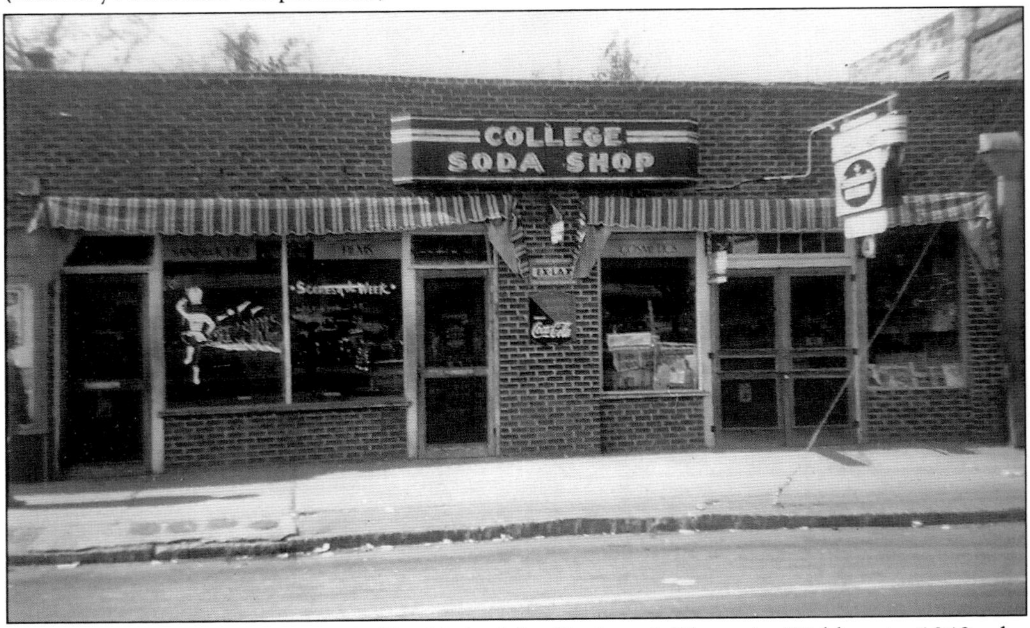

College Soda Shop, c. 1945. Established by Paul and Clemmie Webber in 1942, the College Soda Shop was a popular restaurant and soda shop in the African-American community. It was located on Boulevard across from the Southern Railway depot. (Courtesy Dr. Clemmie Webber.)

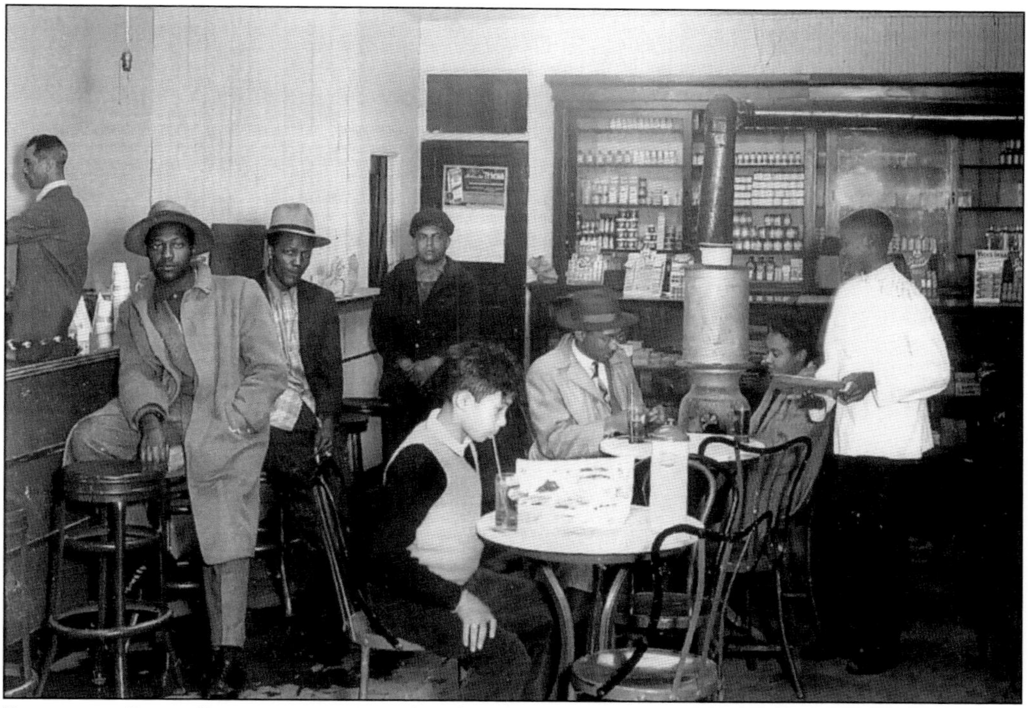

RIVERSIDE SODA SHOP, c. 1946. After being successful with the College Soda Shop, Mr. and Mrs. Webber established the Riverside Soda Shop on the west side of town in 1945 at the corner of Russell and Windsor Streets. Pictured, from left to right, are Paul Webber, Albert Felder, unidentified, Earl Cummings, Paul Webber III, two unidentified people, and Theodore Curry. Note the pot-bellied stove that was common in the past. (Courtesy Dr. Clemmie Webber.)

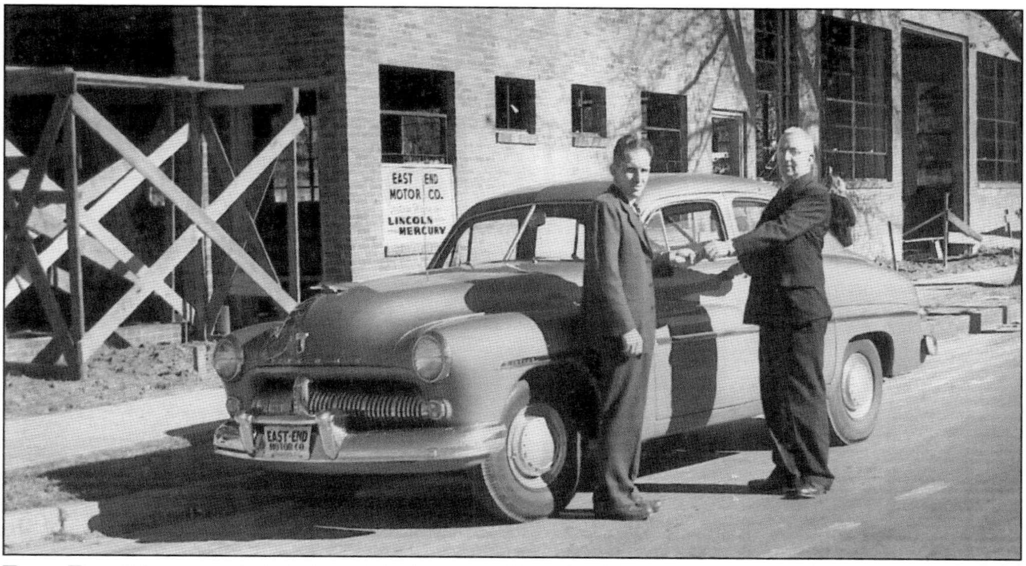

EAST END MOTORS, 1948. In 1948 the new Lincoln Mercury car dealership opened on the corner of Russell Street and Highway 601. Here Cliff Morgan presents the keys to the first car sold at his dealership to Pelham Felder. Note that construction of the building was not even complete when the first sale occurred. (Courtesy Ruth Morgan.)

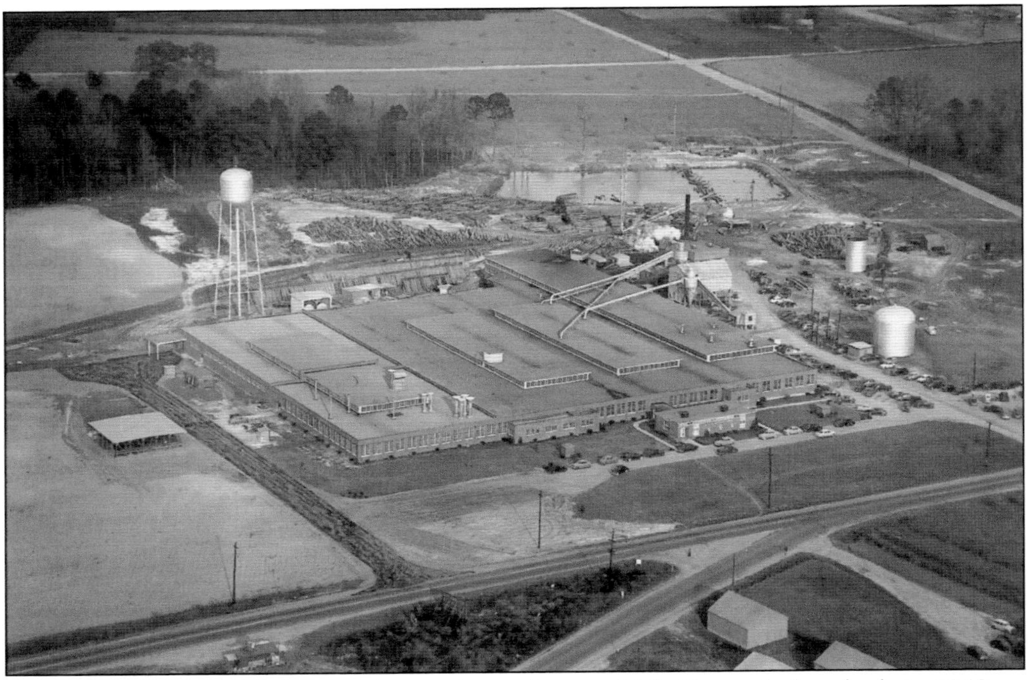

U.S. Plywood, 1951. This aerial view shows the new U.S. Plywood plant built in 1948 on the Five Chop Road. Veneered plywood paneling was the principal product made at this location. Whittaker Elementary School would later be constructed in the upper part of this picture on what would become a new four-lane highway known now as the Bypass. (Courtesy Phil and Gerry Adams.)

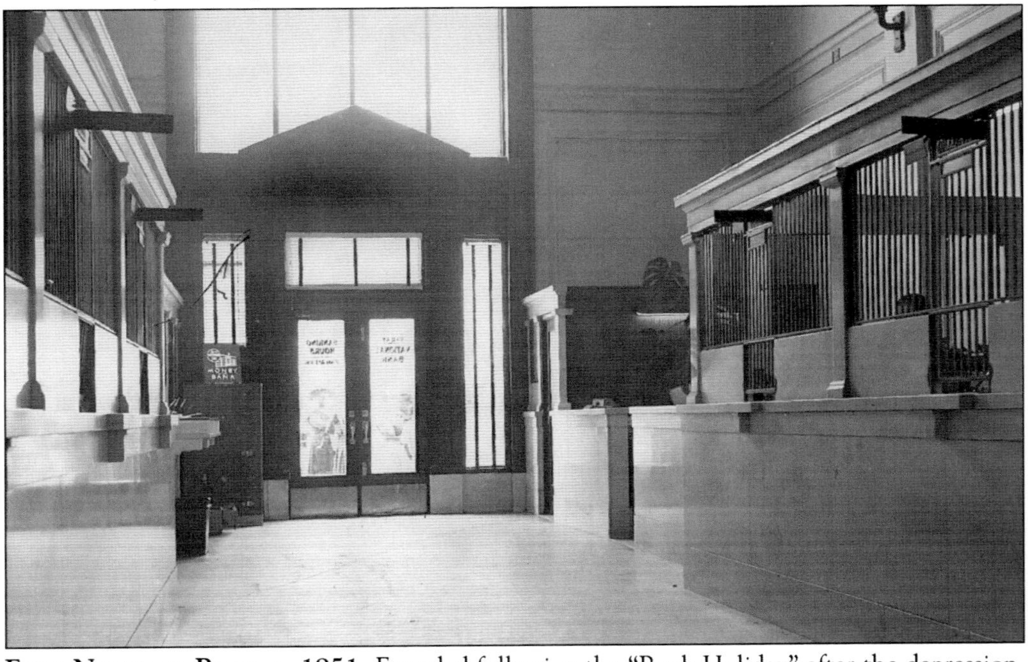

First National Bank, c. 1951. Founded following the "Bank Holiday" after the depression, First National Bank has been a main fixture in the Orangeburg community. Shown here is the interior of its original office building on Russell Street. (Courtesy Catherine Senn.)

Seven

Hospital

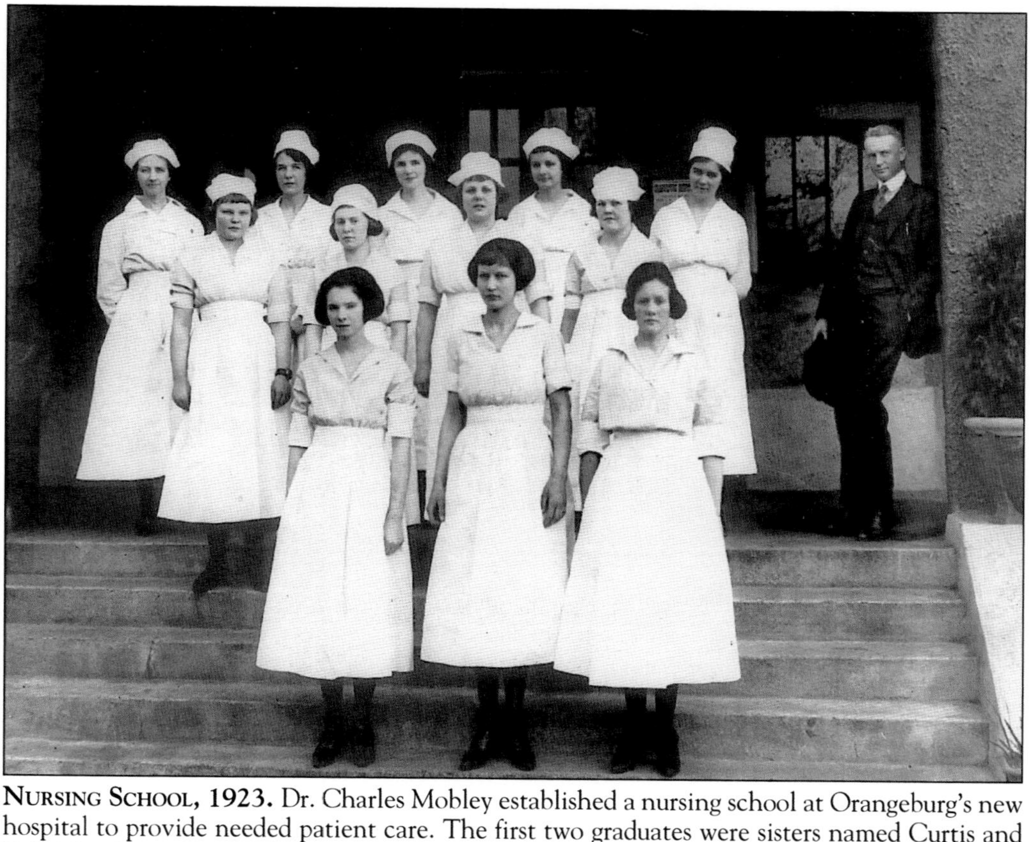

Nursing School, 1923. Dr. Charles Mobley established a nursing school at Orangeburg's new hospital to provide needed patient care. The first two graduates were sisters named Curtis and Eula Mae Carter. Pictured here, from left to right, are (front row) Adelaide Rush, x; Annie Maud Dean, 1924; and Mary Sue Jones, 1926; (middle row) Curtis Carter, 1923; Lillian Geiger, 1924; Eula Mae Carter, 1923; and Minnie Zeigler,1924; (back row) Sally Hicklin, RN, superintendent of nurses; Maude Brasington, RN; Miss Carroll, RN; Mattie Williams, RN; Miss Snell, RN; and Dr. Charles Mobley, founder. (Courtesy The Regional Medical Center.)

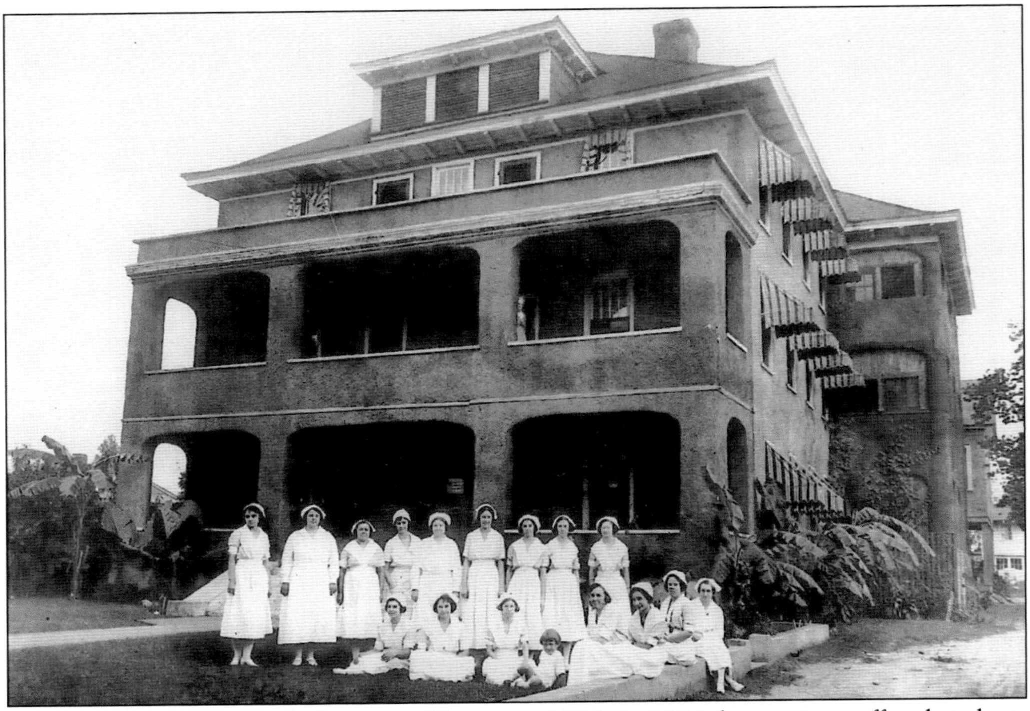

Exterior of Dr. Mobley's Original Hospital, 1924. In 1924 the nursing staff and students pose in front of Dr. Mobley's hospital on Glover Street This building was constructed in the 1890s as a dormitory for the Orangeburg Collegiate Institute, a Baptist-affiliated college. After the college closed in 1914, it became Orangeburg's first sustainable hospital in 1919. The boy in front is "Red" Fairey, the first baby born at the hospital after it opened. (Courtesy The Regional Medical Center.)

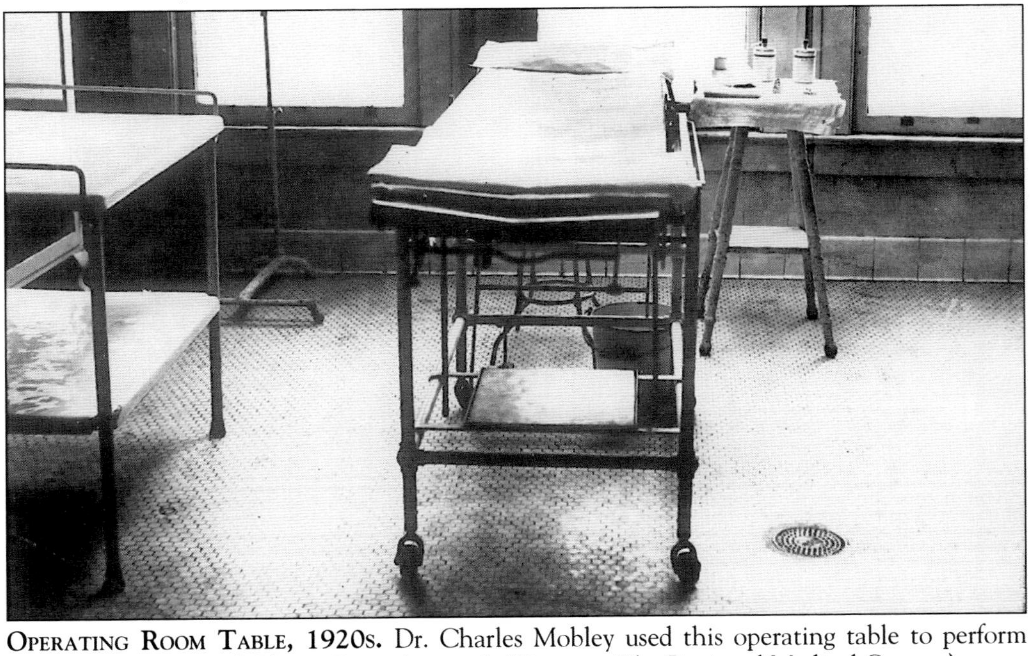

Operating Room Table, 1920s. Dr. Charles Mobley used this operating table to perform surgery in the original Glover Street hospital. (Courtesy The Regional Medical Center.)

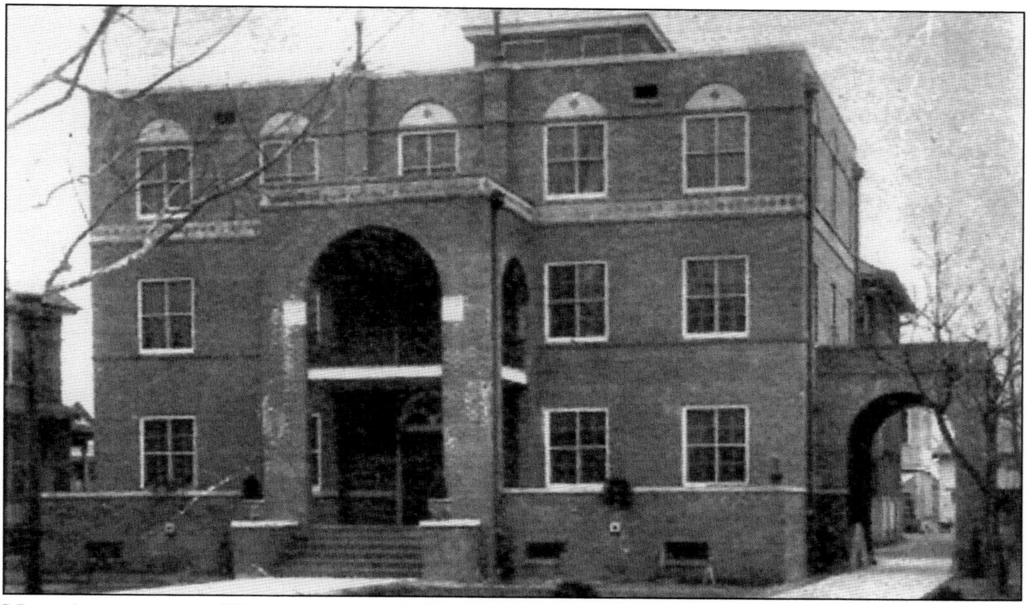

NEW ADDITION TO HOSPITAL, 1926. By 1924 Orangeburg had already outgrown its original hospital facility, so a new addition was constructed in front of the first building. A covered walkway connected the two buildings. (Courtesy Harry Wannamaker III.)

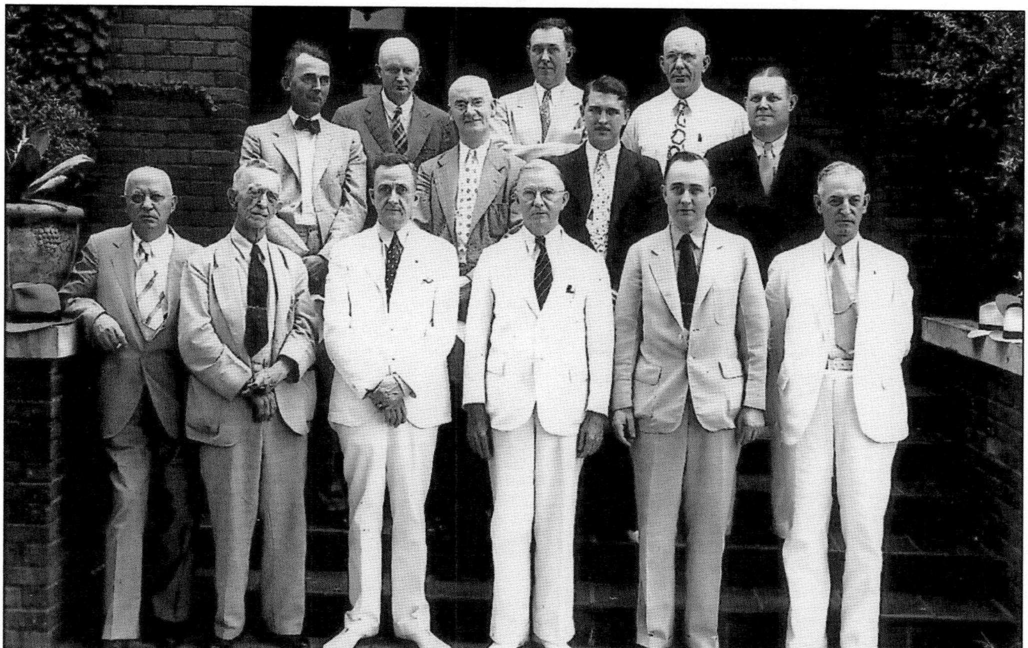

MEDICAL STAFF, 1936. The physicians who served the medical needs of Orangeburg's citizens in 1936 are shown in front of the old hospital. Altogether there were eleven general practitioners and three surgeons. Pictured, from left to right, are (front row) Dr. Lin C. Shecut, Dr. T.A. Jeffords, Dr. Henry Schiffley, Dr. C.I. Green, Dr. Homer Eargle, and Dr. Vance Brabham Sr. (middle row) Dr. W.L. Heaner, Dr. Henry P. Moore Sr., Dr. James W. Harter, Dr. L.P. Thackston Sr. (back row) Dr. Charles A. Mobley, Dr. George Truluck, and Dr. Grover C. Bolin. Dr. James M. Albergotti Jr. was absent. (Courtesy The Regional Medical Center.)

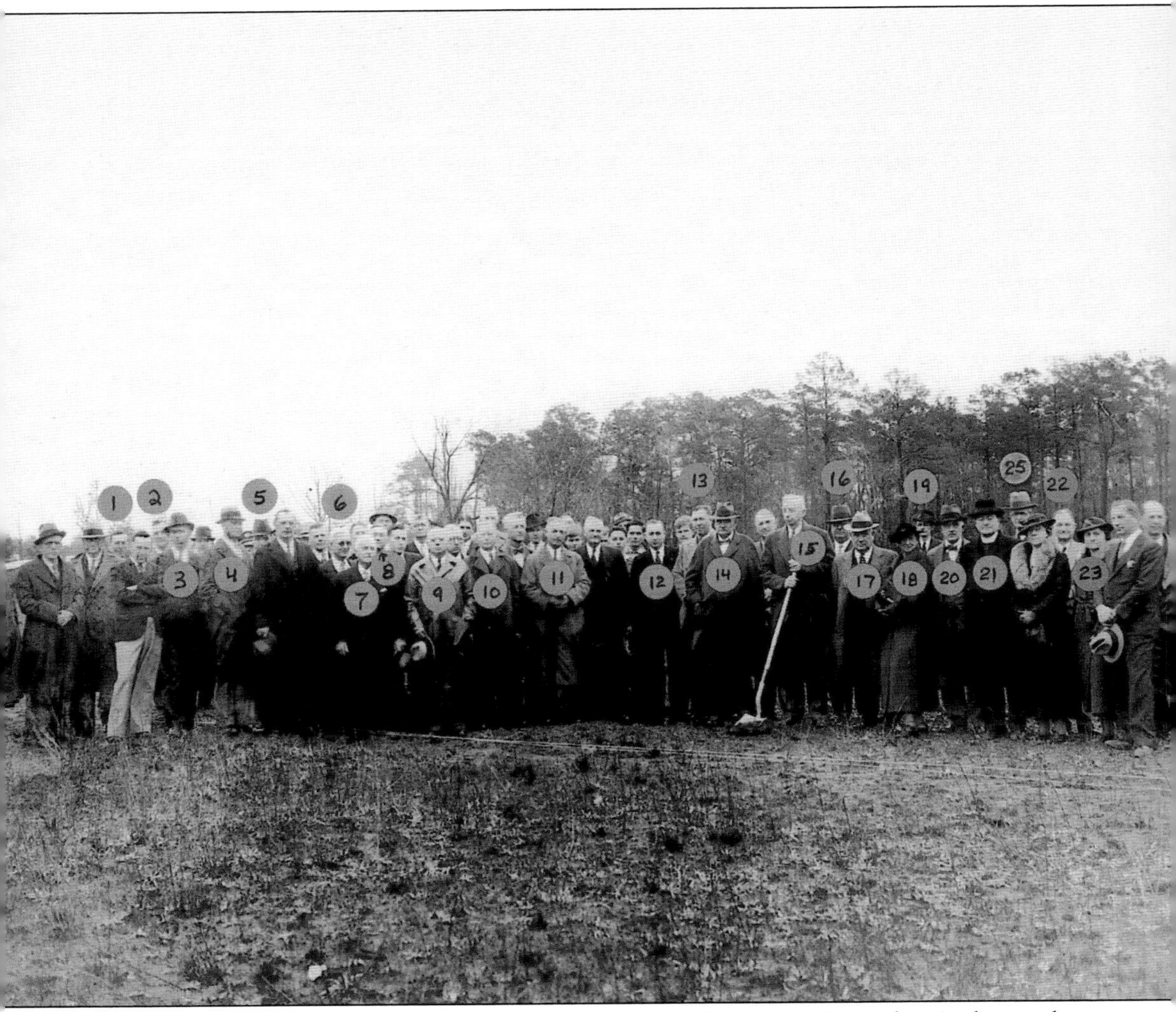

Tri-County Hospital Groundbreaking, 1936. By 1934 Orangeburg's hospital was outdated as well as being too small to meet the public's needs. The newly formed Tri-County Hospital Commission took over the ownership and operations about this time so that federal and foundation funds could be obtained. The groundbreaking ceremony took place on January 15,1936. The man with the shovel is W. Eugene Atkinson, chairman of the hospital commission, which was the board of trustees. As one can see the new site was in the midst of a field in a then undeveloped area. In fact the leaders of the hospital were scolded by many of Orangeburg's citizens for "building the new hospital so far out in the country." Those identified are: 1) John Harley; 2) Orrin Crum; 3) Louis Theiling, city treasurer; 4) Rep. Watt E. Smith; 5) Dr. James M. Albergotti Jr.; 6) C.C. Berry Sr.; 7) Edward Hawes, city engineer; 8) John F. Pearson, DPU manager; 9) Dr. Lin C. Shecut; 10) Dr. C.I. Green; 11) Dr. Vance W. Brabham Sr.; 12) Dr. Homer M. Eargle; 13) Dr. George M. Truluck; 14) Mayor Robert H. Jennings Sr.; 15) W. Eugene Atkinson, board chairman; 16) Marion Felder; 17) Rev. J. Elwood Welsh, board member; 18) Mrs. Robert H. Jennings Sr., board member; 19) Rutledge Osborne; 20) Sen. Robert Lide, board member; 21) Father Thomas J. Cronin, board member; 22) W.E. Bennett, board member; 23) Mrs. L.A. Hartzog, board member; 24) J.F. Cleckley, board member; 25) John M. Sifly, city council. (Courtesy Gene Atkinson.)

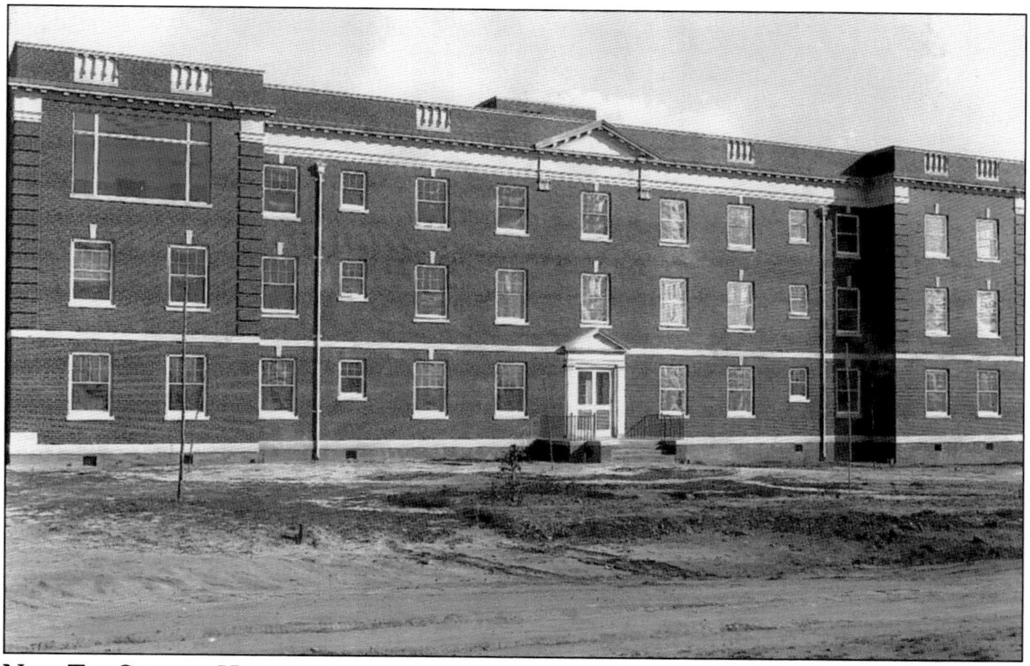

New Tri-County Hospital Nearing Completion, 1937. Construction of Orangeburg's new hospital on Carolina Avenue was nearly complete in this 1937 picture. A grand opening and public tour was held just prior to its occupation on August 17,1937. (Courtesy Cleveland Dempsey.)

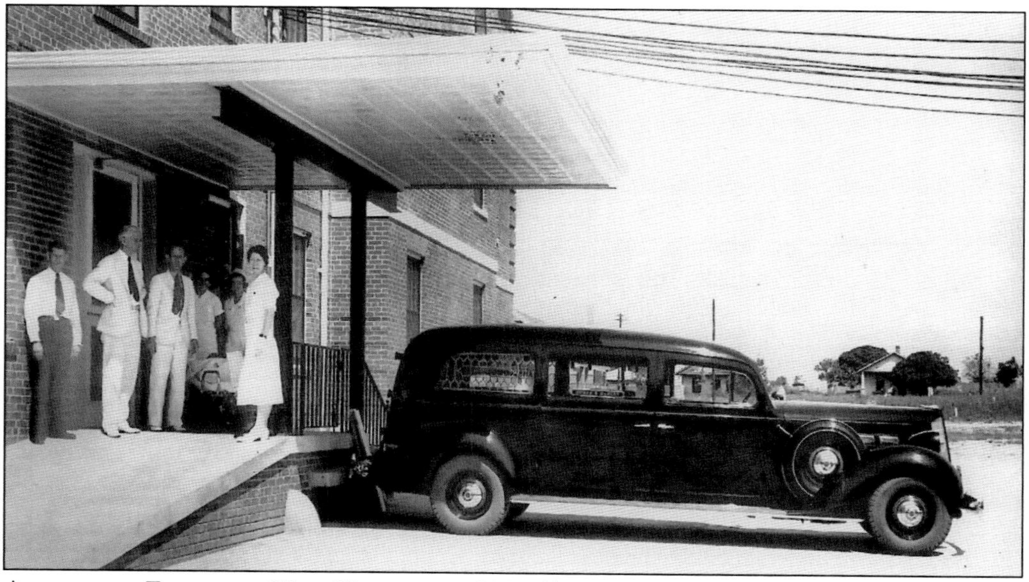

Ambulance Entrance New Hospital, 1937. Shown is an ambulance from Dukes-Harley Funeral Home at the emergency room entrance to the new Tri-County Hospital around 1937. As can be seen in the background, this area was not well developed. In fact many men and boys were disappointed that the hospital was built there as it destroyed their best area for hunting. Shown above, from left to right, are Clifton Harley, Dukes-Harley Funeral Home; W. Eugene Atkinson, hospital commission chairman; W.A. Cooper, hospital superintendent; and Betty Stroble Bozard, RN. (Courtesy The Regional Medical Center.)

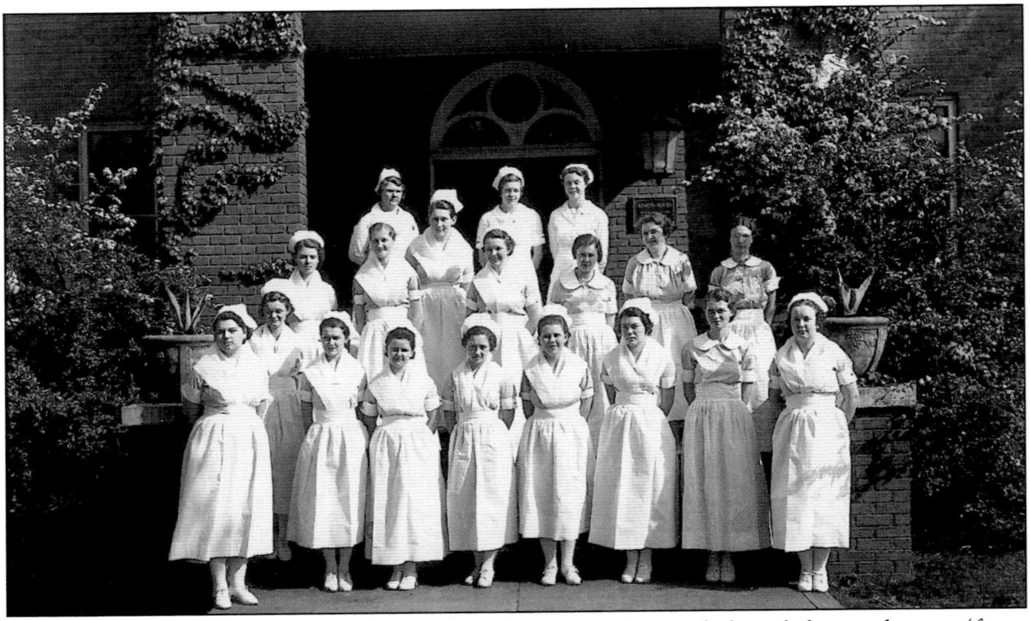

Nursing School Classes of 1935, 1936, and 1937. Pictured, from left to right, are (front row) Emmett Sharpe, 1937; Blanche Jamison,1937; Fannie Mae Kennerly, 1938; Lorene Felder, 1937; Eloise Riley, 1935; Elizabeth Jackson, 1937; Sara Steele, x; and Zola Starnes, 1937; (second row) Emma Guess, x; (third row) Carrie Mae Hartzog, 1937; Helen Creech, 1937; Nellie King, x; Betty Floyd, 1939; Maymie Hall, 1938; and Theresa Bozard, x; (fourth row) Louise Robinson, 1936; (fifth row) Instructors Mae Smith, head nurse; Irene Austin, 1930; and Lillie Inabinet, 1934. (Courtesy The Regional Medical Center.)

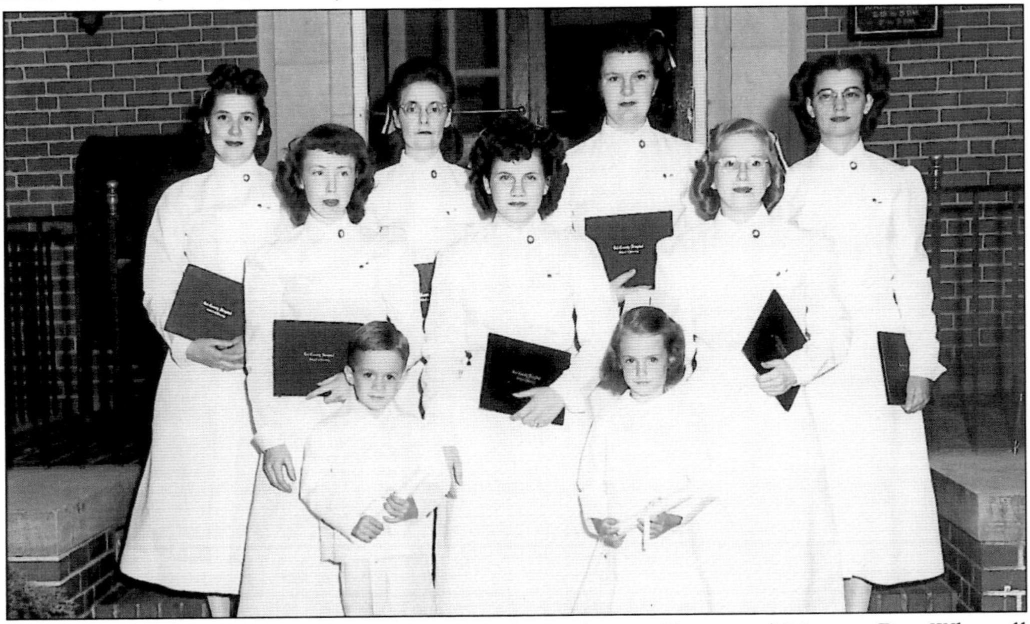

Nursing Class of 1949. Shown here, from left to right, are (front row) Mascots Dan Whetsell and Susan Brabham; (middle row) Louise Shuler, Claudia Fender, and Louise Beasley; (third row) Mazie Thompson, Alice Guess, Juliette West, and Mary Johnson. (Courtesy The Regional Medical Center.)

Eight

Hawthorne and The Methodist Home

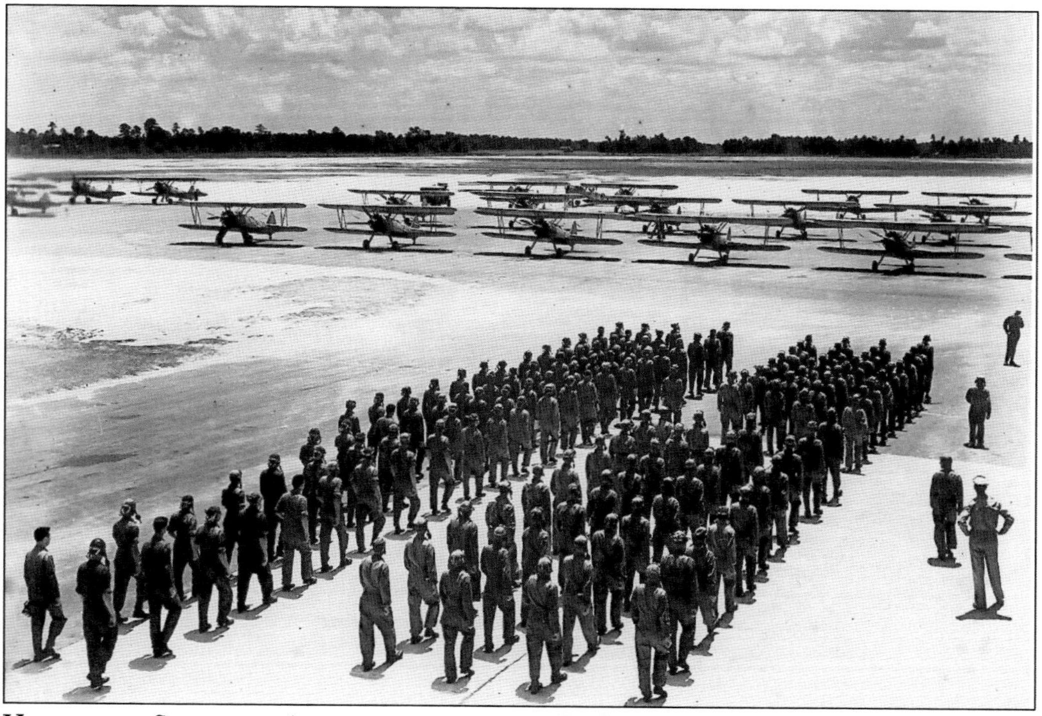

Hawthorne School of Aeronautics, c. 1943. With World War II raging in Europe, the Hawthorne School of Aeronautics was established in Orangeburg to train pilots for America's preparation for the inevitable. This facility was located several miles south of the city. Shown here are several squadrons of cadets in formation near the Stearman planes that were used for this initial pilot training. (Courtesy Al McMichael.)

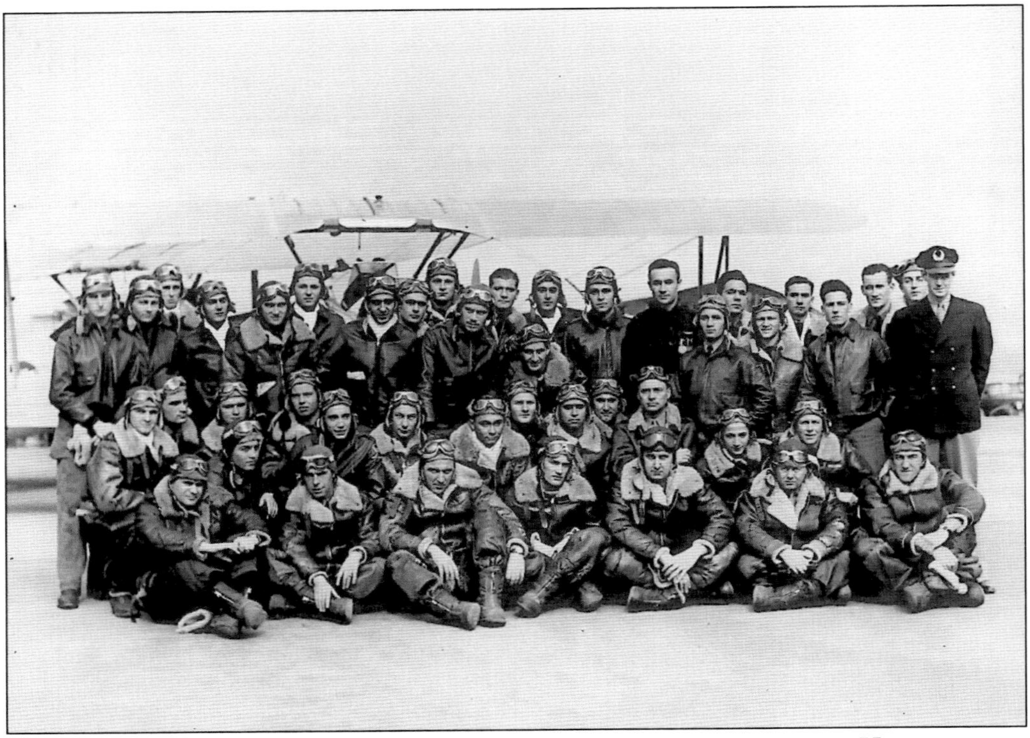

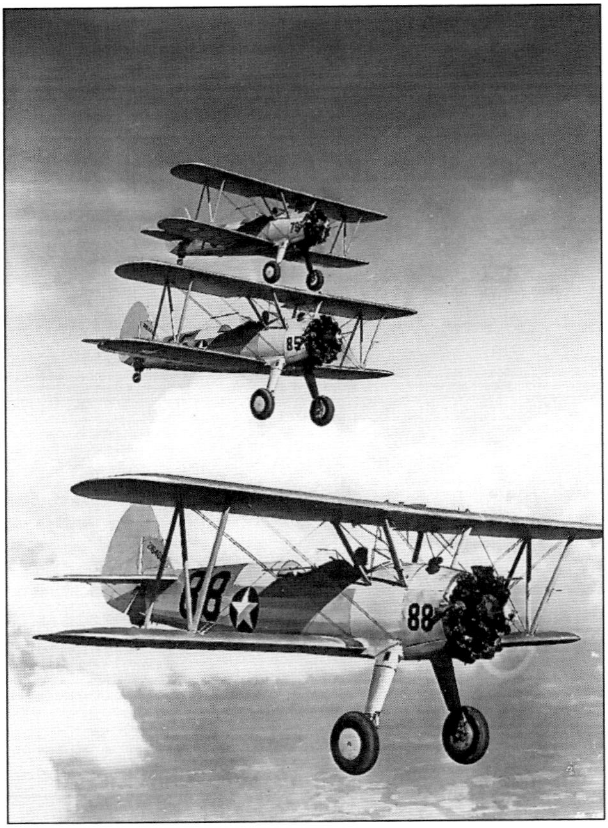

STUDENT PILOTS AT HAWTHORNE, c. 1943. The Hawthorne School of Aeronautics trained more than 4,000 American pilots as well as over 1,600 French pilots during World War II. The primary training school in Orangeburg lasted about three months, after which student pilots were transferred to another base for more advanced training and tactical uses of military aircraft. (Courtesy Mattie W. Wentink.)

STEARMAN PT-17 PLANES, c. 1943. The training of pilots was conducted with the two cockpit open air bi-plane made by Stearman. It featured a 200 horsepower Continental radial engine and had a top speed of about 120 miles per hour. (Courtesy Mattie W. Wentink.)

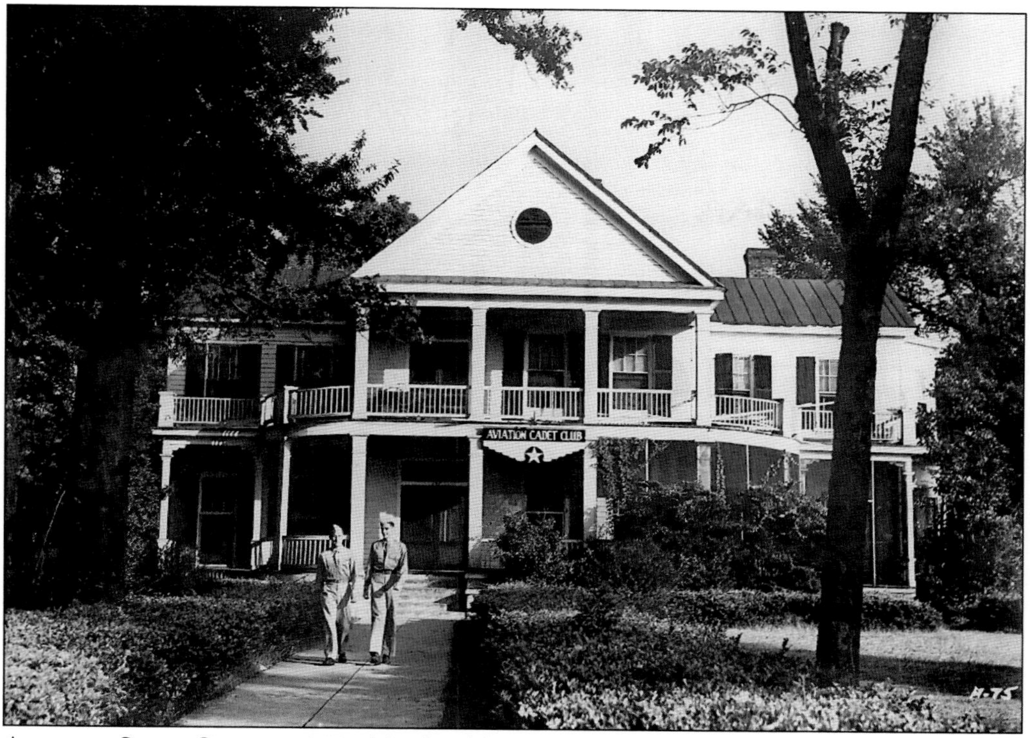

AVIATION CADET CLUB, c. 1943. After hard days and nights of training, cadets were occasionally given some time off on weekends. The old Ed Scoville/W.C. Wannamaker home at the corner of Russell and Doyle Streets was converted into a recreation hall to provide entertainment for these student pilots. (Courtesy Mattie W. Wentink.)

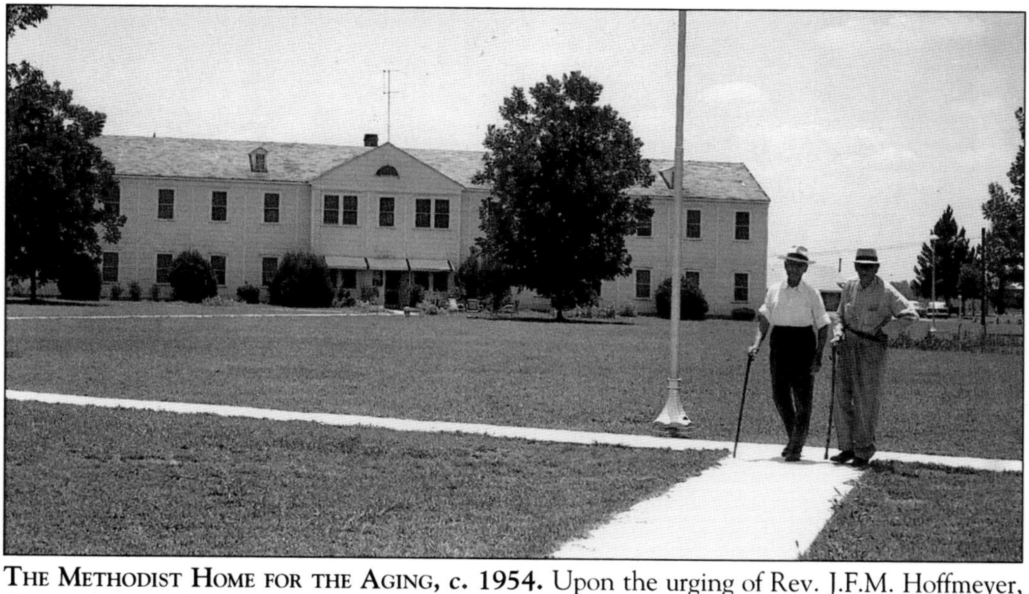

THE METHODIST HOME FOR THE AGING, c. 1954. Upon the urging of Rev. J.F.M. Hoffmeyer, the Methodist Church of South Carolina established The Methodist Home for the Aging in 1953 at the former site of the Hawthorne School of Aeronautics. This bold new concept of providing a retirement home for senior citizens caught on, and many other facilities of this type began to be established in the 1950s and 1960s. (Courtesy The Methodist Oaks.)

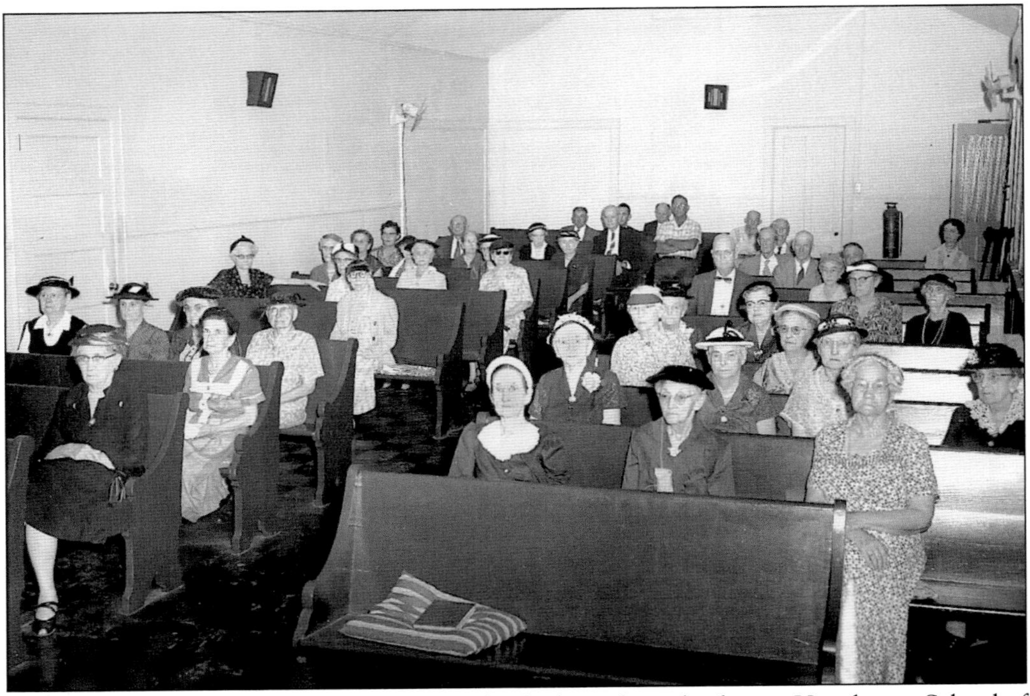

The Methodist Home Chapel, c. 1954. The facilities from the former Hawthorne School of Aeronautics were converted for use as a retirement home. Here is an early photograph showing the residents attending chapel on Sunday. (Courtesy The Methodist Oaks.)

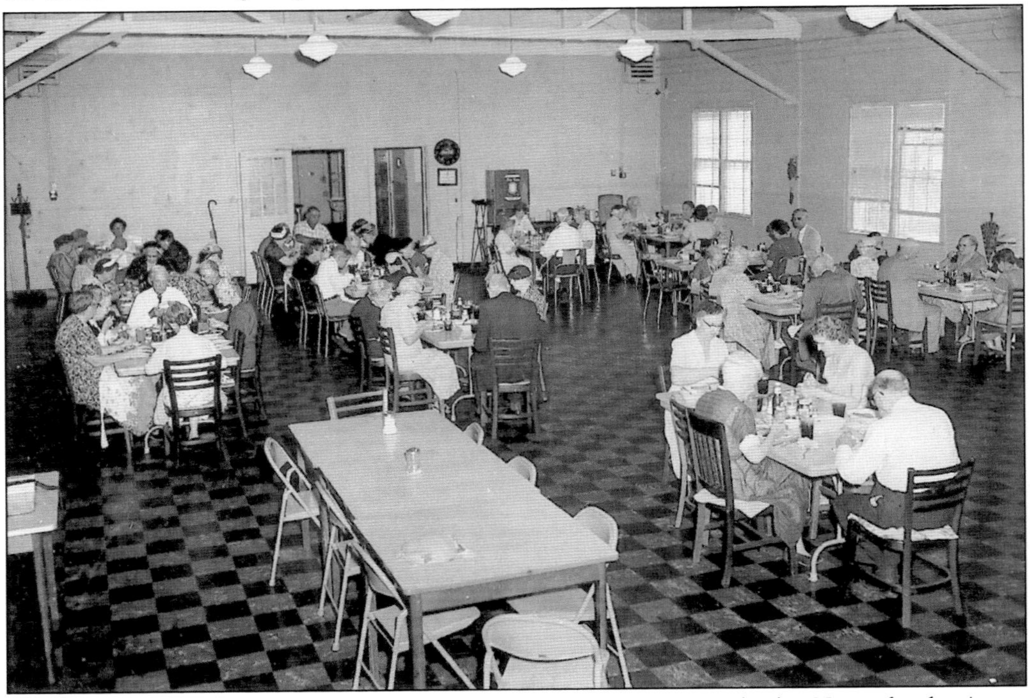

The Methodist Home Dining Hall, c. 1954. Residents of the Methodist Home for the Aging are shown in the dining hall during the first year or so after the facility was opened. (Courtesy The Methodist Oaks.)

Nine

RECREATION

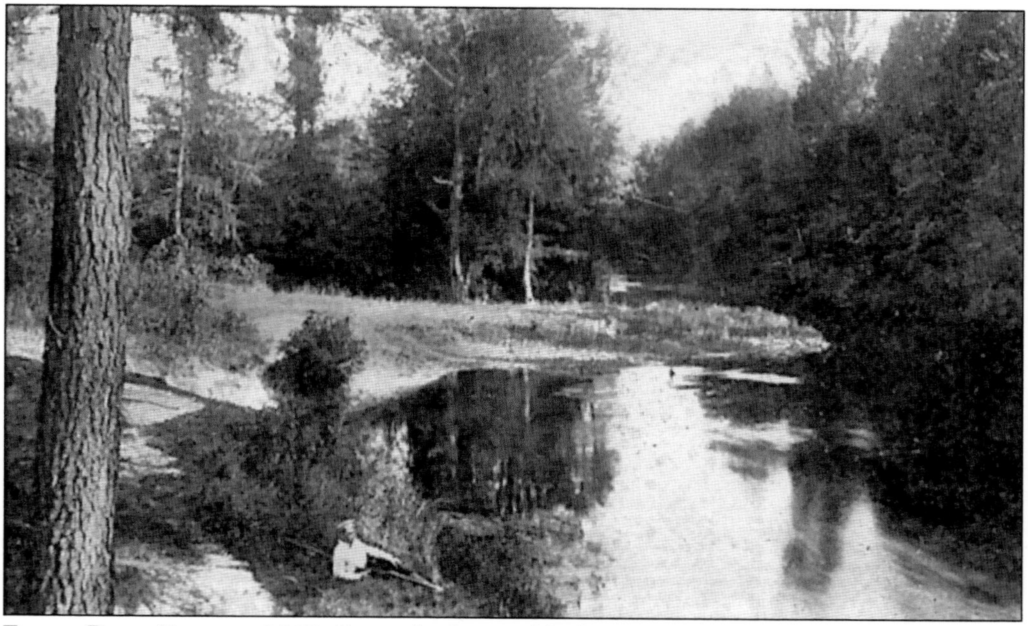

EDISTO RIVER FISHING, 1907. Being the longest black water river in the world, the north fork of the Edisto River has always been a popular fishing and recreation area for local residents. (Courtesy Anna Lou Wolfe.)

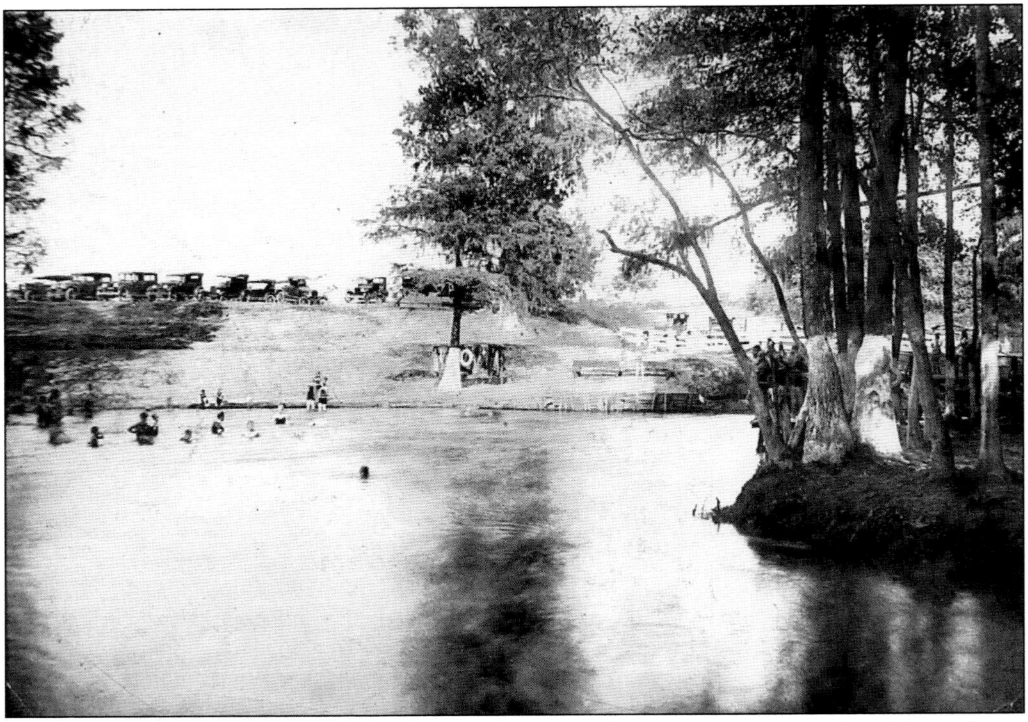

SWIMMING AREA, EDISTO RIVER, 1920S. Cooling off by swimming in the Edisto River has proven to be a popular pastime in the heat of the summer over the years. (Courtesy Cleveland Dempsey.)

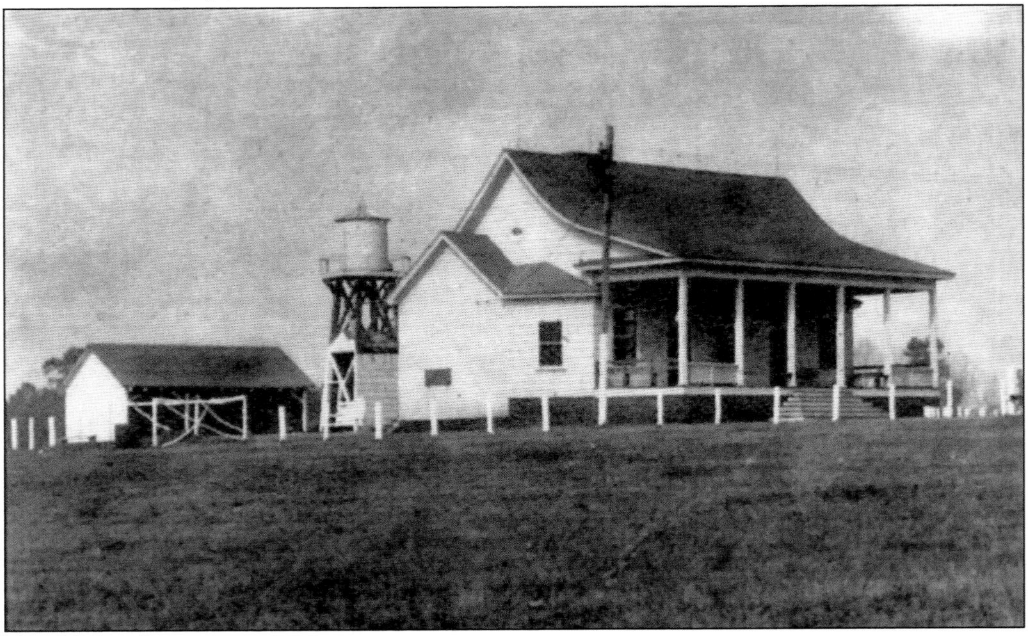

COUNTRY CLUB OF ORANGEBURG CLUB HOUSE, 1926. The Country Club of Orangeburg was founded in 1922, and primarily featured a golf course. Note the water tower in the background as city water was not widely available outside of town in those days. (Courtesy Harry Wannamaker III.)

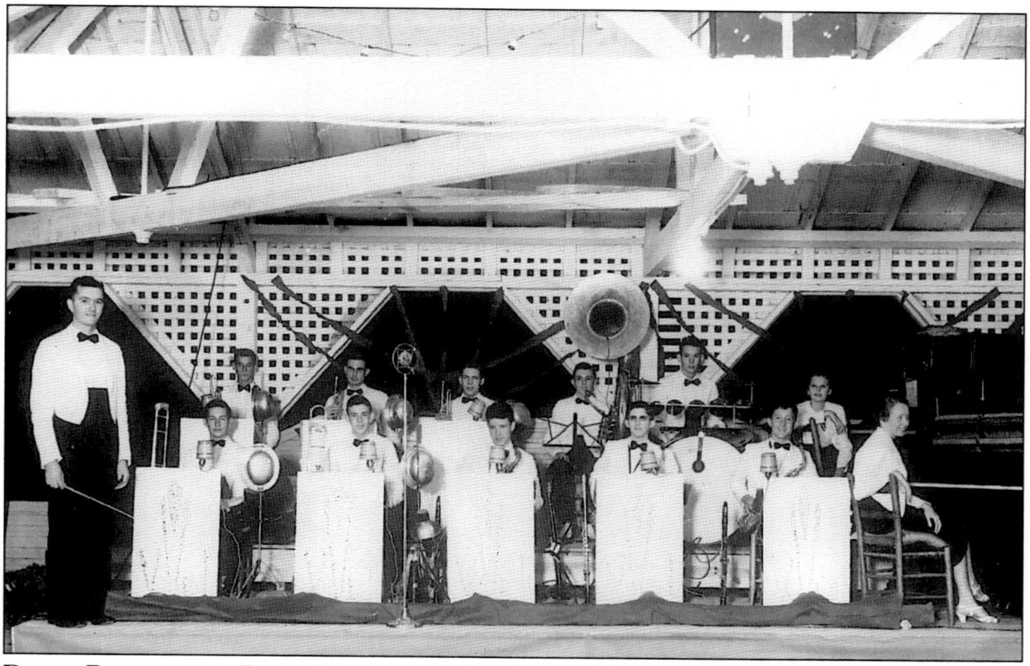

DANCE BAND AT THE RIVER PAVILION, 1935. In the 1930s local musicians would get together and play for dances at the river pavilion. In that day the pavilion consisted of an enclosed ground floor with a snackbar and restrooms, while the upper floor was an open air, roofed dance floor. Pictured from left to right are (front row) Victor Jackson (leader), Henry Wofford, Russell Wolfe, Bruce Berry, Lee Mack, Wilbur Smith, and Boogie Smoak Ziegler, (back row) Walker Limehouse, Harold "Buster" Loring, Dan Dukes, Raymond Smith, Billy Ziegler, and Mable Wannamaker Leadley. (Courtesy W.C. Ziegler.)

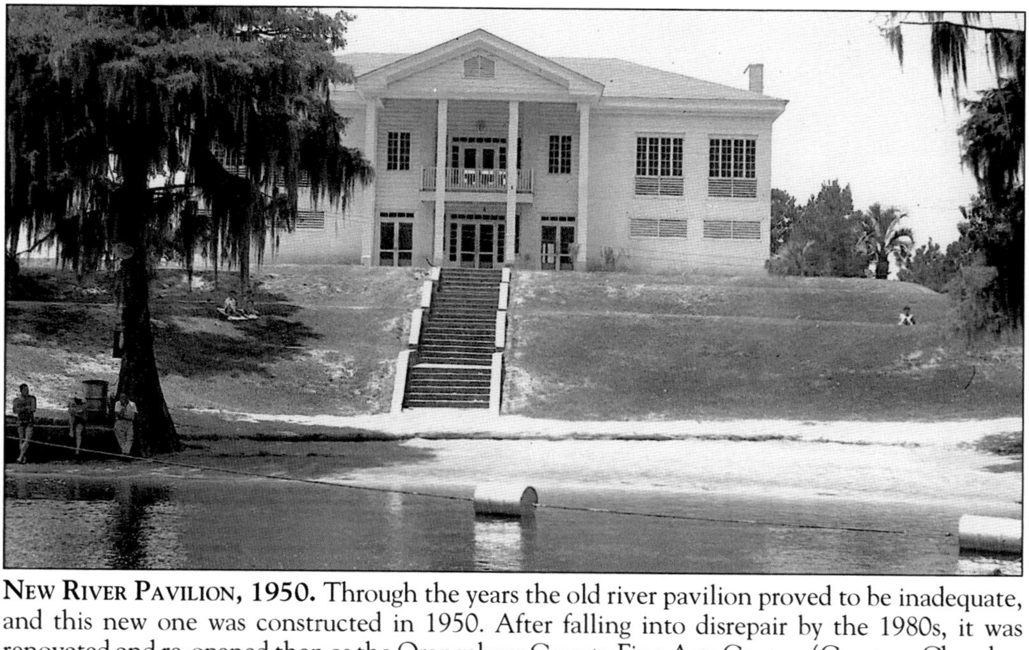

NEW RIVER PAVILION, 1950. Through the years the old river pavilion proved to be inadequate, and this new one was constructed in 1950. After falling into disrepair by the 1980s, it was renovated and re-opened then as the Orangeburg County Fine Arts Center. (Courtesy Chamber of Commerce.)

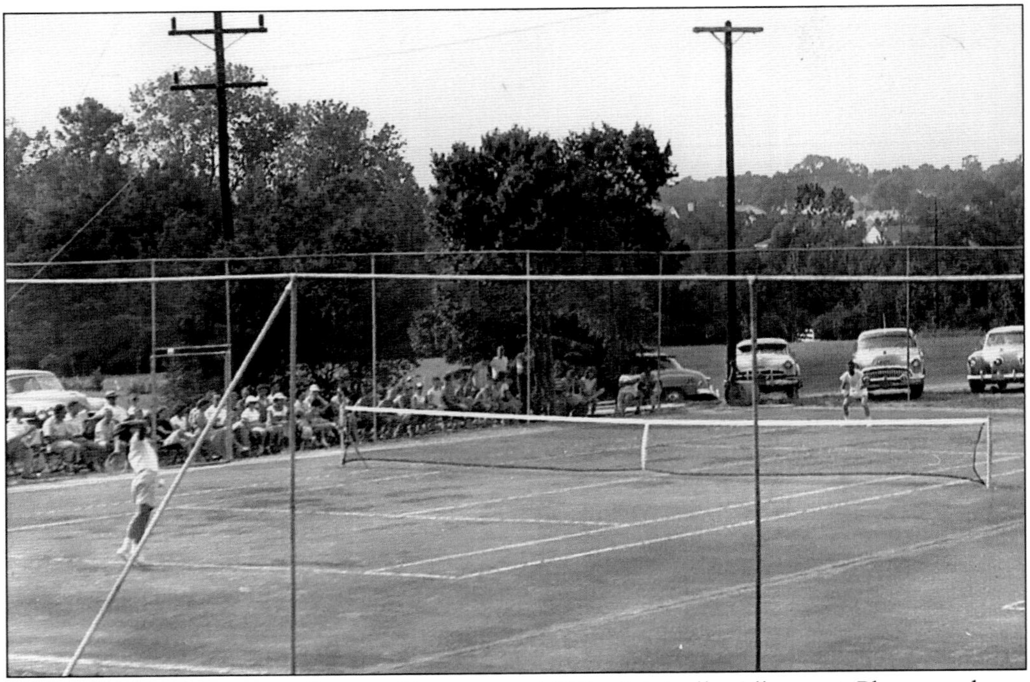

ALBERGOTTI PLAYGROUND TENNIS COURTS, c. 1953. Originally Albergotti Playground was located where the current Rose Garden is in Edisto Memorial Gardens. Funds were given for the establishment of this playground in 1920 by Mr. and Mrs. James M. Albergotti. The area proved to be very low and the ballfield, tennis courts, and playground were often flooded after rains, so they were moved to their current location in 1950. (Courtesy City of Orangeburg.)

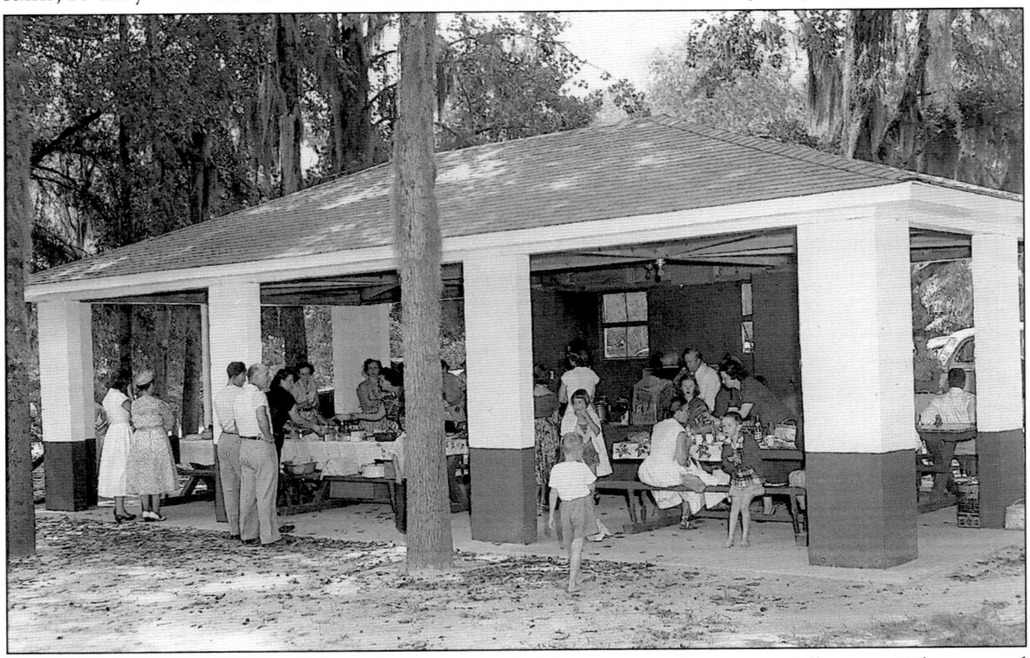

ALBERGOTTI PLAYGROUND PICNIC SHELTER, c. 1953. As part of the new Albergotti Playground recreational complex, a large picnic shelter was built to accommodate group gatherings. (Courtesy City of Orangeburg.)

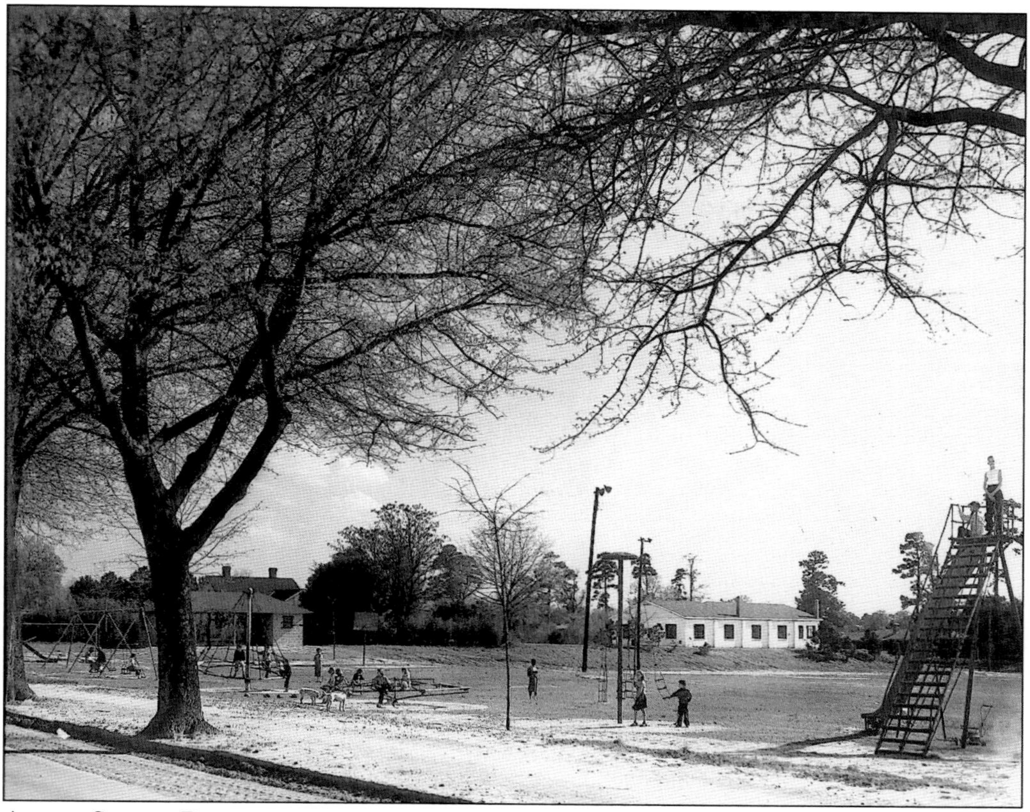

ADDEN STREET PLAYGROUND, C. 1953. Orangeburg is blessed to have many neighborhood playgrounds. The Adden Street Playground was on a site that featured a ballfield for baseball, softball, and football; a youth center known for years as the "Canteen;" and the playground shown here. (Courtesy Chamber of Commerce.)

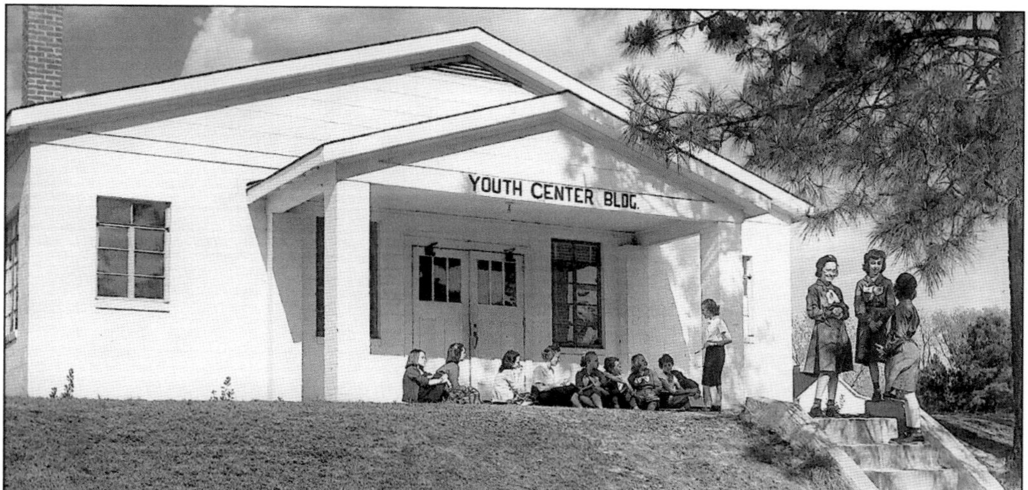

THE CANTEEN YOUTH CENTER, c. 1953. The Canteen has served many purposes through the years: a youth center for hobbies and crafts, a meeting place for youth groups such as the Girl Scouts seen here, a Friday night dance hall, and Parks and Recreation offices. (Courtesy Chamber of Commerce.)

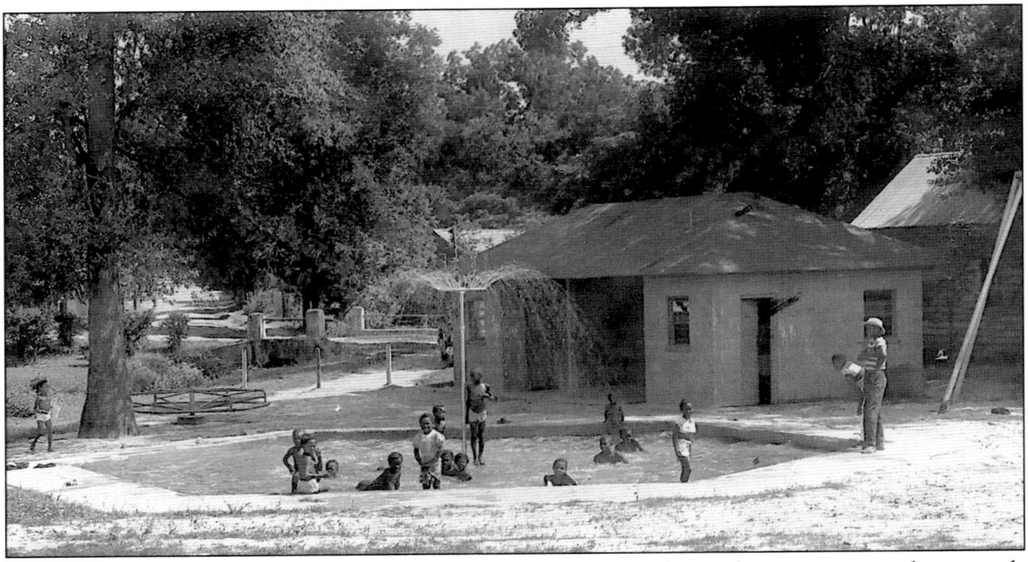

Peasley Street Playground, c. 1953. In the days of racial segregation playgrounds were established in African-American neighborhoods also. Shown here are children playing under a spray fountain to cool off during the summer heat. Through the years Mrs. Geraldyne Zimmerman has been a tremendous neighborhood leader who helped guide and direct the fortune of this playground. In turn the city named the new youth center there the Zimmerman Youth Center in the 1970s for her tireless devotion through the years. (Courtesy City of Orangeburg.)

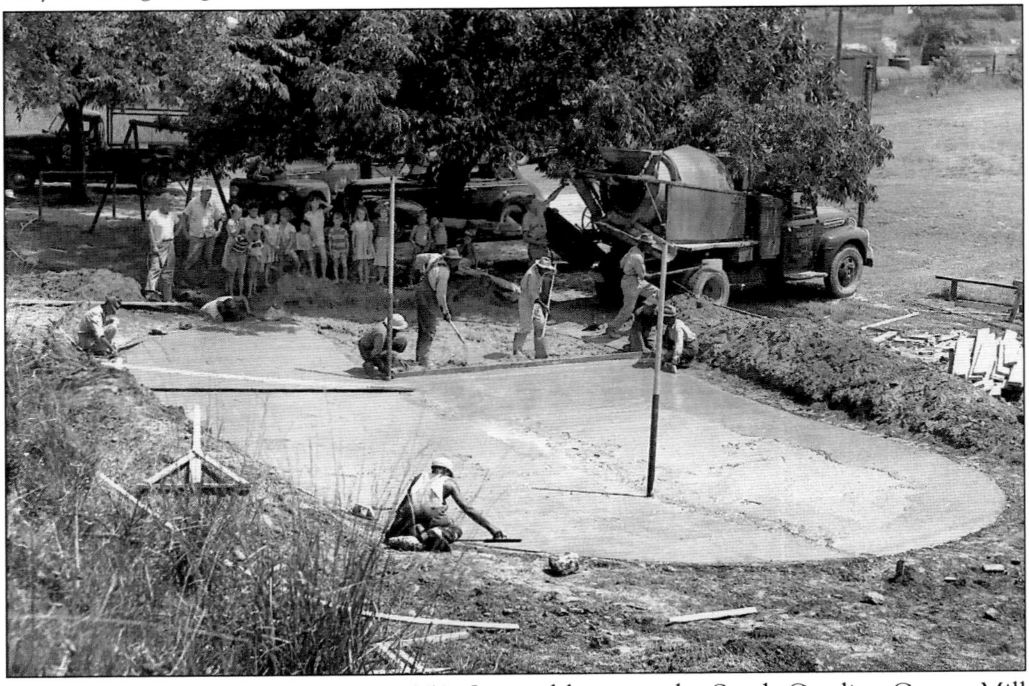

Duncan Street Playground, c. 1953. Located between the South Carolina Cotton Mill (now Zeus Industrial Products) and the fairgrounds is another good example of a neighborhood playground. Here workmen are pouring concrete for a new tetherball court around 1953. (Courtesy City of Orangeburg.)

Ten

Edisto Memorial Gardens

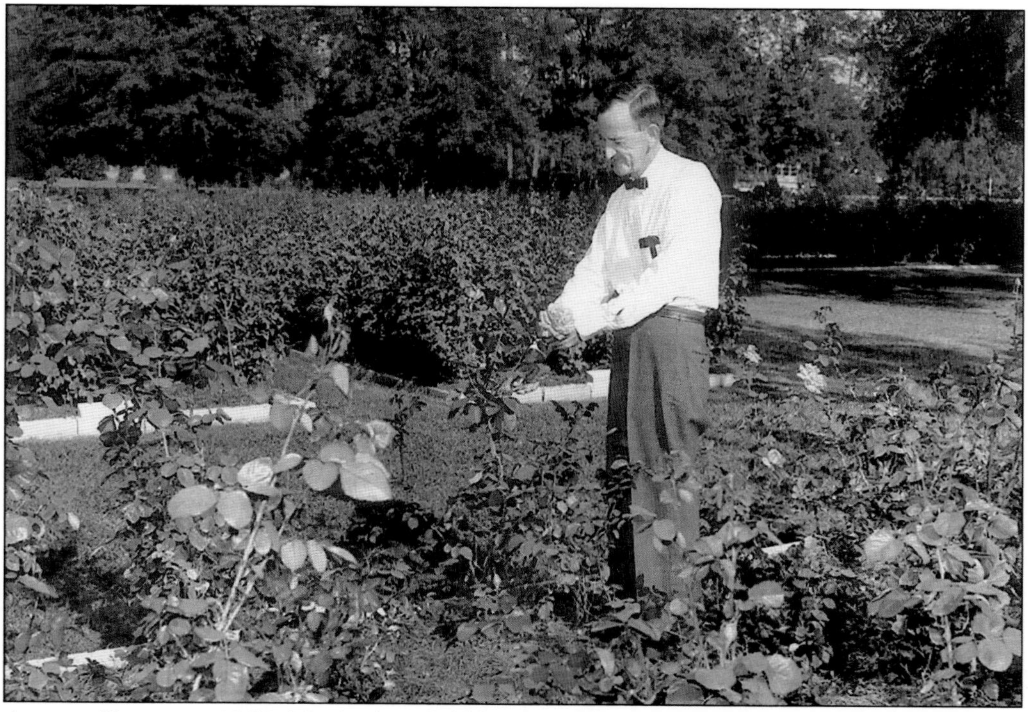

Andrew Dibble, c. 1950. Mr. Andrew Dibble is considered to be the "father of Edisto Memorial Gardens." He served as park superintendent from 1937 to 1964 and designed the gardens as most know it today. Before he took over in 1937 the gardens had floundered somewhat during their initial 11 years. Mr. Dibble did a masterful job in transforming Edisto Memorial Gardens into a horticultural splendor. Today over 600,000 visitors come each year to enjoy the sheer beauty that the gardens exude. (Courtesy Robert Dibble.)

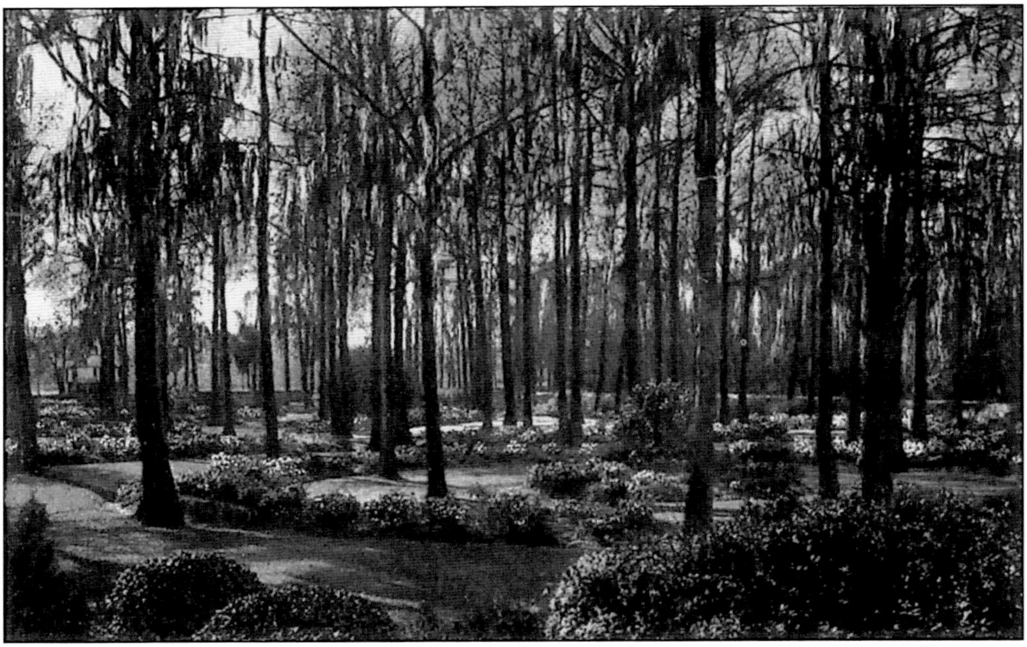

Orangeburg Botanical Gardens, c. 1930s. After being started in 1926 the gardens were originally called the Orangeburg Botanical Gardens for the first five to ten years of existence. (Courtesy Addie Stewart Felkel.)

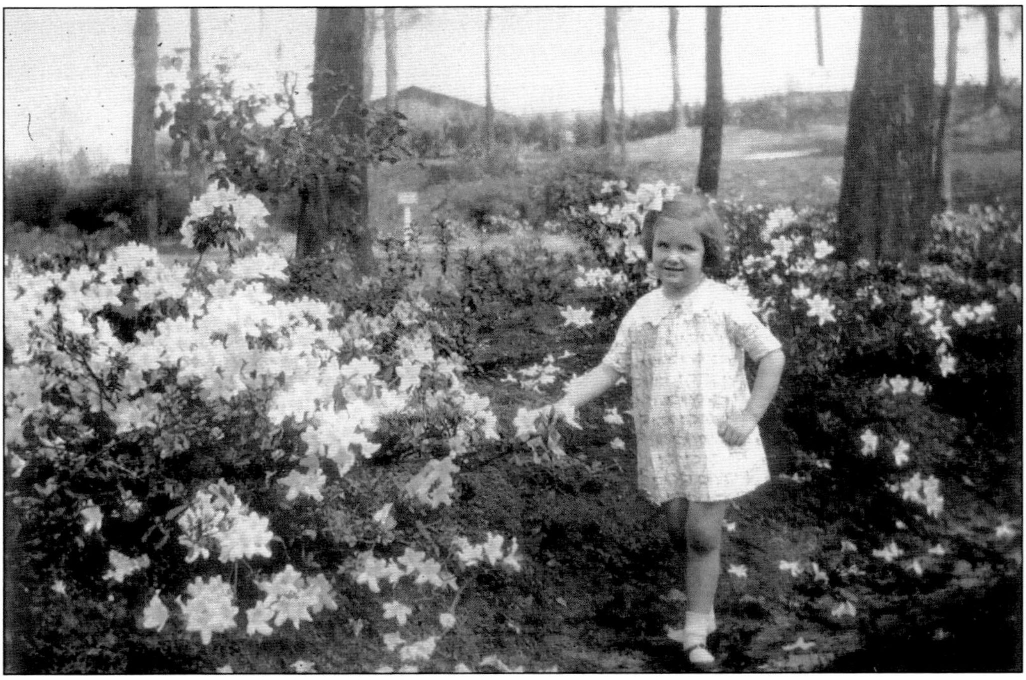

Azalea Gardens, mid 1930s. Bess Wolfe Hill is shown posing beside the beautiful Azalea Gardens as a child. Her father, Col. Russell Wolfe, was very instrumental in several phases of construction at Edisto Memorial Gardens. He was a demolitions expert and was called on from time to time to dynamite stumps out of the ground when an expansion of the gardens would occur. (Courtesy Bess Wolfe Hill.)

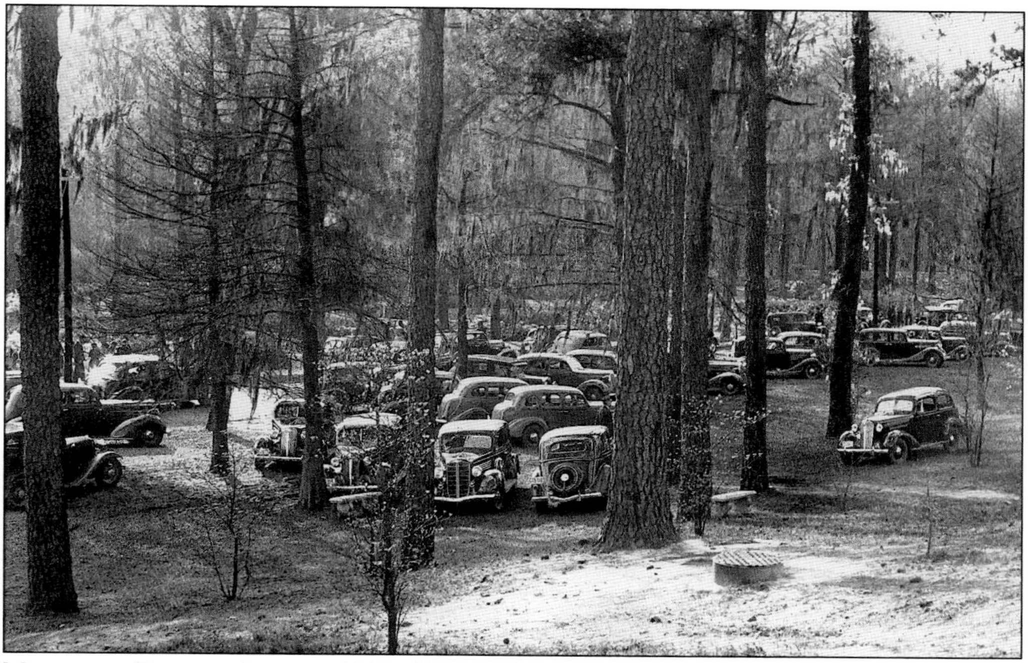

MAKESHIFT PARKING LOT, c. 1937. During the azalea blooming season many people, both local and out of town, came to enjoy the beautiful scenery. At times, there were so many cars that visitors would park wherever they could, as evidenced here. The cars here are in the area where the future scenic garden drive up the hillside would be constructed in 1940 and 1941. The azalea gardens can be seen in the background across the street from these parked vehicles. (Courtesy Chamber of Commerce.)

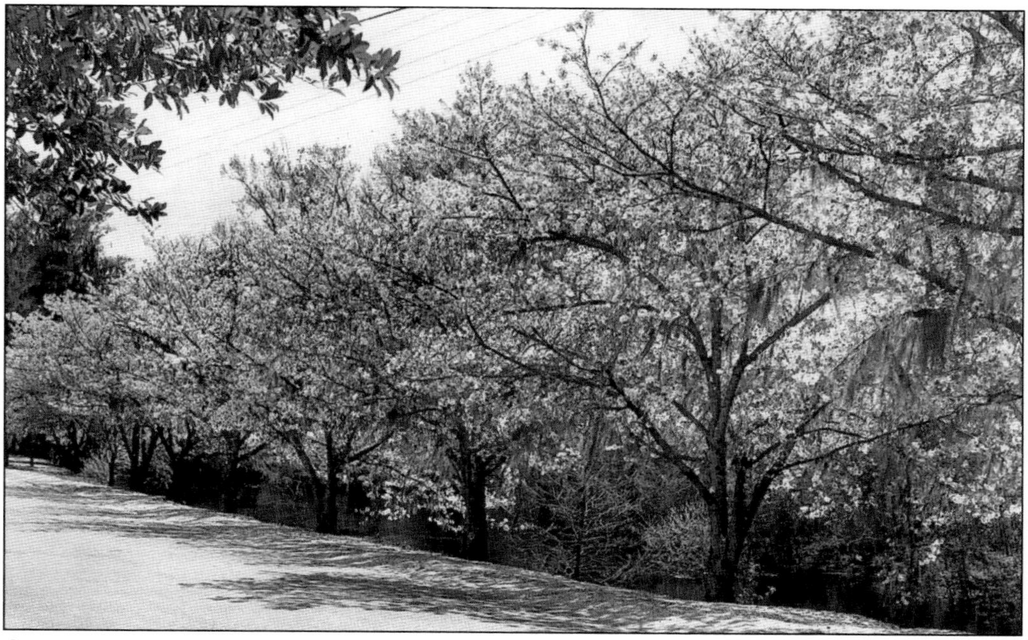

CHERRY TREES, c. 1950. Riverside Drive along the banks of the Edisto River were beautifully lined by colorful cherry trees for many years. The drive along the river during blooming season was absolutely breathtaking. (Courtesy Chamber of Commerce.)

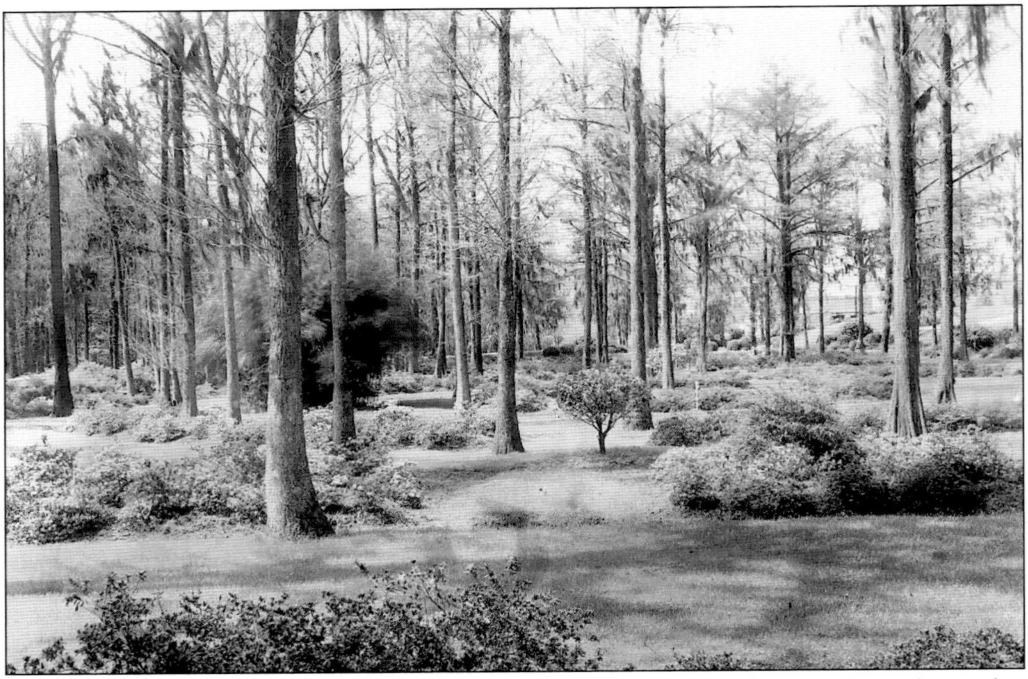

AZALEA GARDENS, 1940s. The initial phase of Edisto Memorial Gardens was the azalea garden area, first planted in 1926. This five acre area previously had been a boggy old dumping ground along the banks of the Edisto River. (Courtesy Chamber of Commerce.)

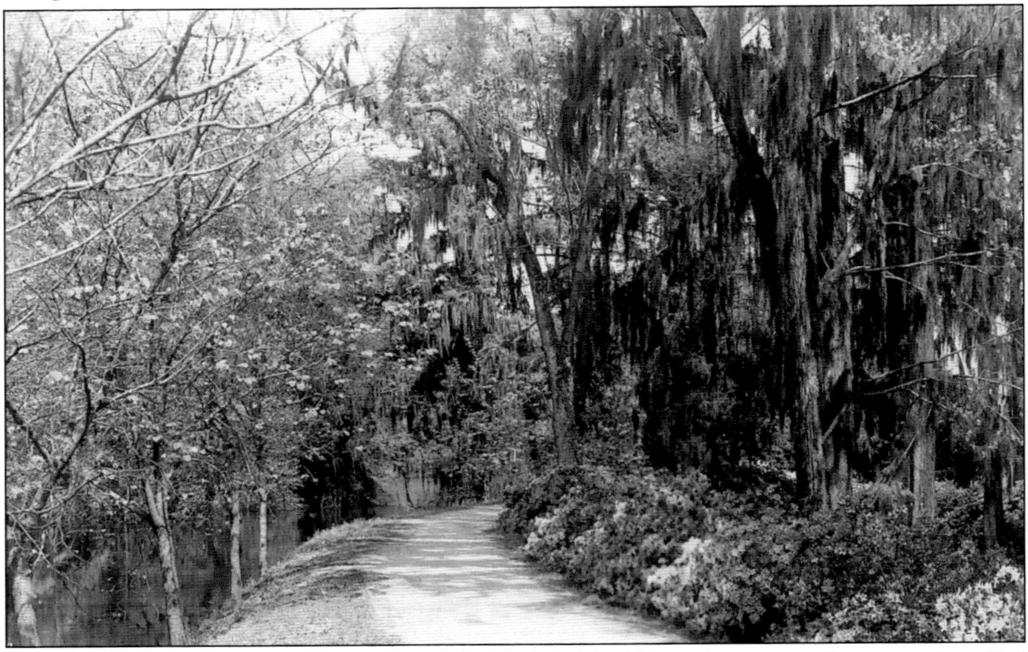

"SHUG LANE," c. 1950. The levee along the banks of the Edisto River was affectionately called "Shug Lane" after the name of the mule used by park employees in the gardens. The dump cart that was harnessed to Shug hauled many a load in the day-to-day maintenance of the gardens. Others have also referred to this levee as "Lovers' Lane" for obvious reasons. (Courtesy Chamber of Commerce.)

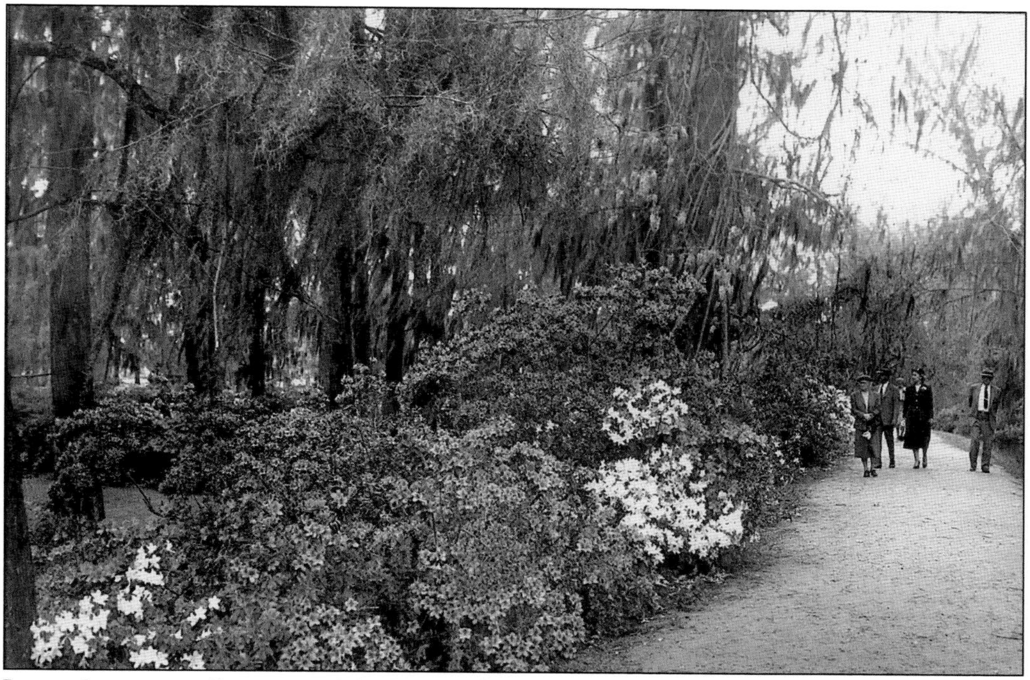

LEVEE ALONG THE RIVER, c. 1950. Visitors here are seen strolling along the banks of the river enjoying the beautiful azaleas in full bloom. (Courtesy Chamber of Commerce.)

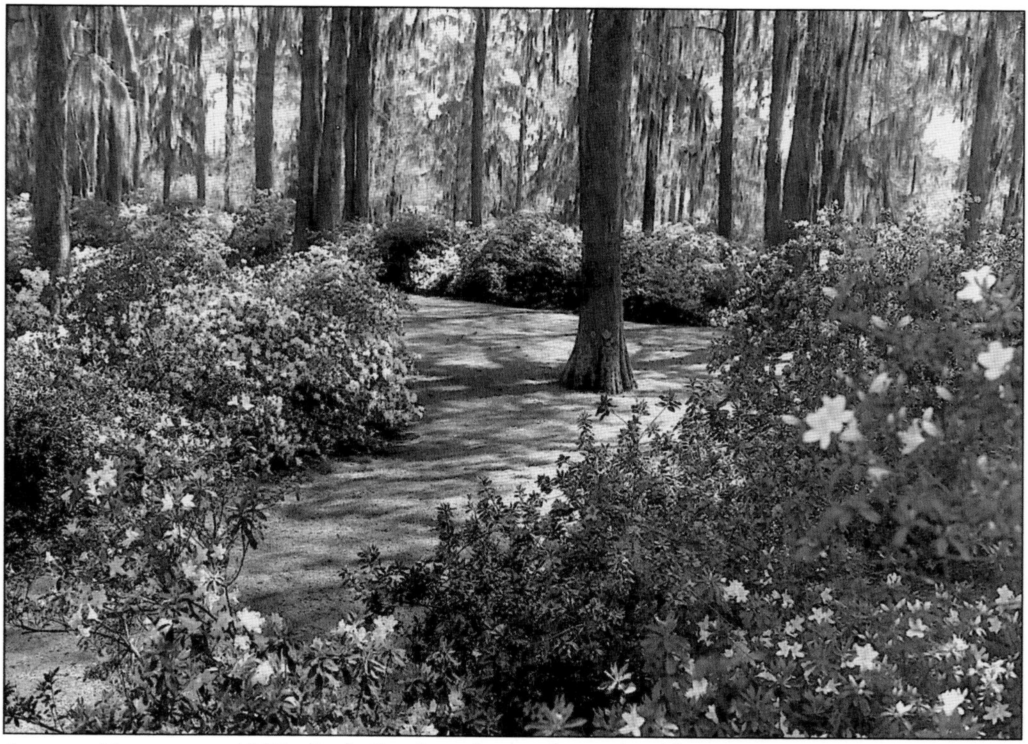

AZALEA GARDEN, c. 1951. Peak Sundays during the azalea blooming season would attract as many as 10,000 people. Policemen had to be stationed for directing traffic to help facilitate the flow of cars through the gardens. (Courtesy Chamber of Commerce.)

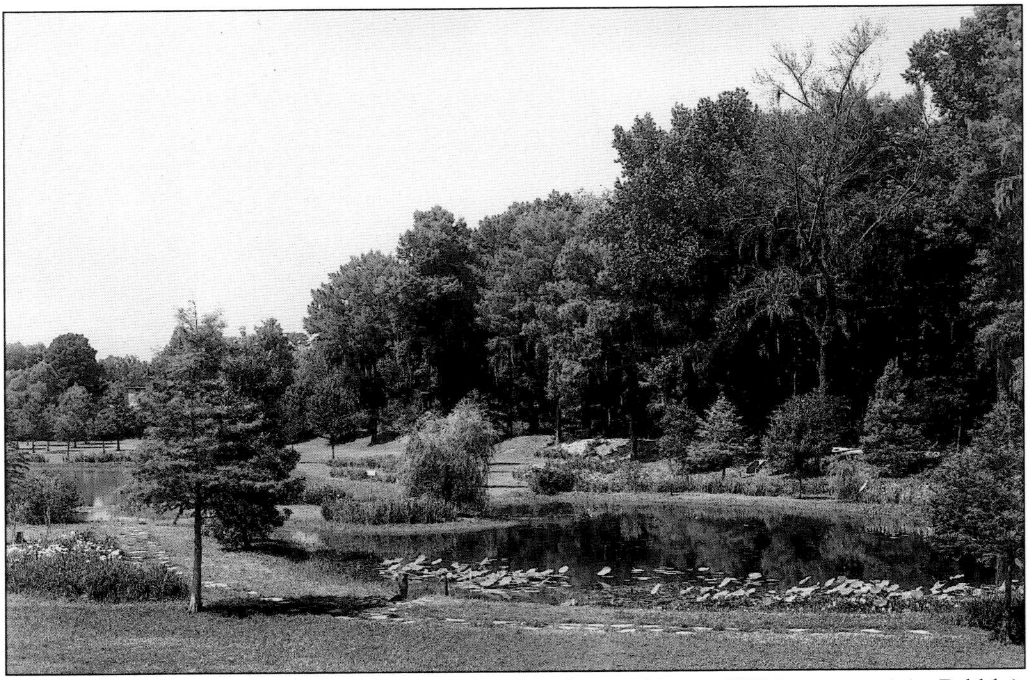

Lake Area, c. 1950. The lake area was developed in 1939 as a WPA project. Mr. Dibble's master plan conceived this area as an "Iris and Water Garden." Many irises, water lilies, and lotuses were used to beautify the surroundings here. (Courtesy Chamber of Commerce.)

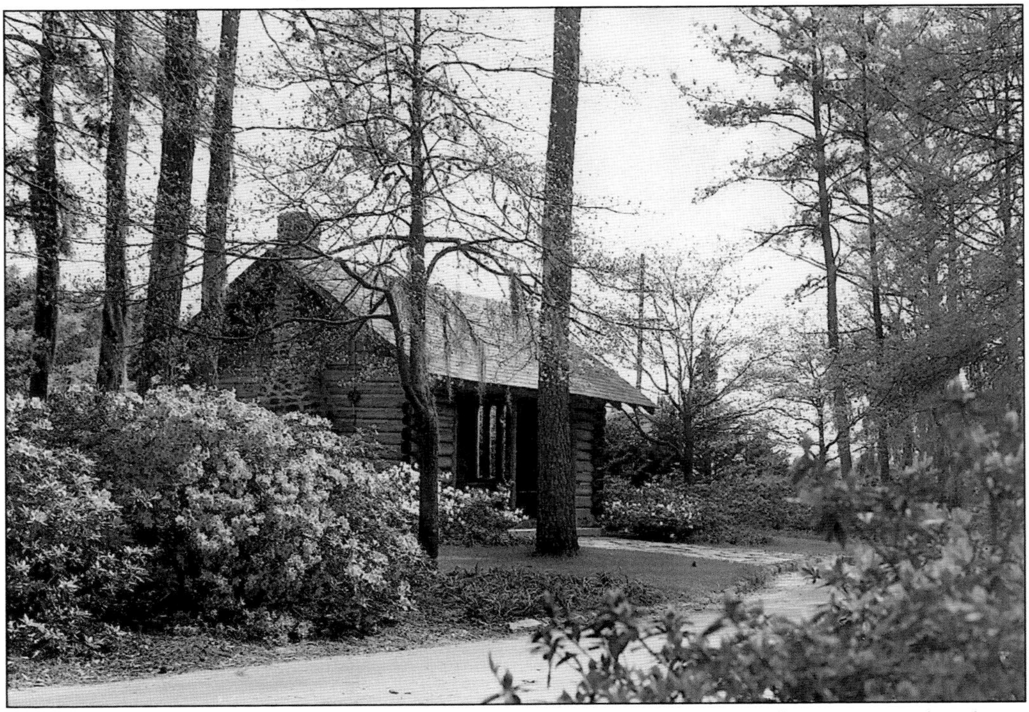

Old Park Office, c. 1952. This log cabin, constructed in 1941 along the scenic garden drive, served as Mr. Andrew Dibble's park office for many years. It was constructed from cypress trees that needed to be removed from the gardens. (Courtesy Chamber of Commerce.)

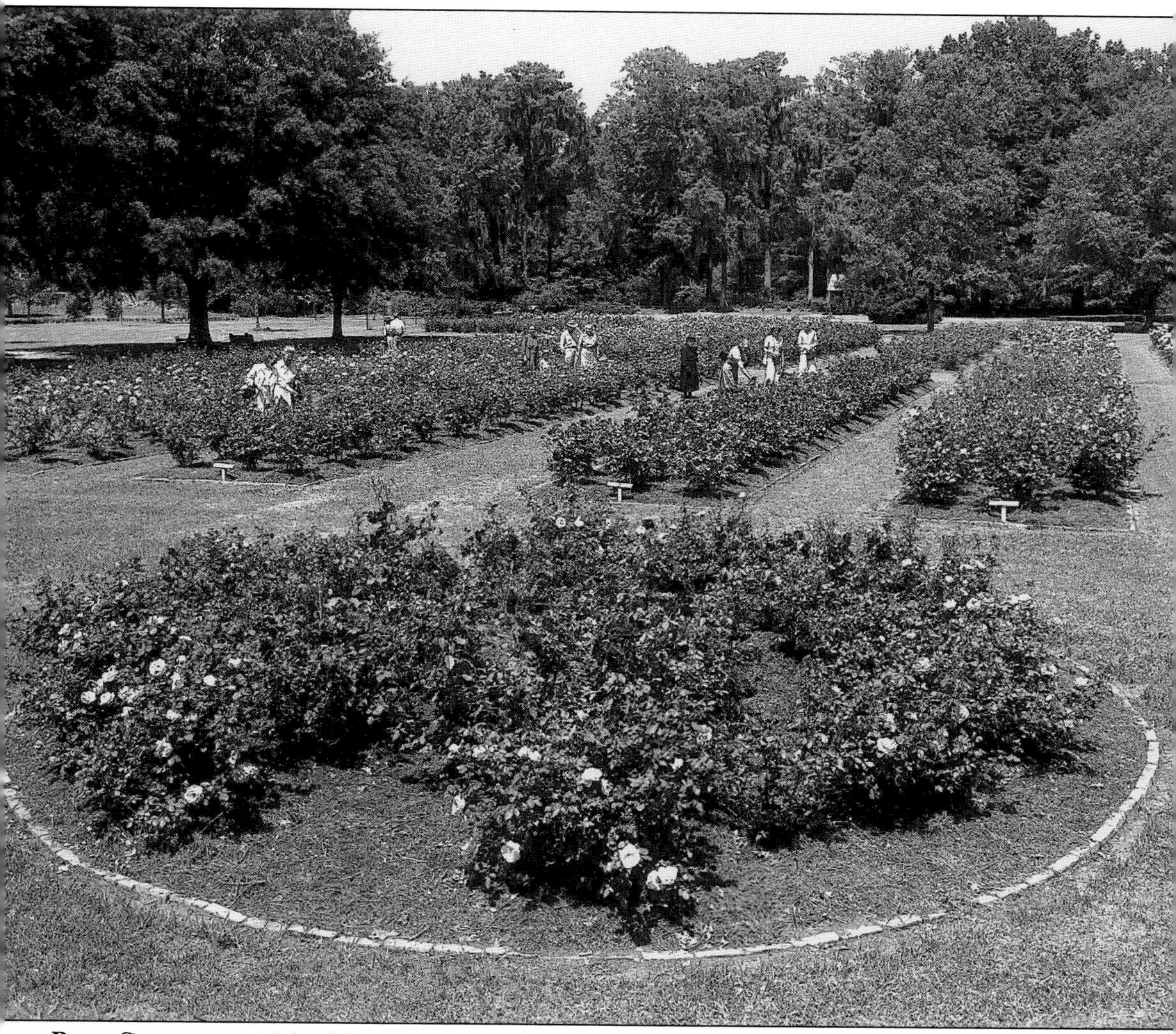

ROSE GARDEN, c. 1953. Visitors are seen here strolling through the rose gardens during the peak blooming season. Thousands of beautiful roses make up this colorful rose haven. Past winners of the All America Rose Selections (AARS) are on display in this paradise. From 1920 to 1950 this same area was the site of Albergotti Playground that contained playground equipment, a ballfield, tennis courts, and a bandstand for musical concerts. (Courtesy Chamber of Commerce.)

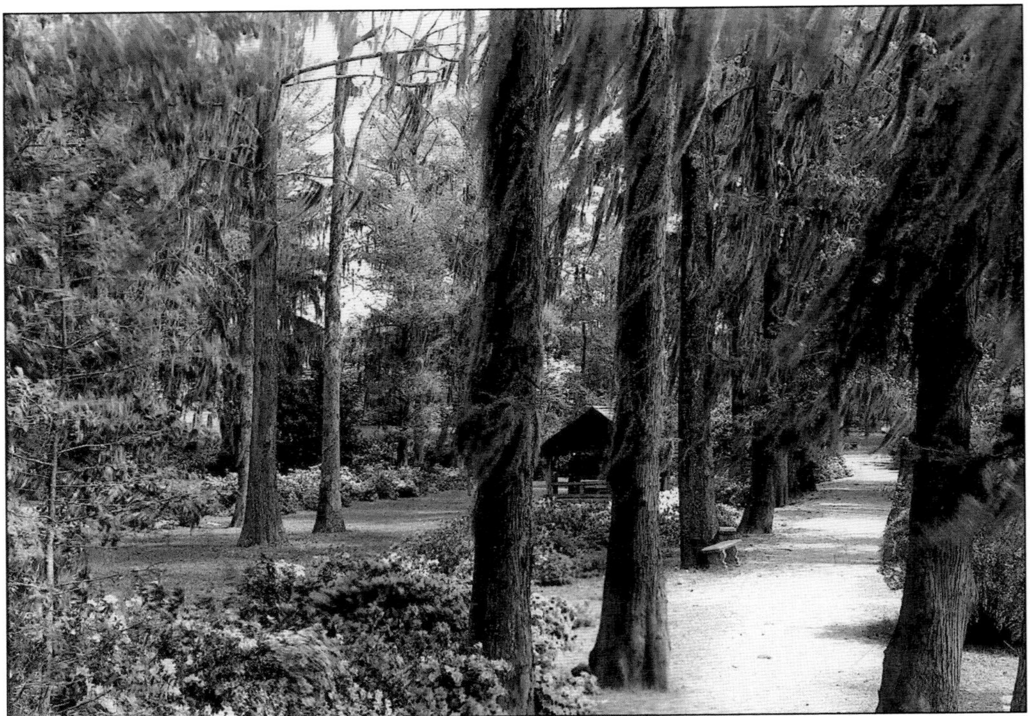

Old Pathway to the Waterwheel, c. 1953. For years this area was the main pathway in the gardens that bisected the Rose Garden and Azalea Garden. It was also a beautiful moss draped tunnel through the tall trees that led to the most recognizable landmark in the gardens, the Chinese Water Wheel. In the mid-1990s this passage was enhanced by building a scenic raised boardwalk along part of its course. (Courtesy Chamber of Commerce.)

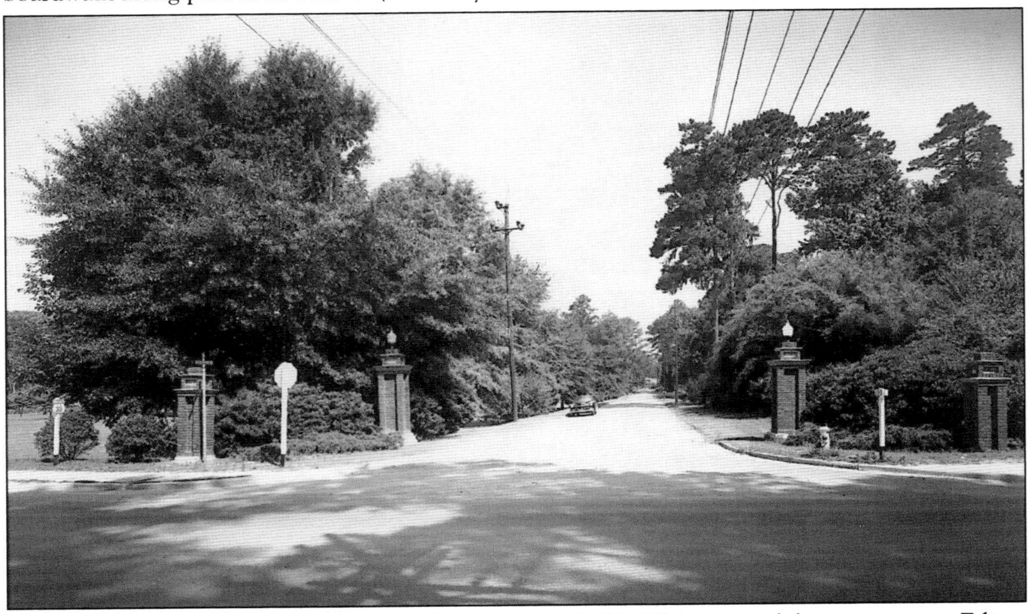

Old Entrance to Edisto Memorial Gardens, c. 1950. This view of the entrance to Edisto Memorial Gardens shows how it appeared for many years before the Ladies' Fountain was relocated from Memorial Plaza to this site in the 1950s. (Courtesy E.J. Lackey.)